CCENT Practice and Study Guide:
Exercises, Activities, and Scenarios to Prepare for the ICND1/CCENT Certification Exam

Allan Johnson

Cisco Press

800 East 96th Street

Indianapolis, Indiana 46240 USA

CCENT Practice and Study Guide: Exercises, Activities, and Scenarios to Prepare for the ICND1/CCENT Certification Exam

Allan Johnson

Published by:
Cisco Press
800 East 96th Street
Indianapolis, IN 46240 USA

Printed in the United States of America

First Printing December 2013

Library of Congress Control Number: 2013953354

ISBN-13: 978-1-58713-345-9
ISBN-10: 1-58713-345-8

Publisher
Paul Boger

Associate Publisher
Dave Dusthimer

Business Operation Manager Cisco Press
Jan Cornelssen

Executive Editor
Mary Beth Ray

Production Manager
Sandra Schroeder

Senior Development Editor
Christopher Cleveland

Project Editor
Mandie Frank

Copy Editor
Keith Cline

Technical Editor
Steve Stiles

Editorial Assistant
Vanessa Evans

Book Designer
Mark Shirar

Composition
Trina Wurst

Proofreader
Megan Wade-Taxter

Trademark Acknowledgments

All terms mentioned in this book that are known to be trademarks or service marks have been appropriately capitalized. Cisco Press or Cisco Systems, Inc., cannot attest to the accuracy of this information. Use of a term in this book should not be regarded as affecting the validity of any trademark or service mark.

Warning and Disclaimer

This book is designed to provide information about networking. Every effort has been made to make this book as complete and as accurate as possible, but no warranty or fitness is implied.

The information is provided on an "as is" basis. The authors, Cisco Press, and Cisco Systems, Inc. shall have neither liability nor responsibility to any person or entity with respect to any loss or damages arising from the information contained in this book or from the use of the discs or programs that may accompany it.

The opinions expressed in this book belong to the author and are not necessarily those of Cisco Systems, Inc.

Corporate and Government Sales

The publisher offers excellent discounts on this book when ordered in quantity for bulk purchases or special sales, which may include electronic versions and/or custom covers and content particular to your business, training goals, marketing focus, and branding interests. For more information, please contact:
U.S. Corporate and Government Sales
1-800-382-3419   corpsales@pearsontechgroup.com

For sales outside the United States please contact:
International Sales   international@pearsoned.com

Feedback Information

At Cisco Press, our goal is to create in-depth technical books of the highest quality and value. Each book is crafted with care and precision, undergoing rigorous development that involves the unique expertise of members from the professional technical community.

Readers' feedback is a natural continuation of this process. If you have any comments regarding how we could improve the quality of this book, or otherwise alter it to better suit your needs, you can contact us through email at feedback@ciscopress.com. Please make sure to include the book title and ISBN in your message.

We greatly appreciate your assistance.

Americas Headquarters	Asia Pacific Headquarters	Europe Headquarters
Cisco Systems, Inc.	Cisco Systems, Inc.	Cisco Systems International BV
170 West Tasman Drive	168 Robinson Road	Haarlerbergpark
San Jose, CA 95134-1706	#28-01 Capital Tower	Haarlerbergweg 13-19
USA	Singapore 068912	1101 CH Amsterdam
www.cisco.com	www.cisco.com	The Netherlands
Tel: 408 526-4000	Tel: +65 6317 7777	www-europe.cisco.com
800 553-NETS (6387)	Fax: +65 6317 7799	Tel: +31 0 800 020 0791
Fax: 408 527-0883		Fax: +31 0 20 357 1100

Cisco has more than 200 offices worldwide. Addresses, phone numbers, and fax numbers are listed on the Cisco Website at **www.cisco.com/go/offices.**

©2008 Cisco Systems, Inc. All rights reserved. CCVP, the Cisco logo, and the Cisco Square Bridge logo are trademarks of Cisco Systems, Inc.; Changing the Way We Work, Live, Play, and Learn is a service mark of Cisco Systems, Inc.; and Access Registrar, Aironet, BPX, Catalyst, CCDA, CCDP, CCIE, CCIP, CCNA, CCNP, CCSP, Cisco, the Cisco Certified Internetwork Expert logo, Cisco IOS, Cisco Press, Cisco Systems, Cisco Systems Capital, the Cisco Systems logo, Cisco Unity, Enterprise/Solver, EtherChannel, EtherFast, EtherSwitch, Fast Step, Follow Me Browsing, FormShare, GigaDrive, GigaStack, HomeLink, Internet Quotient, IOS, IP/TV, iQ Expertise, the iQ logo, iQ Net Readiness Scorecard, iQuick Study, LightStream, Linksys, MeetingPlace, MGX, Networking Academy, Network Registrar, Packet, PIX, ProConnect, RateMUX, ScriptShare, SlideCast, SMARTnet, StackWise, The Fastest Way to Increase Your Internet Quotient, and TransPath are registered trademarks of Cisco Systems, Inc. and/or its affiliates in the United States and certain other countries.

All other trademarks mentioned in this document or Website are the property of their respective owners. The use of the word partner does not imply a partnership relationship between Cisco and any other company. (0609R)

About the Author

Allan Johnson entered the academic world in 1999 after 10 years as a business owner/operator to dedicate his efforts to his passion for teaching. He holds both an MBA and an M.Ed in occupational training and development. He is an information technology instructor at Del Mar College in Corpus Christi, Texas. In 2003, Allan began to commit much of his time and energy to the CCNA Instructional Support Team, providing services to Networking Academy instructors worldwide and creating training materials. He now works full time for Cisco Networking Academy as a learning systems developer.

About the Technical Reviewer

Steve Stiles is a Cisco Network Academy instructor for Rhodes State College and a Cisco certified instructor trainer having earned CCNA Security- and CCNP-level certifications. He was the recipient of the 2012 Outstanding Teacher of the Year award by the Ohio Association of Two-Year Colleges and co-recipient for the Outstanding Faculty of the Year award at Rhodes State College.

Dedication

For my wife, Becky. Without the sacrifices you made during the project, this work would not have come to fruition. Thank you providing me the comfort and resting place only you can give.

Acknowledgments

When I began to think of whom I would like to have as a technical editor for this work, Steve Stiles immediately came to mind. With his instructor and industry background, as well as his excellent work building activities for the new Cisco Networking Academy curriculum, he was an obvious choice. Thankfully, when Mary Beth Ray contacted him, he was willing and able to do the arduous review work necessary to make sure that you get a book that is both technically accurate and unambiguous.

The Cisco Network Academy authors for the online curriculum and series of Companion Guides take the reader deeper, past the CCENT exam topics, with the ultimate goal of not only preparing the student for CCENT certification, but also for more advanced college-level technology courses and degrees, as well. Thank you, especially to Amy Gerrie and her team of authors—Rick Graziani, Wayne Lewis, and Bob Vachon—for their excellent treatment of the material; it is reflected throughout this book.

Mary Beth Rey, executive editor, you amaze me with your ability to juggle multiple projects at once, steering each from beginning to end. I can always count on you to make the tough decisions.

This is my fifth project with Christopher Cleveland as development editor. His dedication to perfection pays dividends in countless, unseen ways. Thank you again, Chris, for providing me with much-needed guidance and support. This book could not be a reality without your persistence.

Contents at a Glance

Contents

Icons Used in This Book

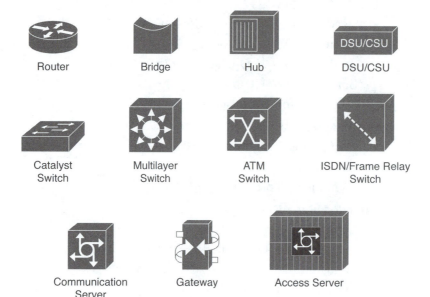

Router   Bridge   Hub   DSU/CSU

Catalyst Switch   Multilayer Switch   ATM Switch   ISDN/Frame Relay Switch

Communication Server   Gateway   Access Server

Command Syntax Conventions

The conventions used to present command syntax in this book are the same conventions used in the IOS Command Reference. The Command Reference describes these conventions as follows:

- **Boldface** indicates commands and keywords that are entered literally as shown. In actual configuration examples and output (not general command syntax), boldface indicates commands that are manually input by the user (such as a **show** command).

- *Italics* indicate arguments for which you supply actual values.

- Vertical bars (|) separate alternative, mutually exclusive elements.

- Square brackets [ ] indicate optional elements.

- Braces { } indicate a required choice.

- Braces within brackets [{ }] indicate a required choice within an optional element.

Introduction

The purpose of this book is to provide you with an extra resource for studying the exam topics of the Interconnecting Cisco Networking Devices Part 1 (ICND1) exam that leads to Cisco Certified Networking Entry Technician (CCENT) certification. This book maps to the first two Cisco Networking Academy courses in the CCNA Routing and Switching curricula: *Introduction to Networks* (ITN) and *Routing and Switching Essentials* (RSE). ITN introduces basic concepts of computer networks including deep dives into the seven layers of the OSI model, IP addressing, and the fundamentals of Ethernet. Successfully completing the course means that you should be able to build small LANs and implement basic addressing and configurations on routers and switches. RSE expands on ITN, taking the student further into basic router and switch configuration. Successfully completing the course means that you should be able to configure and troubleshoot routers and switches using a variety of technologies including RIPv2, single-area OSPF, VLANs, and inter-VLAN routing for both IPv4 and IPv6 networks. To learn more about CCNA Routing and Switching courses and to find an Academy near you, visit http://www.netacad.com (http://www.cisco.com/web/learning/netacad/index.html).

However, if you are not an Academy student but would like to benefit from the extensive authoring done for these courses, you can buy any or all of CCNA Routing and Switching Companion Guides (CG) and Lab Manuals (LM) of the Academy's popular online curriculum. Although you will not have access to the Packet Tracer network simulator software, you will have access to the tireless work of an outstanding team of Cisco Academy instructors dedicated to providing students with comprehensive and engaging CCNA Routing and Switching preparation course material. The titles and ISBNs for the first two courses of the CCNA Routing and Switching CGs and LMs are as follows:

- *Introduction to Networks Companion Guide* (ISBN: 9781587133169)

- *Introduction to Networks Lab Manual* (ISBN: 9781587133121)

- *Routing and Switching Essentials Companion Guide* (ISBN: 9781587133183)

- *Routing and Switching Essentials Lab Manual* (ISBN: 9781587133206)

Goals and Methods

The most important goal of this book is to help you pass the 100-101 Interconnecting Cisco Networking Devices Part 1 (ICND1) exam, which is associated with the Cisco Certified Entry Network Technician (CCENT) certification. Passing the CCENT exam means that you have the knowledge and skills required to successfully install, operate, and troubleshoot a small branch office network. You can view the detailed exam topics any time at http://learningnetwork.cisco.com. They are divided into seven broad categories:

- Operation of IP Data Networks

- LAN Switching Technologies

- IP Addressing for IPv4 and IPv6

- IP Routing Technologies

- IP Services

- Network Device Security

- Troubleshooting

This book offers exercises that help you learn the concepts, configurations, and troubleshooting skills crucial to your success as a CCENT exam candidate. Each chapter differs slightly and includes some or all of the following types of practice:

- Vocabulary Matching Exercises
- Concept Questions Exercises
- Skill-Building Activities and Scenarios
- Configuration Scenarios
- Troubleshooting Scenarios

Audience for This Book

This book's main audience is anyone taking the CCNA Routing and Switching courses of the Cisco Networking Academy curriculum. Many Academies use this Practice Study Guide as a required tool in the course, whereas other Academies recommend the Practice Study Guide as an additional resource to prepare for class exams and the CCENT certification.

The secondary audiences for this book include people taking CCENT-related classes from professional training organizations. This book can also be used for college- and university-level networking courses, as well as anyone wanting to gain a detailed understanding of routing.

How This Book Is Organized

Because the content of the *Introduction to Networks Companion Guide*, the *Routing Switching Essentials Companion Guide*, and the online curriculum is sequential, you should work through this Practice Study Guide in order beginning with Chapter 1.

The book covers the major topic headings in the same sequence as the online curriculum. This book has 22 chapters, with the same names as the online course chapters. However, the numbering is sequential in this book, progressing from Chapter 1 to Chapter 22. The online curriculum starts over at Chapter 1 in Routing and Switching Essentials.

Most of the configuration chapters use a single topology where appropriate. This allows for better continuity and easier understanding of routing and switching commands, operations, and outputs. However, the topology differs from the one used in the online curriculum and the Companion Guide. A different topology affords you the opportunity to practice your knowledge and skills without just simply recording the information you find in the text.

Lab, Packet Tracer, and Video Demonstration Activities

Packet Tracer
☐ Activity

☐ Video
Demonstration

Throughout the book, you will find references to Lab, Packet Tracer, and Video Demonstration activities. These references are provided so that you can, at that point, complete those activities. The Packet Tracer and Video Demonstration activities are only accessible if you have access to the online curriculum. However, the Labs are available in the Lab Manuals previously cited.

Part I: Introduction to Networks

- **Chapter 1, "Exploring the Network":** This chapter provides vocabulary and concept exercises to reinforce your understanding of network components, LANs, WANs, and the Internet. You will also practice classifying network architecture requirements.

- **Chapter 2, "Configuring a Network Operating System":** The exercises in the first part of this chapter are devoted to accessing Cisco devices, navigating the IOS, and learning about command structure. In the second half, you practice configuring and verifying a switch for basic connectivity.

- **Chapter 3, "Network Protocols and Communications":** This chapter's exercises are devoted to protocols, standards, and the two main reference models we use in networking: TCP/IP and OSI. You will also complete activities which focus on data encapsulation and addressing as information moves across a network.

- **Chapter 4, "Network Access":** This chapter is all about how computing devices physically connect to the network. You will complete exercises that focus on physical access including copper, fiber, and wireless media. Then, moving up the OSI model to Layer 2, you will engage in activities that focus on the data link layer protocols and concepts.

- **Chapter 5, "Ethernet":** This chapter continues with the data link layer with exercises devoted to Ethernet concepts and operation, including the Ethernet frame, the MAC address, and ARP. In addition, you will complete activities focused on the operation of the main Layer 2 device: the switch.

- **Chapter 6, "Network Layer":** This chapter starts off with exercises for understanding the operation of the Internet Protocol, both version 4 and version 6. Then the activities move on to routing operations, including how hosts determine a gateway of last resort, and identifying the parts of a routing table. Next, you will engage in exercises that focus on router components and the boot-up process. Finally, you will practice basic router configuration and verification.

- **Chapter 7, "Transport Layer":** Continuing the journey up the OSI model, this chapter's activities focus on the operation of the transport layer, including TCP, UDP, and the three-way TCP handshake.

- **Chapter 8, "IP Addressing":** With the growing adoption of IPv6, networking students now need to be competent in both IPv4 and IPv6. The activities in this chapter focus on the operation, configuration, and verification versions of the Internet Protocol.

- **Chapter 9, "Subnetting IP Networks":** Segmenting IP addresses into logical subnets is the focus of the exercises, activities, and scenarios in this chapter. You will practice subnetting for fixed-length and variable-length subnet masks. In addition, you will practice subnetting IPv6 addresses.

- **Chapter 10, "Application Layer":** This chapter focuses on the layer at which the end user interacts with the network. Exercises are devoted to reinforcing your understanding of common application layer protocols.

- **Chapter 11, "It's a Network":** In this chapter, we step back and see how to assemble these elements together in a functioning network that can be maintained. Activities include small network design considerations, network security concerns, securing remote access with SSH, and verifying basic network performance.

Part II: Routing and Switching Essentials

- **Chapter 12, "Introduction to Switched Networks":** Part II starts off with an introduction to LAN design concepts and a the operation of switches. Exercises focus on identifying network design principles, selecting switch hardware, switch forwarding methods, and the MAC address table.

- **Chapter 13, "Basic Switching Concepts and Configuration":** This chapter is a bit of a review of the content in Part I. Activities focus on the switch boot sequence, configuration, and verification. New activities for Part II include switch port security configuration and verification.

- **Chapter 14, "VLANs":** This chapter focuses on VLAN concepts and configuration. Exercises include VLAN segmentation concepts and implementations. Also, you will practice trunk configuration and complete activities devoted to understanding DTP. The chapter wraps up with activities on VLAN security.

- **Chapter 15, "Routing Concepts":** In this chapter, it's all about the router. Exercises focus on router functions, components, and configuration. You will practice configuring a dual-stack IPv4 and IPv6 one-router, two-PC topology. Then, activities focus on routing decisions, including path determination, administrative distance, switching packets from hop to hop, and analyzing the routing table.

- **Chapter 16, "Inter-VLAN Routing":** This chapter introduces inter-VLAN routing and Layer 3 switching. After an exercise on comparing types of inter-VLAN routing, the bulk of the chapter is devoted to practicing inter-VLAN routing configuration and troubleshooting. The chapter ends with a look at Layer 3 switching concepts, configuration, and troubleshooting.

- **Chapter 17, "Static Routing":** This chapter focuses on manual route configuration using static routes. Exercises focus on comparing static and dynamic routing and the types of static routes. Practice activities focus on configuring and troubleshooting static, default, summary, and floating static routes for both IPv4 and IPv6.

- **Chapter 18, "Routing Dynamically":** To route dynamically, a router needs a routing protocol. The exercises in this chapter are devoted to all the basic routing protocol concepts, including protocol operation and characteristics, how a router learns about networks, and deep dives into distance vector and link-state routing protocols.

- **Chapter 19, "Single-Area OSPF":** This chapter introduces OSPF with exercises for reinforcing your understanding of OSPF operations. In addition, activities allow you to practice configuration and troubleshooting for both single-area OSPFv2 and OSPFv3.

- **Chapter 20, "Access Control Lists":** Understanding and correctly configuring ACLs is one of the most important skills a network administrator can master. Therefore, the exercises and activities in this chapter focus on ACL concepts, configuration, and troubleshooting IPv4 ACLs. There is also a brief section devoted to IPv6 ACL configuration practice.

- **Chapter 21, "DHCP":** When a device boots, it needs IP addressing. Although you can manually configure addressing, most devices obtain addressing dynamically through DHCP. Exercises focus on DHCP concepts, and practice activities focus on DHCP configurations, for both IPv4 and IPv6.

- **Chapter 22, "Network Address Translation for IPv4":** NAT was created to provide a temporary solution to the limited address space in IPv4. Just about every router connected to the network uses NAT or forwards traffic to a NAT-enabled device for address translation. This chapter focuses on exercises to reinforce your understanding of NAT operation and characteristics. Practice activities include configuring, verifying, and troubleshooting static NAT, dynamic NAT, and PAT.

About the Cisco Press Website for This Book

Cisco Press provides additional content that can be accessed by registering your individual book at the ciscopress.com website. Becoming a member and registering is free, and you then gain access to exclusive deals on other resources from Cisco Press

To register this book, go to http://www.ciscopress.com/bookstore/register.asp and enter the book's ISBN located on the back cover of this book. You'll then be prompted to log in or join Ciscopress.com to continue registration.

After you register the book, a link to the supplemental content will be listed on your My Registered Books page.

CHAPTER 1

Exploring the Network

Globally Connected

In today's world, we are connected like never before. People with ideas can communicate instantly with others—next door or halfway around the world. Networks are rapidly transforming our planet into a global village.

Vocabulary Exercise: Matching

Match the definition on the left with a term on the right. This exercise is a one-to-one matching.

Definitions

a. Gives anyone a means to communicate their thoughts to a global audience without technical knowledge of web design.

b. Enable instant real-time communication between two or more people.

c. Web pages that groups of people can edit and view together.

d. Enables people to share files with each other without having to store and download them from a central server.

e. Interactive websites where people and communities create and share user-generated content.

f. Allows people to deliver their recordings to a wide audience.

g. Gives people the opportunity to work together without the constraints of location or time zone, often across real-time interactive video.

Terms

____ collaboration tools

____ social media

____ blogs

____ P2P file sharing

____ podcasting

____ IM/texting

____ wikis

Completion Exercise

_____ come in all sizes. They can range from simple configurations consisting of two computers to complex topologies connecting millions of devices. Simple networks installed in _____ enable sharing of resources, such as printers, documents, pictures, and music between a few local computers.

In businesses and large organizations, networks can be used to provide access to information centrally located on network _____. In addition to the many internal organizational benefits, companies often use their networks to provide products and services to customers through their connection to the Internet. The _____ is the largest network in existence and means a "network of networks."

All computers connected to a network that participate directly in network communication are classified as _____ or end _____. They can act as a _____, a _____, or both. The software installed on the computer determines which role the computer plays. _____ are hosts that have software installed that enable them to provide information, like email or web pages, to other hosts on the network. _____ are computer hosts that have software installed that enable them to request and display the information obtained from servers.

The simplest peer-to-peer network consists of _____ using a wired or wireless connection. Multiple PCs can also be connected to create a larger peer-to-peer network, but this requires a network device, such as a ____, to interconnect the computers.

In Table 1-1, list the advantages and disadvantages of peer-to-peer networking.

Table 1-1   Advantages and Disadvantages of Peer-to-Peer Networking

Advantages	Disadvantages

Lab - Researching Network Collaboration Tools

LANs, WANs, and the Internet

The path that a message takes from source to destination can be as simple as a single cable connecting one computer to another or as complex as a network that literally spans the globe. LANs, WANs, and the Internet provide the basic framework for that interconnectedness.

Completion Exercise

The network infrastructure contains three categories of network components: devices, media, and services. _____ and _____ are the physical elements, or hardware, of the network. Hardware is often the visible components of the network platform. Some components may not be so visible, such as _____ media. _____ are the communication programs, called software, that run on the networked devices.

The network devices that people are most familiar with are called ___ _____, or _____. These devices form the interface between users and the underlying communication network.

List at least five examples of end devices:

A host device is either the _____ or destination of a message transmitted over the network. Each host on a network is identified by an _____.

_____ devices interconnect end devices and can connect multiple individual networks to form an _____. These devices use the destination host _____ to determine the path that messages should take through the network.

List three examples of intermediary network devices:

List at least three of the main functions of intermediary devices:

Communication across a network is carried on a _____ (singular form of the word media), which provides the channel over which the message travels from source to _____.

List the three types of media used to interconnect devices:

On metallic wires, the data is encoded into _____ _____ that match specific patterns. Fiber-optic transmissions rely on _____. In a wireless transmission, patterns of _____ depict the various bit values.

List the four criteria for choosing network media:

When conveying complex information such as displaying all the devices and medium in a large internetwork, it is helpful to use visual representations known as _____ diagrams. They provide visual maps of how the network is connected.

There are two types of _____ diagrams:

_____ identify the physical location of intermediary devices, configured ports, and cable installation.

_____ identify devices, ports, and IP addressing schemes.

Classify and Identify Network Components

In Figure 1-1, label the three major classifications of network components. Then, underneath each icon, label the network component.

Figure 1-1   Common Network Component Icons

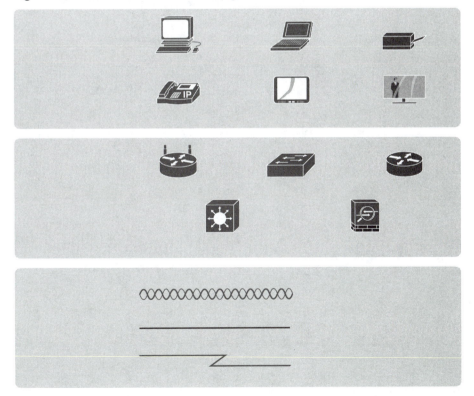

Compare LANs and WANs

In Table 1-2, indicate whether the feature is a LAN feature or a WAN feature by marking the appropriate column.

Table 1-2   LAN and WAN Features

LANs	WANs	LAN or WAN Feature
		Interconnect end devices in a limited area such as a home, a school, an office building, or a campus
		Typically provide slower speed links between networks
		Provide high-speed bandwidth to internal end devices and intermediary devices
		Interconnect networks over wide geographic areas such as between cities, states, provinces, countries, or continents
		Usually administered by multiple service providers
		Usually administered by a single organization or individual

Vocabulary Exercise: Matching

Match the definition on the left with a term on the right. This exercise is a one-to-one matching.

Definitions

a. Similar to a LAN but wirelessly interconnects users and end points in a small geographic area.

b. Requires a clear line of sight, installation costs can be high, and connections tend to be slower and less reliable than its terrestrial competition.

c. Also called a LAN adapter, it provides the physical connection to the network at the PC or other host device.

d. Available from a provider to the customer premise over a dedicated copper or fiber connection providing bandwidth speeds of 10 Mbps to 10 Gbps.

e. The availability of this type of Internet access is a real benefit in those areas that would otherwise have no Internet connectivity at all, or for those constantly on the go.

f. Provide the interface between users and the underlying communication network.

g. A network infrastructure that provides access to users and end devices in a small geographic area.

These devices interconnect end devices.

h. Reserved circuits that connect geographically separated offices for private voice and/or data networking. In North America, circuits include T1 (1.54 Mbps) and T3 (44.7 Mbps); in other parts of the world, they are available in E1 (2 Mbps) and E3 (34 Mbps).

i. A private connection of LANs and WANs that belongs to an organization—basically an internetwork that is usually only accessible from within the organization.

j. An inexpensive, very low-bandwidth option to connect to the ISP and should only be considered as a backup to other higher-speed connection options.

k. Data signal is carried on the same coaxial media that delivers the television signal. It provides a high-bandwidth, always-on connection to the Internet.

l. Provides secure and safe access to individuals who work for a different organizations but require access to the company's data.

m. A network infrastructure that is larger than a LAN but smaller than a WAN and are usually operated by a single organization.

n. Provides the channel over which the message travels from source to destination.

o. A network infrastructure that provides access to other networks over a wide geographic area.

p. Provides a high-bandwidth, always-on connection that runs over a telephone line, with the line split into three channels.

q. A network infrastructure designed to support file servers and provide data storage, retrieval, and replication.

Terms

_____ DSL

_____ medium

_____ metropolitan-area network (MAN)

_____ network interface card

_____ Metro Ethernet

_____ wireless LAN (WLAN)

_____ dedicated leased line

_____ satellite

_____ wide-area network (WAN)

_____ intranet

_____ storage-area network (SAN)

_____ cellular

_____ dial-up telephone

_____ cable

_____ local-area network (LAN)

_____ end devices

_____ intermediary devices

_____ extranet

Lab - Researching Converged Network Services (ITN 1.2.3.3/NB 1.2.1.3)

 Packet Tracer - Network Representation (ITN 1.2.4.4/NB 1.3.4.4)

The Network as a Platform

The converged network is capable of delivering voice, video streams, text, and graphics between many different types of devices over the same communication channel and network structure. This platform provides access to a wide range of alternative and new communication methods that enable people to interact directly with each other almost instantaneously.

The converged network must support a wide range of applications and services, and must operate over many different types of cables and devices that make up the physical infrastructure. As networks evolve, we are discovering that the underlying architectures need to address four basic characteristics to meet user expectations:

- Fault tolerance
- Scalability
- Quality of service (QoS)
- Security

Classify Network Architecture Requirements

In Table 1-3, select the appropriate column to classify each of the network architecture requirements.

Table 1-3   Reliable Network Features

Requirement	Characteristic			
	Fault Tolerance	Scalability	Quality of Service	Security
Many tools and procedures are being implemented to address the need to exchange confidential and business-critical information.				
Common network standards allow hardware and software vendors to focus on product improvements and services.				
Different types of Internet service providers can affect the quality of network data delivery.				
Networks can grow or expand with minimal impact on performance.				

Requirement	Characteristic			
	Fault Tolerance	Scalability	Quality of Service	Security
Types of network equipment, how they are identified (IP address/MAC address), and how they are named can have an impact on the growth of a network.				
Networks should always be available.				
Compromising the integrity of crucial business and personal assets could have serious repercussions.				
Types of network connectivity can affect delivery of information.				
Business and personal network equipment must be protected.				
Traffic delay and data loss should be considered when setting up delivery through priority queuing.				
Priority queues are implemented when demand for network bandwidth exceeds supply.				
Full memory queues mean packets must be dropped.				
Data can travel through more than one route for delivery from a remote source.				
Priority for queuing packets is based on the type of data sent and how important it may be.				
Developing a plan for priority queuing is a strategy for quality delivery of information.				
Business and personal data must be protected.				

 Lab - Mapping the Internet (ITN 1.3.1.3/NB 1.3.3.3)

The Changing Network Environment

Before the Internet became so widely available, businesses largely relied on print marketing to make consumers aware of their products. Compare that to how consumers are reached today. Most businesses have an Internet presence where consumers can learn about their products, read reviews from other customers, and order products directly from the website. As new technologies and end-user devices come to market, businesses and consumers must continue to adjust to this ever-changing environment.

Completion Exercise

The concept of any device, to any content, in any way is a major global trend that requires significant changes to the way devices are used. This trend is known as _____ _____.

_____ tools give employees, students, teachers, customers, and partners a way to instantly connect, interact, and conduct business, through whatever communications channels they prefer, and achieve their objectives.

_____ calls and _____ conferencing are proving particularly powerful for sales processes and for doing business.

_____ computing is the use of computing resources (hardware and software) that are delivered as a service over a network. A company uses the hardware and software in the _____, and a service fee is charged.

List at least four major components associated with data centers:

_____ networking is not designed to be a substitute for dedicated cabling for data networks. However, it is an alternative when data network cables or wireless communications are not a viable option.

Although many homes connect to the Internet either through a cable or DSL service provider, wireless is another option. Briefly describe two types of wireless (not satellite) options for the home:

1.

2.

Network Security Terminology

Provide the security term that matches the definition.

_____ refers to a network attack triggered by date.

_____ is arbitrary code running on user devices.

_____ block unauthorized access to your network.

_____ is an attack that slows down or crashes equipment and programs.

_____ filter network access and data traffic.

 Lab - Researching IT and Networking Job Opportunities (ITN 1.4.4.3/NB 1.4.3.6)

CHAPTER 2

Configuring a Network Operating System

The Cisco Internetwork Operating System (IOS) is a generic term for the collection of network operating systems used on Cisco networking devices. Cisco IOS is used for most Cisco devices regardless of the type or size of the device. This chapter focuses on gaining proficiency using basic IOS commands and configuring switches.

IOS Bootcamp

The user can interact with the shell of an operating system using either the command-line interface (CLI) or graphical user interface (GUI).

Completion Exercise

When a computer is powered on, it loads the operating system into _____ (acronym). When using the ___ (acronym), the user interacts directly with the system in a text-based environment by entering commands on the keyboard at a command prompt. The ___ (acronym) allows the user to interact with the system in an environment that uses graphical images, multimedia, and text.

In Table 2-1, identify the term for the description of each part of an operating system.

Table 2-1   Three Major Parts of an Operating System

Term	Description
	Communicates between the hardware and software and manages how hardware resources are used to meet software requirements
	The user interface that allows users to request specific tasks for the OS, either through the CLI or GUI
	The physical part of the computer including underlying electronics

The operating system on home routers is usually called ___ware. The most common method for configuring a home router is using a _____ to access an easy-to-use ___ (acronym).

The network operating system used on Cisco devices is called the Cisco _____ (___). The most common method of accessing these devices is using a _____ (acronym).

The IOS file itself is several megabytes in size and is stored in a semi-permanent memory area called _____, which provides nonvolatile storage. When referring to memory, what does the term *nonvolatile* mean?

_____

In many Cisco devices, the IOS is copied from flash into _____ (____) when the device is powered on. RAM is considered _____ memory because data is lost during a power cycle.

Cisco IOS routers and switches perform functions that network professionals depend upon to make their networks operate as expected. List at least four major functions performed or enabled by Cisco routers and switches.

_____

_____

_____

_____

_____

_____

_____

**Video Demonstration - CCO Accounts and IOS Image Exploration
(ITN 2.1.1.5/NB 2.1.1.4)**

Accessing a Cisco IOS Device

You can access the CLI environment on a Cisco IOS device in several ways. In Table 2-2, indicate which access method is most appropriate for the given scenario.

Table 2-2   Methods for Accessing a Cisco IOS Device

Console	Telnet/SSH	AUX	Scenario
			You call your manager to tell him you cannot access your switch or router in another city over the Internet. He provides you with the information to access the switch through a telephone connection.
			You physically cable access to the switch, are not prompted for a password, and can access the IOS. This is the default operation.
			You are on vacation and need to check on one of your switches. The only access you have is your cellular phone.
			The password for a device was changed. No one knows what the new password is, and you need to reset a new password.
			Your manager gives you a rollover cable and tells you to use it to configure the switch.
			The device you are configuring cannot be accessed by cable because you are not in the building. You use a telephone to dial in to it.
			You are in the equipment room with a new switch that needs to be configured.
			You access the IOS by using another intermediary device over a network connection.
			You do not need remote-access services to the networking device to configure it because the device is physically accessible to you.
			You use a password-encrypted connection to remotely access a device over a network.

Navigating the IOS Matching Exercise

Match the definition on the left with a term on the right. This exercise is a one-to-one matching. Each definition has exactly one matching term.

Definitions

    a. Scrolls down through the commands in the history buffer.

    b. Privileged EXEC mode.

    c. Moves the cursor to the beginning of the command line.

    d. Interface Configuration mode.

    e. Has the same effect as using the key combination Ctrl+Z.

    f. When in any configuration mode, ends the configuration mode and returns to privileged EXEC mode.

    g. User EXEC mode.

    h. Returns the user to the previous configuration mode. Can also end the console session.

    i. Moves the cursor to the end of the command line.

    j. All-purpose break sequence. Use to abort DNS lookups.

    k. Completes a partial command name entry.

    l. Global configuration mode.

    m. Scrolls up through the commands in the history buffer.

Terms

_____ Switch>

_____ up arrow

_____ down arrow

_____ Ctrl+A

_____ Switch(config-if)#

_____ end

_____ Ctrl+Shift+6

_____ Tab

_____ exit

_____ Router(config)#

_____ Ctrl+E

_____ Ctrl+Z

_____ Router#

Lab - Establishing a Console Session with Tera Term (ITN/NB 2.1.4.9)

Packet Tracer ☐ Activity

Packet Tracer - Navigating the IOS (ITN/NB 2.1.4.8)

☐ Video Demonstration

Video Demonstration - Navigating the IOS (ITN/NB 2.1.3.6)

Basic Device Configuration

Now that we reviewed accessing and navigating the IOS, we are ready to review initial switch configuration, including setting a name for the switch, limiting access to the device configuration, configuring banner messages, and saving the configuration. We will also review configuring the switch for remote management by adding IP addressing and default gateway.

Applying a Basic Configuration

The following exercise walks you through a basic configuration.

First, enter global configuration mode for the switch:

```
Switch#
```

Next, apply a unique hostname to the switch. Use S1 for this example:

```
Switch(config)#
```

Now, configure the encrypted password that is to be used to enter privileged EXEC mode. Use class as the password:

```
S1 (config)#
```

Next, configure the console and vty lines with the password cisco. The console commands follow:

```
S1(config)#
S1(config-line)#
S1(config-line)#
```

The vty lines use similar commands:

```
S1(config-line)#
S1(config-line)#
S1(config-line)#
```

Return to global configuration mode:

```
S1(config-line)#
```

From global configuration mode, configure the message-of-the-day banner. Use the following text: Authorized Access Only. A delimiting character such as a # is used at the beginning and at the end of the message:

```
S1(config)#
```

What is the purpose of the message of the day?

_____

_____

What is the command to enter VLAN interface configuration mode for S1?

```
S1(config)#
```

Enter the command to configure the IP address 10.1.1.11 and subnet mask 255.255.255.0:

```
S1(config-if)#
```

Enter the command to activate the VLAN interface:

```
S1(config-if)#
```

Configure S1 with the default gateway address 10.1.1.1:

```
S1(config)#
```

Return to the privileged EXEC prompt:

```
S1(config)#
```

What command saves the current configuration?

```
S1#
```

What command displays the current configuration?

```
S1#
```

 Lab - Building a Simple Network (ITN/NB 2.3.3.4)

Lab - Configuring a Switch Management Address (ITN/NB 2.3.3.5)

 Packet Tracer - Implementing Basic Connectivity (ITN/NB 2.3.2.5)

Packet Tracer - Skills Integration Challenge (ITN/NB 2.4.1.2)

CHAPTER 3

Network Protocols and Communications

The network industry has adopted a framework that provides a common language for understanding current network platforms as well as facilitates the development of new technologies. Central to this framework is the use of generally accepted models that describe network rules and functions.

Rules of Communication

Networks can vary in size, shape, and function. However, simply having the physical connection between end devices is not enough to enable communication. For communication to occur, devices must follow precise rules.

Vocabulary Exercise: Matching

Match the definition on the left with a term on the right. This exercise is a one-to-one matching. Each definition has exactly one matching term.

Definitions

a. Used by source and destination to negotiate correct timing for successful communication.

b. One-to-many delivery of a message.

c. The size restrictions of frames require the source host to break a long message into individual pieces that meet both the minimum and maximum size requirements.

d. The format each computer message is encapsulated in before it is sent over the network.

e. When this occurs, hosts on the network have rules that specify what action to take if no reply is received.

f. The process of converting information into another, acceptable form, for transmission.

g. The process of converting transmitted information into an understandable form.

h. One-to-all delivery of a message.

i. Needed by hosts on the network to know when to begin sending messages and how to respond when errors occur.

j. The process of placing one message format inside another message format.

k. One-to-one delivery of a message.

Terms

____ broadcast

____ frame

____ segmentation

____ unicast

____ encoding

____ multicast

____ decoding

____ response timeout

____ flow control

____ encapsulation

____ access method

Network Protocols and Standards

For networked devices to successfully communicate, a network protocol suite must describe precise requirements and interactions. Networking protocols define a common format and set of rules for exchanging messages between devices. A group of interrelated protocols necessary to perform a communication function is called a protocol suite. In this section, we review the TCP/IP protocol suite, investigate standards organizations, and compare the OSI and TCP/IP models.

Protocol Definitions: Matching

Match the definition on the left with a protocol acronym on the right. This exercise is a one-to-one matching. Each definition has exactly one matching protocol.

Definitions   Terms

a. Dynamically assigns IP addresses to client sta-   ____ TCP
tions at startup
                                                                    ____ ICMP
b. Translates domain names, such as cisco.com,
into IP addresses   ____ FTP

c. Uses composite metric based on bandwidth,   ____ EIGRP
delay, load, and reliability
                                                                    ____ ARP
d. Does not confirm successful datagram trans-
mission   ____ UDP

e. Enables clients to send email to a mail server   ____ POP

f. Set of rules for exchanging text, graphic imag-   ____ HTTP
es, sound, video, and other multimedia files
on the World Wide Web   ____ NAT

g. Enables clients to retrieve email from a mail   ____ DHCP
server
                                                                    ____ IP
h. Translates IP addresses from a private network
into globally unique public IP addresses   ____ SMTP

i. Addresses packets for end-to-end delivery   ____ DNS
over an Internetwork
                                                                    ____ OSPF
j. Provides dynamic address mapping between
an IP address and a hardware address

k. Link-state routing protocol

l. A reliable, connection-oriented, and acknowledged file delivery protocol

m. Reliable, acknowledged transmissions that
confirm successful delivery

n. Provides feedback from a destination host to
a source host about errors in packet delivery

Mapping the Protocols of the TCP/IP Suite

In Table 3-1, indicate the layer to which each protocol belongs.

Table 3-1   **Protocols of the TCP/IP Suite**

Protocol	Application	Transport	Internet	Network Access
POP				
PPP				
FTP				
DHCP				
IMAP				
IP				
TCP				
ICMP				
ARP				
HTTP				
TFTP				
Ethernet				
Interface drivers				
OSPF				
UDP				
DNS				
EIGRP				
SMTP				

Explore the Purpose of Standards Organizations

The following six standards organizations are responsible for creating, developing, and monitoring many of the protocols and standards used in today's communications networks:

- IANA: http://www.iana.org/
- ICANN: http://www.icann.org/en/about/welcome
- IEEE: http://standards.ieee.org/develop/index.html
- IETF: http://www.ietf.org/newcomers.html#whither
- ITU: http://www.itu.int/en/about/Pages/whatwedo.aspx
- TIA: http://www.tiaonline.org/standards/strategic-initiatives

Investigate each organization's website at the address listed next to the acronym. Read the information provided. In Table 3-2, match the standards organization to its description.

Note: Web addresses can often change. If the above links are broken, try using your favorite search engine to find the information.

Table 3-2   Standards Organization Descriptions

Description	IANA	ICANN	IEEE	IETF	ITU	TIA
Uses communications standards to predict famines and global climate changes.						
Manages the DNS root zone standards and the .int registry.						
Coordinates unique international Internet addresses for site names and IP addresses.						
Develops standards for homeland security/emergency response teams.						
Standards are developed using a six-stage lifecycle diagram.						
Provides a space where Internet protocols are set and maintained.						
"Makes the Internet work better," using an engineering approach.						
Serves as the central repository for protocol name and number registries.						
Creates standards for worldwide cabling infrastructure.						
Provides wireless standards for IPTV.						
Official standards products are RFC documents, published free of charge.						
Defines policies describing how "names and numbers" of the Internet operate.						
Supports "bridge the digital divide" initiatives.						
Manages the DNS, IP addresses, and protocol identifier assignments.						
Offers online tools and resources for standards and developers.						
Creates standards for wired and wireless technologies .						
Develops standards/protocols affecting cloud computing.						
Supports navigation and online maps via radio/satellite transmissions.						
Standardizes the IP to applications' protocol layers.						

 Lab - Researching Networking Standards (ITN 3.2.3.6/NB 3.1.3.6)

OSI Reference Model Layers: Matching

Match the definition on the left with layer on the right. This exercise is a one-to-one matching. Each definition has exactly one matching layer.

Definitions

a. Provides services to exchange the individual pieces of data over the network between identified end devices

b. Describes methods for exchanging data frames between devices over a common media

c. Provides for common representation of the data transferred between application layer services

d. Describe the mechanical, electrical, functional, and procedural means to activate, maintain, and deactivate physical connections for bit transmission to and from a network device

e. Provides services to the presentation layer to organize its dialogue and to manage data exchange

f. Defines services to segment, transfer, and reassemble the data for individual communications between the end devices

g. Provides the means for end-to-end connectivity between individuals in the human network using data networks

Layers

____ presentation

____ transport

____ network

____ application

____ session

____ physical

____ data link

TCP/IP Model Layers: Matching

Match the definition on the left with layer on the right. This exercise is a one-to-one matching. Each definition has exactly one matching layer.

Definitions

a. Determines the best path through the network

b. Represents data to the user, plus encoding and dialog control

c. Controls the hardware devices and media that make up the network

d. Supports communications between diverse devices across diverse networks

Layers

____ transport

____ network access

____ application

____ Internet

Mapping the Layers of the OSI and TCP/IP Models

In Figure 3-1, label the layers for each model.

Figure 3-1   The Layers of the OSI and TCP/IP Model

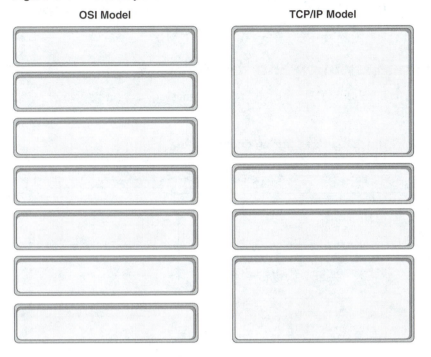

 Packet Tracer - Investigating the TCP/IP and OSI Models in Action (ITN 3.2.4.6/NB 3.1.4.6)

Lab - Researching RFCs (ITN 3.2.4.7/NB 3.2.2.3)

Moving Data in the Network

The data for one transmission—a file, a text, a picture, a video—does not travel from source to destination in one massive, uninterrupted stream of bits. In this section, we review protocol data units (PDUs), encapsulation, and the addressing that makes segmentation of a transmission possible.

Data Encapsulation and the PDUs

In Figure 3-2, label the PDUs at each layer as a message is sent "down the stack" in preparation for transmission.

Figure 3-2   The PDUs Used During Encapsulation

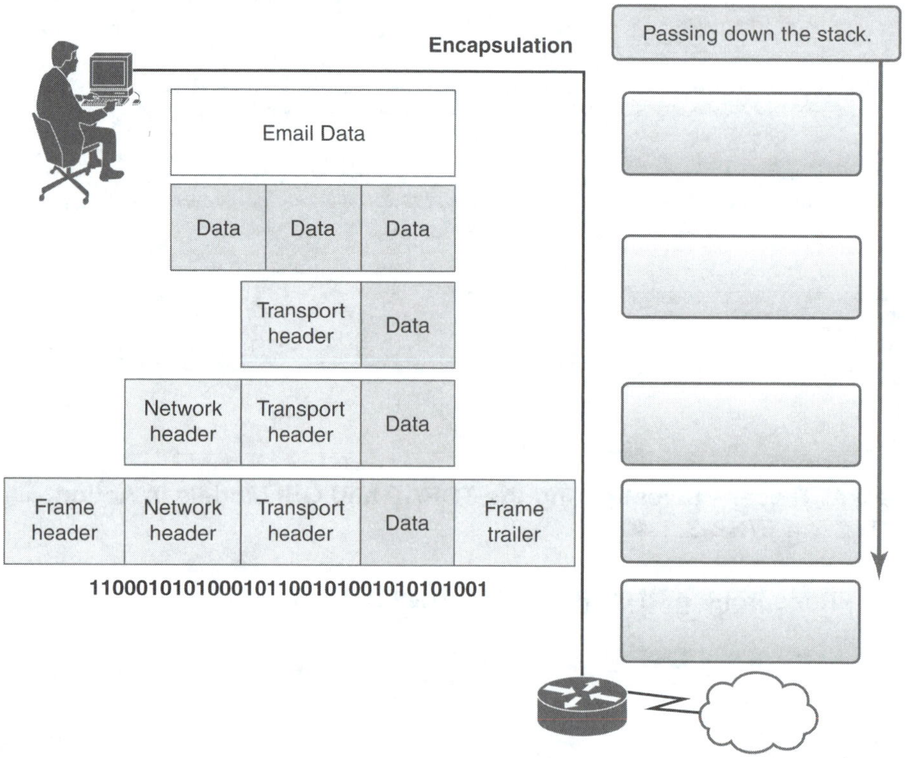

The Role of Addressing in Network Communications

Briefly describe the role of Layer 3 IP addresses.

Briefly describe the purpose of Layer 2 MAC addresses.

Briefly describe the purpose of the default gateway.

Lab - Using Wireshark to View Network Traffic (ITN/NB 3.3.3.4)

Packet Tracer - Explore a Network (ITN/NB 3.3.3.3)

CHAPTER 4

Network Access

Two layers within the OSI model are so closely tied that according to the TCP/IP model they are in essence one layer. In this chapter, we review the general functions of the physical and data link layers.

Physical Layer Protocols

Before any network communications can occur, a physical connection to a local network must be established first. A physical connection can be a wired or a wireless connection. The type of connection depends totally on the setup of the network.

Completion Exercise

_____ (NICs) connect a device to the network. Ethernet NICs are used for a wired connection, whereas _____ (WLAN NICs) are used for wireless.

Explain the difference between wired and wireless access to the media.

The process that data undergoes from source to destination is as follows:

- The ____ is _____ by the _____ layer, placed into _____ by the _____ layer, and further encapsulated as _____ by the data link layer.

- The _____ layer encodes the _____ and creates the electrical, optical, or radio wave signals that represent the ___.

- These signals are then sent on the _____ one at a time.

- The destination's _____ layer retrieves these individual signals from the _____, restores them to their bit representations, and passes the bits up to the _____ layer as a complete _____.

There are three basic forms of network media:

- _____: The signals are patterns of electrical pulses.

- _____: The signals are patterns of light.

- _____: The signals are patterns of microwave transmissions.

List at least four organizations responsible for defining and governing the physical layer hardware, media, encoding, and signaling standards.

- ■

- ■

- ■

- ■

- ■

-
-
-
-
-

Encoding is a method of converting a stream of data bits into a predefined "code." Common encoding methods include the following:

- _____: A 0 is represented by a high to low voltage transition, and a 1 is represented as a low to high voltage transition.

- _____ (NRZ): A 0 may be represented by one voltage level on the media, and a 1 might be represented by a different voltage on the media.

The method of representing the bits is called the _____ method. Signals can be transmitted in one of two ways:

- _____: Data signals are transmitted without an associated clock signal. Therefore, frames require start and stop indicator flags.

- _____: Data signals are sent along with a clock signal that occurs at evenly spaced time durations referred to as the bit time.

_____ is the process by which the characteristic of one wave (the signal) modifies another wave (the carrier). The following techniques have been widely used in transmitting data on a medium:

- _____ (___): A method of transmission in which the carrier frequency varies in accordance with the signal

- _____ (___): A transmission technique in which the amplitude of the carrier varies in accordance with the signal

- _____ (____): A technique in which an analog signal, such as a voice, is converted into a digital signal by sampling the signal's amplitude and expressing the different amplitudes as a binary number

Different physical media support the transfer of bits at different speeds. Data transfer is usually discussed in terms of _____ and _____.

_____ is the capacity of a medium to carry data and is usually measured in kilobits per second (Kbps) or megabits per second (Mbps). _____ is the measure of the transfer of bits across the media over a given period of time. Due to a number of factors, _____ usually does not match the specified _____ in physical layer implementations. Many factors influence throughput, including the following:

- The amount of _____

- The type of _____

- The _____ created by the number of network devices encountered between source and destination

_____ refers to the amount of time for data to travel from one given point to another.

Vocabulary Exercise: Matching

Match the definition on the left with a term on the right. This exercise is a one-to-one matching. Each definition has exactly one matching term.

Definitions

a. How 1s and 0s are represented on the media varies depending on encoding scheme.

b. How much useable data is transferred over a given amount of time.

c. The actual measure of data bits over a given period of time.

d. A method for converting streams of data bits into groupings of bits (predefined).

e. Arbitrarily spaced time duration for signals.

f. Evenly spaced time duration for signals.

g. Amount of data that is allowed by the medium to flow during a given set of time.

h. A technique to convert voice analog to digital signals.

i. Transmission method where the carrier frequency varies according to the signals sent.

k. Hardware devices, media, and connectors which transmit and carry bit signals.

Terms

____ asynchronous

____ signaling method

____ frame encoding

____ bandwidth

____ synchronous

____ frequency modulation

____ throughput

____ physical components

____ goodput

____ Pulse-code Modulation

Lab - Identifying Network Devices and Cabling (ITN 4.1.2.4/NB 9.3.1.4)

Network Media

The three major media used in today's networks are copper, fiber, and wireless. Copper media includes UTP, STP, and coaxial cable. Fiber-optic media includes single mode and multimode. Wireless media includes WiFi, Bluetooth, and WiMAX.

Copper Cabling Completion Exercise

Copper cabling is susceptible to what three types of interference?

-
-
-

What three strategies can reduce copper's susceptibility to interference?

-
-
-

What are the three major types of copper media?

-
-
-

_____-___ (___) cabling is the most common networking media. UTP cabling, terminated with _____ connectors, is used for interconnecting network hosts with intermediate networking devices, such as switches and routers.

_____ _____-___ (___) provides better noise protection than ____ cabling. However, compared to UTP cable, STP cable is significantly more _____ and difficult to _____. Like ____ cable, ___ uses an _____ connector.

_____ cable design has been adapted for use in the following:

- Wireless installations: Carries radio frequency (RF) energy between the antennas and the radio equipment

- Cable Internet installations: Currently used for the final connection to the customer's location and the wiring inside the customer's premises

Compare UTP, STP, and Coaxial Characteristics

In Table 4-1, indicate the cable type to which each characteristic belongs. Some characteristics may belong to more than one cable.

Table 4-1   Copper Media Characteristics

Characteristics	UTP	STP	Coaxial
Most common network media.			
Attaches antennas to wireless devices (can be bundled with fiber-optic cabling for two-way data transmission).			
Uses RJ-45 connectors and 4 pairs of wires to transmit data.			
Terminates with BNC N-type and F-type connectors.			
The new Ethernet 10-GB standard uses this form of copper media.			
Counters EMI and RFI by using shielding techniques and multiple twisted copper wires.			

UTP Cabling Completion Exercise

Explain the two ways UTP cable can limit the negative effect of crosstalk.

1. Cancellation: When two wires in an electrical circuit are placed close together, their magnetic fields are the exact opposite of each other and cancel each other out.

2. Varying the number of twists per wire pair: UTP cable must follow precise specifications governing how many twists or braids are permitted per meter (3.28 feet) of cable.

In Table 4-2, indicate which category of UTP cabling best fits the description.

Table 4-2   UTP Cable Categories

Description	Cat 3	Cat 5	Cat 5e	Cat 6
Supports 1000 Mbps.				
Most often used for phone lines.				
Supports 100 Mbps and can support 1000 Mbps, but it is not recommended.				
An added separator is between each pair of wires, allowing it to function at higher speeds.				
Supports 1000 Mbps to 10 Gbps, though 10 Gbps is not recommended.				
Used for voice communication.				
Used for data transmission. (Select more than one category.)				

Different situations may require UTP cables to be wired according to different wiring conventions. List and describe the three main cable types that use specific wiring conventions.

-

-

-

UTP Cable Pinouts

In Table 4-3, indicate the appropriate pin number for each wire color for the T568A and T568B standards.

Table 4-3   Compare UTP Cable Pinouts

T568A	T568B	Wire Color
		Green
		Green-white
		Brown
		Brown-white
		Orange
		Orange-white
		Blue
		Blue-white

Fiber-Optic Cabling Completion Exercise

Unlike copper wires, fiber-optic cable can transmit signals with less attenuation and is completely immune to ____ and ___ (acronyms).

List and describe the four types of networks that currently use fiber-optic cabling:

-

-

-

-

Although an optical fiber is very thin, it is composed of two kinds of glass and a protective outer shield. Specifically, these are the

- _____: Consists of pure glass and is the part of the fiber where light is carried.

- _____: The glass that surrounds the inner glass and acts as a mirror. This keeps the light pulses contained in the fiber in a phenomenon known as _____.

- _____: Typically a PVC covering that protects fiber.

Light pulses representing the transmitted data as bits on the media are generated by either

-

-

List, describe, and identify the color of the two major types of fiber optic.

-

■

List the three most popular network fiber-optic connectors.

■ _____: An older bayonet-style connector with a twist locking mechanism widely used with multimode fiber

■ _____: Widely adopted LAN and WAN connector that uses a push-pull mechanism to ensure positive insertion

■ _____: Sometimes called a little or local connector, is quickly growing in popularity due to its smaller size

Incorrect termination of fiber-optic media will result in diminished signaling distances or complete transmission failure. Three common types of fiber-optic termination and splicing errors are as follows:

■ _____: The fiber-optic media is not precisely aligned to one another when joined.

■ _____: The media does not completely touch at the splice or connection.

■ _____: The media ends are not well polished, or dirt is present at the termination.

What is a quick and inexpensive field test to find a broken fiber?

Describe three issue with fiber implementations:

■

■

■

Compare Single-Mode and Multimode Fiber

In Table 4-4, indicate whether the description applies the multimode or single-mode fiber.

Table 4-4   Multimode and Single-Mode Fiber

Fiber Optics Description	Multimode	Single Mode
Can help data travel approximately 1.24 miles or 2km/550 meters		
Used to connect long-distance telephony and cable TV applications		
Can travel approximately 62.5 miles or 100km/100,000 meters		
Uses LEDs as a data light source transmitter		
Uses lasers in a single stream as a data light source transmitter		
Used within a campus network		

Wireless Media Completion Exercise

Wireless media carry electromagnetic signals that represent the binary digits of data communications using radio or microwave frequencies. Wireless media provides the greatest mobility options of all media. However, wireless does have some areas of concern. Briefly describe each.

- Coverage area:

- Interference:

- Security:

List and describe the three common data communications standards that apply to wireless media:

-

-

-

A common wireless data implementation is enabling devices to wirelessly connect via a LAN. List and describe the two devices required for WLAN connectivity.

-

-

In Table 4-5, list the maximum speed and frequency of the 802.11 standards.

Table 4-5   802.11 Speed and Frequency

Standard	Maximum Speed	Frequency(ies)
802.11a		
802.11b		
802.11g		
802.11n		
802.11ac		
802.11ad		

Data Link Layer Protocols

The data link layer is responsible for the exchange of frames between nodes over a physical network media. It allows the upper layers to access the media and controls how data is placed and received on the media.

The Sublayers of the Data Link Layer

List and describe the two sublayers of the data link layer.

-

-

Label the Generic Frame Fields

There are several frame types, but all of them have some generic features in common. In Figure 4-1, label the generic frame fields.

Figure 4-1   Fields in the Generic Frame

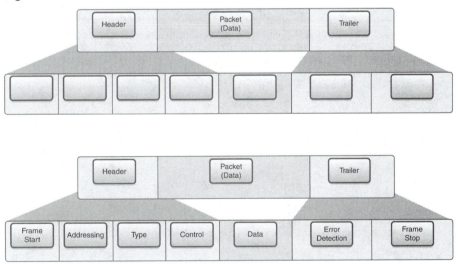

Identify the Data Link Layer Standards Organization

In Table 4-6, identify the organization responsible for the data link layer standard.

Table 4-6   Organizations Responsible for Data Link Standards

Standard	IEEE	ITU-T	ISO	ANSI
HDLC				
802.3 Ethernet				
ADSL				
ISDN				

Standard	IEEE	ITU-T	ISO	ANSI
802.15 Bluetooth				
802.11 Wireless				
FDDI MAC				
FDDI				

Media Access Control

Regulating the placement of data frames onto the media is controlled by the media access control sublayer. There are different ways to regulate placing frames onto the media. The protocols at the data link layer define the rules for access to different media.

Topologies and Access Methods Completion Exercise

Among the different implementations of the data link layer protocols, there are different methods of controlling access to the media. These media access control techniques define whether and how the nodes share the media. The actual media access control method used depends on the following:

- _____: How the connection between the nodes appears to the data link layer.

- _____: How the nodes share the media. The media sharing can be point to point, such as in WAN connections, or shared, such as in LAN networks.

Describe the two types of topologies:

- Physical topology:

- Logical topology:

List and describe the main WAN physical topologies:

-

-

-

-

In point-to-point networks, data can flow in one of two ways:

- _____: Both devices can both transmit and receive on the media but cannot do so simultaneously.

- _____: Both devices can transmit and receive on the media at the same time.

List and describe the main physical topologies used in shared media LANs.

■

■

■

■

Rules govern how devices share media. List and describe the two basic media access control methods for shared media:

■

■

When using a nondeterministic contention-based method, a network device can attempt to access the medium whenever it has data to send. To prevent complete chaos on the media, these methods use a _____ (   ) process to first detect whether the media is carrying a signal.

List and describe the two CSMA methods used for resolving media contention. Include an example of each.

■

■

Label the Ethernet Frame Fields

In Figure 4-2, label the Ethernet frame fields.

Figure 4-2   Fields in the Ethernet Frame

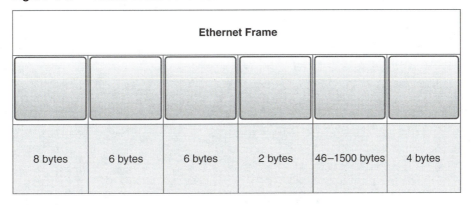

Label the PPP Frame Fields

In Figure 4-3, label the PPP frame fields.

Figure 4-3   Fields in the PPP Frame

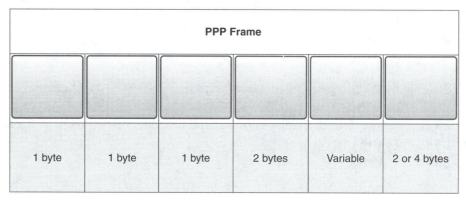

PPP Frame					
1 byte	1 byte	1 byte	2 bytes	Variable	2 or 4 bytes

Label the 802.11 Wireless Frame Fields

In Figure 4-4, label the 802.11 frame fields.

Figure 4-4   Fields in the 802.11 Frame

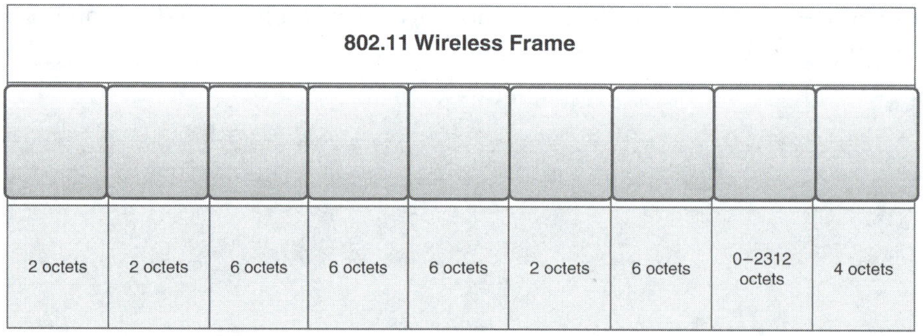

802.11 Wireless Frame								
2 octets	2 octets	6 octets	6 octets	6 octets	2 octets	6 octets	0–2312 octets	4 octets

CHAPTER 5

Ethernet

Ethernet is now the dominant LAN technology. Ethernet operates in the data link layer and the physical layer. Ethernet standards define both the Layer 2 protocols and the Layer 1 technologies. In this chapter, we review the characteristics and operation of Ethernet.

Ethernet Protocol

In this section, we review the Ethernet protocol, its operation, frame format, and the relationship between the MAC and IP addresses.

Ethernet Operation Completion Exercise

List and describe the two primary responsibilities of the Ethernet MAC sublayer:

-

-

List and describe the three primary functions of data encapsulation:

-

-

-

In your own words, explain the operation of CSMA/CD.

Describe the structure of a MAC address including the two major parts, the number of bits, the number of bytes, and the number of hexadecimal digits.

In Table 5-1, indicate which sublayer the characteristic describes.

Table 5-1   MAC and LLC Characteristics

Characteristic	MAC	LLC
Controls the network interface card through software drivers		
Works with hardware to support bandwidth requirements (checks for errors in bits sent and received)		
Remains relatively independent of physical equipment		
Controls access to the media through signaling and physical media standards requirements		
Supports Ethernet technology by using CSMA/CD or CSMA/CA		
Works with the upper layers to add application information for delivery of data to higher-level protocols		

Identify the Ethernet Frame Attributes: Matching

Match the Ethernet frame attribute on the left with a field on the right. This exercise is a one-to-one matching. Each attribute has exactly one matching field.

Frame Attributes

a. Synchronizes sending and receiving devices for frame delivery

b. Detects errors in an Ethernet frame

c. Describes which higher-level protocol has been used

d. Notifies destinations to get ready for a new frame

e. The frame's originating NIC or interface MAC address

f. Uses Pad to increase this frame field to at least 64 bytes

g. Assists a host in determining if the frame received is addressed to them

Fields

____ Type

____ Source Address

____ Start of Frame Delimiter

____ Frame Check Sequence

____ Preamble

____ Destination Address

____ 802.2 Header and Data

Comparing Decimal, Binary, and Hexadecimal Digits

MAC addresses and IPv6 addresses are both represented in hexadecimal digits. As a networking student, you should become fluent in conversion between decimal, binary, and hexadecimal digits. In Table 5-2, list the equivalent value of each decimal digit in the Binary and Hexadecimal columns. Then list the equivalent value of each decimal digit in the Binary and Hexadecimal columns.

Table 5-2   Decimal, Binary, and Hexadecimal Digits

Decimal	Binary	Hexadecimal
0	0000	0
1		
2		
3		
4		
5		
6		
7		
8		
9		
10		
11		
12		
13		
14		
15		

Lab - Using Wireshark to Examine Ethernet Frames (ITN 5.1.4.3/NB 10.1.4.3)

Packet Tracer - Identify MAC and IP Addresses (ITN 5.1.4.4/NB 10.1.4.4)

Address Resolution Protocol

In Ethernet LAN environments, a device must first know the destination MAC address before it can send data. The Address Resolution Protocol (ARP) provides rules for how a device learns the destination MAC address.

Completion Exercise

List the two basic functions of ARP:

■

■

For a frame to be placed on the LAN media, it must have a _____ MAC address. When a packet is sent to the data link layer to be encapsulated into a frame, the node refers to the _____ table or _____ cache in its memory to find the data link layer address that is mapped to the _____ IPv4 address. If this mapping is found in the table, the node can encapsulate the _____ and send out the frame.

The ARP table is maintained dynamically. Briefly explain the two ways a device can gather MAC addresses.

-

-

Entries in the ARP table are time stamped. What happens when the time stamp expires?

What command(s) will display the ARP table on a Cisco router?

What command will display the ARP table on a Windows 7 PC?

Two issues with ARP operation are overhead and security. Briefly describe each.

Overhead on the Media

Security

Identify the MAC and IP Addresses

In Figure 5-1, PC1 is sending data to PC2. Fill in the appropriate addresses that will be encapsulated in the frame when PC1 sends the frame out.

Figure 5-1   MAC and IP Addresses in the Frame

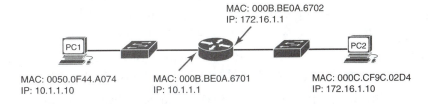

MAC: 000B.BE0A.6702
IP: 172.16.1.1

MAC: 0050.0F44.A074
IP: 10.1.1.10

MAC: 000B.BE0A.6701
IP: 10.1.1.1

MAC: 000C.CF9C.02D4
IP: 172.16.1.10

Destination MAC Address	Source MAC Address	Source IP Address	Destination IP Address	Data	Trailer

Lab - Observing ARP with the Windows CLI, IOS CLI, and Wireshark (ITN 5.2.1.7/NB 10.2.1.8)

Packet Tracer - Examine the ARP Table (ITN 5.2.1.7/NB 10.2.1.7)

LAN Switches

A Layer 2 LAN switch performs switching and filtering based only on the OSI data link layer (Layer 2) MAC address. A switch is completely transparent to network protocols and user applications. A Layer 2 switch builds a MAC address table that it uses to make forwarding decisions. Layer 2 switches depend on routers to pass data between independent IP subnetworks.

Building the MAC Address Table

Referring to Figure 5-2, circle the correct word in the following steps that explain the process of how a switch builds its MAC address table.

Figure 5-2   Switch and Two PC Topology

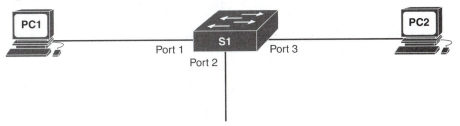

Port 1   S1   Port 3
Port 2

Step 1.   The switch receives a (unicast/broadcast) frame from PC1 on Port 1.

Step 2.   The switch enters the (source/destination) (MAC/IP) address of (PC1/PC2) and the switch port that received the frame into the address table.

Step 3.   Because the destination address is a (unicast/broadcast), the switch floods the frame to all ports, except the port on which it received the frame.

Step 4.   The destination device replies to the (unicast/broadcast) with a (unicast/broadcast) frame addressed to PC1.

Step 5.   The switch enters the (source/destination) (MAC/IP) address of (PC1/PC2) and the port number of the switch port that received the frame into the address table. The destination address of the frame and its associated port is found in the MAC address table.

True or False: The switch can now forward frames between source and destination devices without flooding because it has entries in the address table that identify the associated ports.

Switching Concepts Completion Exercise

Explain the difference between half duplex and full duplex.

What are the three duplex settings supported by Cisco switches? What are the default settings for various port speeds?

What is the purpose of the switch interface configuration command **mdix auto**?

Describe the two basic switch forwarding methods. Include a description of the two variants of one of the methods.

■

■

List and explain the difference between the two methods of memory buffering.

Comparing Switch Forwarding Methods

In Table 5-3, indicate which forwarding method applies to the characteristic described.

Table 5-3   Frame Forwarding Methods

Switch Frame Forwarding Methods Descriptions	Store-and-Forward	Cut-Through
No error checking on frames is performed by the switch before releasing the frame out of its ports.		
The destination network interface card (NIC) discards any incomplete frames using this frame forwarding method.		
Buffers frames until the full frame has been received by the switch.		
Checks the frame for errors before releasing it out of its switch ports; if the full frame was not received, the switch discards it.		
The faster switching method, but may produce more errors in data integrity; therefore, more bandwidth may be consumed.		
A great method to use to conserve bandwidth on your network.		

Forward the Frame

Use the information in the following three figures to answer the questions.

Note: For simplicity, the MAC addresses are simulated using only two hexadecimal digits instead of the full six hexadecimal digits.

In Figure 5-3, PC 0F is sending a frame to PC 0C. Based on the MAC table entries, answer the questions that follow.

Figure 5-3   Switch Frame Forwarding: Scenario 1

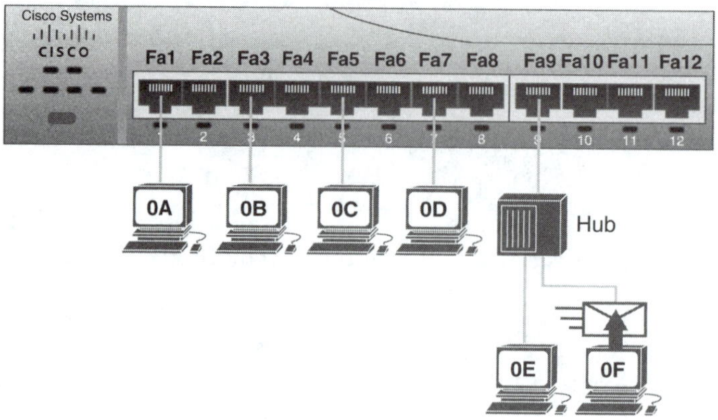

Frame

Preamble	Destination MAC	Source MAC	Length Type	Encapsulated Data	End of Frame
	0C	0F			

MAC Table

Fa1	Fa2	Fa3	Fa4	Fa5	Fa6	Fa7	Fa8	Fa9	Fa10	Fa11	Fa12
								0E 0F			

The switch will forward the frame out which port?

Indicate which of the following statements are true when the switch forwards the frame in Figure 5-3.

Statement	True?
The switch adds the source MAC address to the MAC table.	
The frame is a broadcast frame and will be forwarded to all ports.	
The frame is a unicast frame and will be sent to a specific port only.	
The frame is a unicast frame and will be flooded out all ports.	
The frame is a unicast frame, but it will be dropped by the switch.	

In Figure 5-4, PC 0E is sending a frame to PC 0F. Based on the MAC table entries, answer the questions that follow.

Figure 5-4   Switch Frame Forwarding: Scenario 2

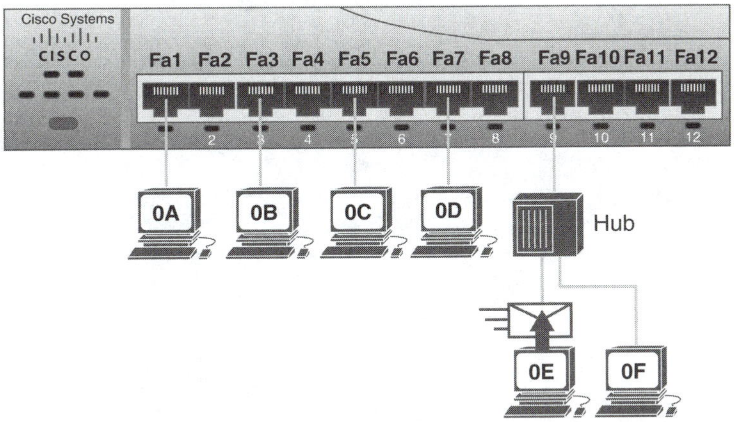

Frame

Preamble	Destination MAC	Source MAC	Length Type	Encapsulated Data	End of Frame
	0F	0E			

MAC Table

Fa1	Fa2	Fa3	Fa4	Fa5	Fa6	Fa7	Fa8	Fa9	Fa10	Fa11	Fa12
						0D		0F			

The switch forwards the frame out which port?

_____

Indicate which of the following statements are true when the switch forwards the frame in Figure 5-4.

Statement	True?
The switch adds the source MAC address to the MAC table.	
The frame is a broadcast frame and will be forwarded to all ports.	
The frame is a unicast frame and will be sent to a specific port only.	
The frame is a unicast frame and will be flooded out all ports.	
The frame is a unicast frame, but it will be dropped by the switch.	

In Figure 5-5, PC 0A is sending a frame to PC 0E. Based on the MAC table entries, answer the questions that follow.

Figure 5-5   Switch Frame Forwarding: Scenario 3

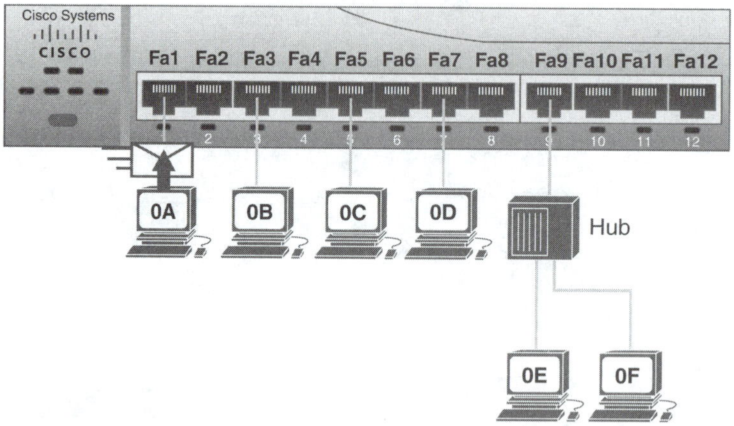

Frame

Preamble	Destination MAC	Source MAC	Length Type	Encapsulated Data	End of Frame
	0E	0A			

MAC Table

Fa1	Fa2	Fa3	Fa4	Fa5	Fa6	Fa7	Fa8	Fa9	Fa10	Fa11	Fa12
		0B						0E	0F		

The switch forwards the frame out which port? ___

Indicate which of the following statements are true when the switch forwards the frame in Figure 5-5.

Statement	True?
The switch adds the source MAC address to the MAC table.	
The frame is a broadcast frame and will be forwarded to all ports.	
The frame is a unicast frame and will be sent to a specific port only.	
The frame is a unicast frame and will be flooded out all ports.	
The frame is a unicast frame, but it will be dropped by the switch.	

Lab - Viewing the Switch MAC Address Table (ITN 5.3.1.10/NB 10.3.1.10)

Layer 3 Switching Concepts Completion Exercise

Briefly explain the difference between a Layer 2 and a Layer 3 switch.

Briefly explain the operation of Cisco Express Forwarding (CEF).

■

■

Describe the three major types of Layer 3 interfaces.

■ Switch Virtual Interface (SVI):

■ Routed Port:

■ Layer 3 EtherChannel:

Layer 3 Switch Configuration

In Figure 5-6, PC1 and PC2 are attached to L3Sw1, which is a Catalyst 3560 Layer 3 switch. L3Sw1 is connected to the gateway router that provides connectivity to the Internet.

Figure 5-6   Layer 3 Switch Topology

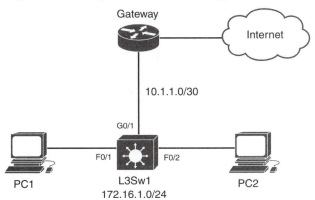

L3Sw1 is already configured with the following commands:

```
interface vlan 1
ip address 172.16.1.1 255.255.255.0
no shutdown
```

These commands configure L3Sw1 as a Layer 3 device on the 172.16.1.0/24 network. Assuming PC1 and PC2 are configured, they can both ping L3Sw1 at 172.16.1.1. However, L3Sw1 is connected to the Gateway router on the 10.1.1.0/30 network, which is a different network than 172.16.1.0/24. PC1 and PC2 cannot access the Internet. L3Sw1 will have to be configured as a Layer 3 switch to route between these two networks.

What global configuration command enables Layer 3 switching on L3Sw1?

```
L3Sw1(config)#
```

What commands will configure L3Sw1 to be a part of the 10.1.1.0/30 network? Assume L3Sw1 will use the IP address 10.1.1.2.

```
L3Sw1(config)#
L3Sw1(config-if)#
L3Sw1(config-if)#
L3Sw1(config-if)#
```

With these commands PC1 and PC2 should be able to access the Internet (assuming the gateway router is correctly configured).

Packet Tracer
☐ Activity

Packet Tracer - Configure Layer 3 Switches (ITN 5.3.3.5/NB 10.3.3.5)

CHAPTER 6

Network Layer

The protocols of the OSI model network layer specify addressing and processes that enable transport layer data to be packaged and transported. The network layer encapsulation enables data to be passed to a destination within a network (or on another network) with minimum overhead. In this chapter, we review the role of the network layer including the protocols, basic routing concepts, the role of the router, and configuring a Cisco router.

Network Layer Protocols

The network layer provides services to allow end devices to exchange data across the network. To accomplish this end-to-end transport, the network layer uses a set of protocols.

The Processes of the Network Layer

Describe the four basic processes of the network layer.

- Addressing end devices:

- Encapsulation:

- Routing:

- De-encapsulation:

Characteristics of the IP Protocol

In Table 6-1, indicate to which category the characteristic of the IP protocol belongs.

Table 6-1   IP Protocol Characteristics

Characteristic	Connectionless	Best-Effort Delivery	Media Independent
No contact is made with the destination host before sending a packet.			
Packet delivery is not guaranteed.			
Will adjust the size of the packet sent depending on what type of network access will be used.			
Fiber-optic cabling, satellites, and wireless can all be used to route the same packet.			
Will send a packet even if the destination host is not able to receive it.			
Does not guarantee that the packet will be delivered without errors.			

Fields of the IPv4 Packet: Matching

Match the IPv4 packet attribute on the left with a field on the right. This exercise is a one-to-one matching. Each attribute has exactly one matching field.

IPv4 Packet Attributes

    a. Maximum value is 65535 bytes.

    b. Identifies the IP address of the recipient host.

    c. Commonly referred to as hop count.

    d. Always set to 0100 for IPv4.

    e. Identifies the number of 32-bit words in the header.

    f. Error-checks the IP header (if incorrect, discards the packet).

    g. Identifies the priority of each packet.

    h. Identifies the IP address of the sending host.

    i. Identifies the upper-layer protocol to be used next.

Fields

____ Differentiated Services

____ Internet Header Length

____ Header Checksum

____ Time-To-Live

____ Version

____ Protocol

____ Destination IP Address

____ Total Length

____ Source IP Address

Fields of the IPv6 Packet: Matching

Match the IPv6 packet attribute on the left with a field on the right. This exercise is a one-to-one matching. Each attribute has exactly one matching field.

IPv6 Packet Attributes

    a. Can be set to use the same pathway flow so that packets are not reordered upon delivery.

    b. Defines the application type to the upper-layer protocol.

    c. Defines the packet fragment size.

    d. When this value reaches 0, the sender is notified that the packet was not delivered.

    e. Classifies packets for congestion control.

    f. Identifies the packet under a field set to 0110.

Fields

____ Version

____ Hop Limit

____ Flow Label

____ Payload Length

____ Next Header

____ Traffic Class

Routing

Routing is the network layer process responsible for forwarding packets from the source to the destination based on the IPv4 or IPv6 address in the packet header. Routers perform this function by looking up the destination network in a routing table. Hosts also have a routing table.

How a Host Routes Packets Completion Exercise

A host can send a packet to itself at IP address _____, to a ____ host if the host is on the same network, or to a _____ host that does not share the same network address. How does a host determine if the packet is local or remote?

When a source device sends a packet to a remote destination device, then the help of routers and routing is needed. The router connected to the local network segment is referred to as the _____.

IPv4 hosts have a routing table they use to route packets. Example 6-1 shows the routing table for a Windows 7 PC.

Example 6-1   Windows 7 PC Routing Table

```
C:\>
<output omitted>
IPv4 Route Table
===========================================================================
Active Routes:
Network Destination          Netmask          Gateway        Interface    Metric
          0.0.0.0            0.0.0.0         10.10.10.1     10.10.10.112      10
       10.10.10.0      255.255.255.0         On-link        10.10.10.112     266
     10.10.10.112    255.255.255.255         On-link        10.10.10.112     266
     10.10.10.255    255.255.255.255         On-link        10.10.10.112     266
        127.0.0.0          255.0.0.0         On-link           127.0.0.1     306
        127.0.0.1    255.255.255.255         On-link           127.0.0.1     306
  127.255.255.255    255.255.255.255         On-link           127.0.0.1     306
        224.0.0.0          240.0.0.0         On-link           127.0.0.1     306
        224.0.0.0          240.0.0.0         On-link        10.10.10.112     266
  255.255.255.255    255.255.255.255         On-link           127.0.0.1     306
  255.255.255.255    255.255.255.255         On-link        10.10.10.112     266
===========================================================================
<output omitted>
```

What Windows 7 commands will display this table?

Which entry in the routing table is the default route?

Which entries in the routing table are loopback addresses?

Which entry in the routing table is the address of the host that is displaying the routing table shown in Example 6-1?

Which entry in the routing table is the network address for the host?

In Table 6-1, indicate to which column the following descriptions refer.

Table 6-1   The Columns of a Windows PC Routing Tabling

Column	Description
	Lists the cost of each route and is used to determine the best route to a destination.
	Lists a subnet mask that informs the host how to determine the network and the host portions of the IP address.
	Lists the address used by the local computer to get to a remote network destination. If a destination is directly reachable, it will show as "on-link" in this column.
	Lists the reachable networks.
	Lists the address of the physical interface used to send the packet to the gateway that is used to reach the network destination.

Routing Table Entry: Matching

Refer to the following routing table entry:

```
D 10.1.1.0/24 [90/2170112] via 209.165.200.226, 00:00:05, Serial0/0/0
```

Match the description on the left with the entry section on the right. This exercise is a one-to-one matching. Each description has exactly one matching entry section.

Item Description

  a. Metric: Identifies the value assigned to reach the remote network. Lower values indicate preferred routes.

  b. Destination network: Identifies the address of the remote network.

  c. Outgoing interface: Identifies the exit interface to use to forward a packet toward the final destination.

  d. Next hop: Identifies the IP address of the next router to forward the packet.

  e. Administrative distance: Identifies the trustworthiness of the route source.

  f. Route time stamp: Identifies when the route was last heard from.

  g. Route source: Identifies how the route was learned.

Item Within Route Entry

____ 10.1.1.0/24

____ D

____ 90

____ 209.165.200.226

____ Serial0/0/0

____ 2170112

____ 00:00:005

 Lab - View Host Routing Tables (ITN/NB 6.2.2.8)

Routers

Regardless of their function, size, or complexity, all router models are essentially computers that require an operating system (OS), a central processing unit (CPU), random-access memory (RAM), and a boot process.

Identify Router Components

Match the function/description on the left with the router component on the right. This exercise is a one-to-one matching. Each function/description has exactly one matching router component.

Function/Description

  a. A way to remotely access the CLI across a network interface

  b. Connects routers to external networks, usually over a large distance

  c. A local port which uses USB or low-speed, serial connections to manage network devices

  d. A port to manage routers (using telephone lines and modems)

  e. Connects computers, switches, and routers for internal networking

Router Component

____ AUX port

____ WAN interface

____ LAN interface

____ Console port

____ Telnet or SSH

Lab - Exploring Router Physical Characteristics (ITN/NB 6.3.1.9)

Packet Tracer - Exploring Internetworking Devices (ITN/NB 6.3.1.10)

Router Boot Process Exercise

Figure 6-1 displays an incomplete diagram of the default boot sequence of a router. Provide details where information is missing.

Figure 6-1   Diagram of the Router Boot Sequence

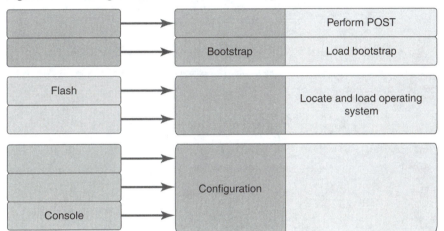

Interpreting the show version Command Exercise

Figure 6-2 displays the output from the **show version** command with parts of the output numbered. Choose the correct label description for each number shown in the figure.

Figure 6-2 **show version Command**

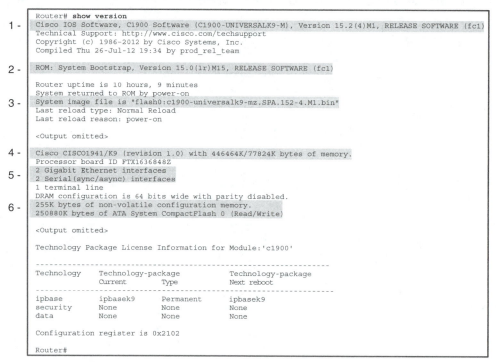

Figure 6-2 Label Description

_____ Cisco IOS software currently in RAM

_____ Displays the type of CPU on this router and the amount of DRAM

_____ Displays the physical interfaces on the router

_____ Displays where the bootstrap program is located and loaded the Cisco IOS

_____ Displays the amount of NVRAM and flash memory on the router

_____ Software initially used to boot the router

Configuring a Cisco Router

Cisco routers and Cisco switches have many similarities. They support a similar modal operating system, support similar command structures, and support many of the same commands. In addition, both devices have identical initial configuration steps when implementing them in a network.

Basic Router Configuration Exercise

When designing a new network or mapping an existing network, it is important to document the network. At a minimum, the documentation should include a topology map of the network and an addressing table that lists the following information:

- Device names

- Interface

- IP address and subnet mask

- Default gateway address for end devices such as PCs

Refer to the topology shown in Figure 6-3 and the addressing scheme in Table 6-2 that follows it to complete this basic configuration exercise.

Figure 6-3   Chapter 6 Topology

Table 6-2   Addressing Table for Chapter 6 Topology

Device	Interface	IP Address	Subnet Mask	Default Gateway
R1	G0/0	172.16.0.1	255.255.0.0	N/A
	S0/0/0	172.17.0.1	255.255.0.0	N/A
R2	G0/0	172.18.0.1	255.255.0.0	N/A
	S0/0/0	172.17.0.2	255.255.0.0	N/A
PC1	NIC	172.16.0.10	255.255.0.0	172.16.0.1
PC2	NIC	172.18.0.10	255.255.0.0	172.18.0.1

When configuring a router, certain basic tasks are performed, including the following:

- Naming the router

- Setting passwords

- Configuring interfaces

- Configuring a banner

- Saving changes on a router

- Verifying basic configuration and router operations

The first prompt is at user mode and will allow you to view the state of the router. What major limitation does this mode have?

What is the router prompt for this mode?

The **enable** command is used to enter the privileged mode. What is the major difference between this mode and the previous mode?

What is the router prompt for this mode?

Applying a Basic Configuration

The following exercise walks you through a basic configuration.

First, enter global configuration mode:

```
Router#
```

Next, apply a unique host name to the router. Use R1 for this example.

```
Router(config)#
```

Now, configure the encrypted password that is to be used to enter privileged EXEC mode. Use **class** as the password.

```
Router(config)#
```

Next, configure the console and Telnet lines with the password cisco. The console commands follow:

```
R1(config)#
R1(config-line)#
R1(config-line)#
```

The Telnet lines use similar commands:

```
R1(config)#
R1(config-line)#
R1(config-line)#
```

From global configuration mode, configure the message-of-the-day banner. Use the following text: Authorized Access Only. A delimiting character such as a # is used at the beginning and at the end of the message.

```
R1(config)#
```

What is the purpose of the message of the day?

Refer to Figure 6-3 for the correct interface designations. What is the command to enter interface configuration mode for R1's serial interface?

```
R1(config)#
```

Enter the command to configure the IP address using the address in Table 6-2:

```
R1(config-if)#
```

Describe the interface with the following text: Link to R2.

```
R1(config-if)#
```

Activate the interface:

```
Router(config-if)#
```

Now enter the commands to configure and activate the Gigabit Ethernet interface on R1. Use the following description text: R1 LAN.

```
R1(config)#
R1(config-if)#
R1(config-if)#
R1(config-if)#
```

What command will save the current configuration?

```
Router#
```

Verifying Basic Router Configuration

Basic configurations can be verified using a few basic **show** commands. In Table 6-3, list the command in the left column that fits the description in the right column.

Table 6-3   Basic Router Configuration Verification Commands

Command	Description
	Displays the current running configuration that is stored in RAM
	Displays the startup configuration file stored in NVRAM
	Displays the routing table that the IOS is currently using to choose the best path to its destination networks
	Displays all the interface configuration parameters and statistics
	Displays abbreviated interface configuration information, including IP address and interface status

Lab - Initializing and Reloading a Router and Switch (ITN/NB)

Video Demonstration - The Router Boot Process (ITN/NB 6.3.2.5)

Packet Tracer - Configure Initial Router Settings (ITN/NB 6.4.1.2)

Packet Tracer - Connect a Router to a LAN (ITN/NB 6.4.3.3)

Packet Tracer - Troubleshooting Default Gateway Issues (ITN/NB 6.4.3.4)

Packet Tracer - Skills Integration Challenge (ITN/NB 6.4.3.5)

CHAPTER 7

Transport Layer

On a single device, people can use multiple applications and services such as email, the Web, and instant messaging to send messages or retrieve information. The transport layer enables these multiple applications to send data over the network at the same time and ensures that, if necessary, all the data is received by the destination. In this chapter, we review the role of the transport layer in encapsulating application data for use by the network layer.

Transport Layer Protocols

The transport layer is responsible for establishing a temporary communication session between two applications and delivering data between them. In TCP/IP, this process is handled by two very different transport layer protocols: Transmission Control Protocol (TCP) and User Datagram Protocol (UDP).

Transportation of Data Completion Exercise

The primary responsibilities of transport layer protocols are

- Tracking the individual communication between _____ on the source and destination hosts

- _____ data for manageability and reassembling _____ data into streams of application data at the destination

- Identifying the proper _____ for each communication stream

Briefly explain how the transport layer can handle delivery of a video stream while you are also sending an email and chatting with your friends.

TCP/IP provides two transport layer protocols. ____ is considered a _____, full-featured transport layer protocol, which ensures that all the data arrives at the destination. In contrast, UDP is a very simple transport layer protocol that does not provide for any _____.

What are the three basic TCP operations that ensure reliability?

-

-

-

List two examples of applications that use TCP.

Briefly explain what is meant by best-effort delivery and give an example.

Introducing TCP and UDP

TCP is a _____-oriented protocol that negotiates and establishes a permanent _____ _____ between source and destination. The _____ is terminated only after all communication is completed.

TCP can implement a method to ensure _____ delivery of the data. In networking terms, _____ means ensuring that each piece of data that the source sends arrives at the destination. TCP can ensure that all pieces reach their destination by having the source device _____ lost or corrupted data.

Why might data arrive at the destination in the wrong order?

How does TCP ensure data is reassembled in order?

Explain the purpose of flow control.

In Table 7-1, indicate which transport layer protocol is described by the characteristic.

Table 7-1   TCP and UDP Characteristics

Characteristic	TCP	UDP
Flow control		
Ordered delivery		
No ordered delivery		
Sequenced message segments		
Three-way handshake		
Less overhead		
Fast transmission requirements		
Guaranteed delivery		
No acknowledgement of receipt		
Connectionless		

TCP and UDP

The key distinction between TCP and UDP is reliability. TCP uses connection-oriented sessions. The main purpose of these sessions is to ensure that the destination receives all the data intact. UDP, in contrast, is a simple protocol that provides the basic transport layer functions without all the overhead of TCP because it is not connection oriented and does not offer the sophisticated retransmission, sequencing, and flow-control mechanisms that provide reliability.

TCP Communication

To establish a TCP connection, the source and destination perform a three-way handshake, which does the following:

- Establishes that the destination device is present on the network

- Verifies that the destination device has an active service and is accepting requests on the port number that the source intends to use for the session

- Informs the destination device that the source client intends to establish a communication session on that port number

In Figure 7-1, fill in the four blanks with one of the following options. Not all options are used:

- Send ACK

- Send SYN

- SYN received

- Established, ACK

- ACK received

- SYN, ACK received

- Send SYN, ACK

Figure 7-1   The TCP Three-Way Handshake

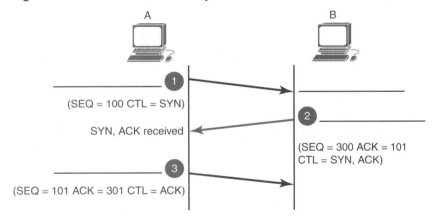

To terminate a single conversation supported by TCP, four exchanges are needed to end both sessions, as shown in Figure 7-1. Fill in the eight blanks with one of the following options. Not all options are used. Options may be used more than once:

- Send ACK

- Send FIN

- Send SYN

- ACK received

- FIN received

- SYN received

Figure 7-2   The TCP Session-Termination Process

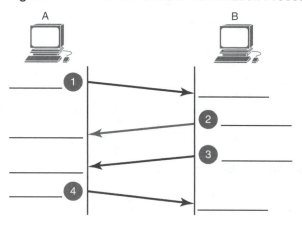

 Lab - Using Wireshark to Observe the TCP 3-Way Handshake (ITN 7.2.1.8/NB 5.2.1.8)

UDP Communication

Directions: In the following paragraphs, circle the correct answer.

UDP is a [simple/complex] protocol that provides the basic transport layer functions. It has much [higher/lower] overhead than TCP because it is does not offer the sophisticated retransmission, sequencing, and flow-control mechanisms that provide reliability. UDP makes it very desirable for applications that are [sensitive/not sensitive] to delays in the transmission of data.

Because UDP is [connectionless/connection oriented], sessions are [established/not established] before communication takes place.

When multiple datagrams are sent to a destination, they may take different paths and arrive in the wrong order. UDP [has no way to reorder/reorders] datagrams into their transmission order because it [does not track/tracks] sequence numbers.

Lab - Using Wireshark to Examine a UDP DNS Capture (ITN 7.2.3.5/NB 5.2.3.5)

TCP or UDP, That Is the Question

In Table 7-1, indicate which transport protocol is used by each of the application layer protocols.

Table 7-1   Classifying Transport Layer Protocols

Application	TCP	UDP	Both
SNMP			
FTP			
IPTV			
HTTP			
DNS			
DHCP			
Telnet			
VoIP			
TFTP			
SMTP			

Lab - Using Wireshark to Examine FTP and TFTP Captures (ITN 7.2.4.3/NB 5.2.4.3

CHAPTER 8

IP Addressing

Designing, implementing, and managing an effective IP addressing plan ensures that networks can operate effectively and efficiently. Addressing is a key function of network layer protocols that enables data communication between hosts. Both Internet Protocol Version 4 (IPv4) and Internet Protocol Version 6 (IPv6) provide hierarchical addressing for packets that carry data. In this chapter, we review the structure of IP addresses and their application to the construction and testing of IP networks and subnetworks.

IPv4 Network Addresses

At the most basic level, all data is represented in <u>binary digits</u> or bits. Therefore, both IPv4 and IPv6 addresses are simply a series of 1s and 0s that, when grouped logically, can be used to represent the location of a specific device or a grouping of devices—a network. Because numbering systems are foundational to computer and networking code, your ability to convert between binary, hexadecimal, and decimal numbering systems is an essential skill.

IPv4 Address Structure

In IPv4, addresses are ___-bit binary numbers. However, for ease of use by people, binary patterns representing IPv4 addresses are expressed as _____. This is first accomplished by separating each _____ (8 bits) of the ___-bit binary pattern, called an _____, with a dot. It is called an _____ because each decimal number represents 1 _____ or 8 bits.

In Table 8-1, convert the binary addresses into their dotted-decimal equivalent.

Table 8-1   Binary to Decimal IPv4 Address Conversion

IPv4 Binary Representation	IPv4 Dotted-Decimal Representation
11000000 10101000 00001010 00110010	
10101100 00010000 00100011 00010111	
00001010 01100100 11001000 00110010	
01000000 01100110 00010110 10000010	
11010001 10100101 11001111 11110101	

In Table 8-2, convert the dotted-decimal addresses into their binary equivalent.

Table 8-2   Decimal to Binary IPv4 Address Conversion

IPv4 Binary Representation	IPv4 Dotted-Decimal Representation
	198.133.219.15
	192.127.7.63
	128.107.25.100
	172.31.32.64
	10.86.175.27

With your Cisco user login, you have access to the Binary Game at The Cisco Learning Network in either PC format

https://learningnetwork.cisco.com/docs/DOC-1803

or for mobile devices (shown in Figure 8-1):

https://learningnetwork.cisco.com/docs/DOC-11119

This game is a fun and effective way to learn to convert 8-bit binary numbers.

Figure 8-1   Binary Game for Mobile Devices

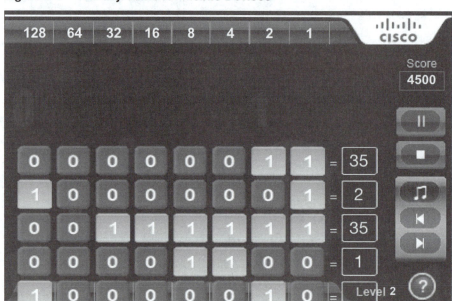

IPv4 Subnet Mask

Understanding binary notation is important when determining whether two hosts are in the same network. Within the 32-bit IPv4 address, a portion of the far-left bits makes up the network and the remainder of the far-right bits makes up the host. The subnet mask is used to mark this network|host bit boundary. Starting from the far-left bits, the subnet mask is represented by a series of 1s. A 1 indicates a network bit. Where the series of 1s ends and the series of 0s begins marks the bit boundary, as shown in Example 8-1.

Example 8-1   Bit Boundaries for IPv4 Address 10.32.48.240/11

```
IPv4 Address:              00001010.00100000.00110000.11110000
Subnet Mask:               11111111.11100000.00000000.00000000
Network Address:           00001010.00100000.00000000.00000000
```

The dotted-decimal format for a /11 subnet mask is 255.224.0.0 because /11 means that the first 11 far-left bits are 1s. Converted to dotted decimal, /11 is 255.224.0.0. The 224 is called the last nonzero octet in the subnet mask. You should know by now how to convert all the possible nonzero octets in a subnet mask from binary to decimal.

The Last Nonzero Octet

Fill in Table 8-3 with the correct decimal value for each bit position and for the last nonzero octet in a subnet mask.

Table 8-3   The Last Nonzero Octet in a Subnet Mask

Decimal Value	128 Bit Value							
255	1	1	1	1	1	1	1	1
	1	1	1	1	1	1	1	0
	1	1	1	1	1	1	0	0
	1	1	1	1	1	0	0	0
	1	1	1	1	0	0	0	0
	1	1	1	0	0	0	0	0
	1	1	0	0	0	0	0	0
	1	0	0	0	0	0	0	0

ANDing to Determine the Network Address

The bitwise AND operation is used by computers and networking devices to determine the network address from a given host address and subnet mask comparison. An AND operation is the comparison of two bits. Fill in the correct results for each of the following bitwise AND operations.

1 AND 1 = _

0 AND 1 = _

0 AND 0 = _

1 AND 0 = _

In Table 8-4, convert the prefix notion for a subnet mask to the dotted-decimal format. Then use the AND operation to determine the network address. For now, leave the Broadcast Address column empty.

Table 8-4   Determine the Network Address

Host Address/Prefix	Subnet Mask in Dotted Decimal	Network Address	Broadcast Address
192.168.1.10/24	255.255.255.0	192.168.1.0	192.168.1.255
192.168.25.130/27			
192.168.35.162/30			
192.168.1.137/23			
172.16.23.76/20			
172.31.254.172/15			
10.50.160.63/18			
10.220.100.9/17			
10.152.112.66/12			

The broadcast address for a given network address is the last available address in the range of addresses. For example, the broadcast address for 192.168.1.0/24 is 192.168.1.255. Now complete Table 8-4, filling in the broadcast address for each network.

Note: Plenty of calculators are available on the Internet that you can use to check your answers (for example, http://www.subnetmask.info). However, you will not be able to use a calculator while taking any Cisco exam. So, you should practice these problems without a calculator. Make these conversions on your own, and then use a calculator to check your answers.

 Lab - Using the Windows Calculator with Network Addresses (ITN 8.1.2.7/NB 7.1.2.7)

Lab - Converting IPv4 Addresses to Binary (ITN 8.1.2.8/NB 7.1.2.8)

IPv4 Unicast, Broadcast, and Multicast

In an IPv4 network, the hosts can communicate one of three ways:

- _____: The process of sending a packet from one host to another individual host

- _____: The process of sending a packet from one host to all hosts in the network

- _____: The process of sending a packet from one host to a selected group of hosts, possibly in different networks

In an IPv4 network, the _____ addresses applied to an end device are referred to as the host address. A _____ broadcast is sent to all hosts on a nonlocal network. The _____ broadcast is used for communication with hosts on the same local network. These packets always use a destination IPv4 address _____.

Explain why broadcast traffic should be limited.

IPv4 has a block of addresses reserved for addressing multicast groups: _____ to _____. The IPv4 multicast addresses _____ to _____ are reserved link-local addresses. The globally scoped addresses are _____ to _____. They may be used to multicast data across the Internet.

Packet Tracer
☐ **Activity**

Packet Tracer - Investigate Unicast, Broadcast, and Multicast Traffic (ITN 8.1.3.8/NB 7.1.3.8)

Types of IPv4 Addresses

Private Addresses

Private addresses are defined in RFC ____, *Address Allocation for Private Internets*. The private address blocks are as follows:

- __.0.0.0 to __.255.255.255 (__.0.0.0/__)

- ___.__.0.0 to ___.__.255.255 (___.__.0.0/__)

- ___.___.__.0 to ___.___.__.255 (___.___.__.0/__)

What distinguishes a private address from a public address?

Loopback Addresses

Explain the purpose of the loopback address ___.0.0._.

Link-Local Addresses

IPv4 addresses in the address block ___.___._._ to ___.___.___.___ (___.___.0.0/__) are designated as link-local addresses.

When would an IPv4 link-local address be used by a host?

What is the major limitation to link-local addresses?

Test-Net Addresses

The address block ___._._._ to ___._._.___ (___._.0/__) is set aside for teaching and learning purposes. These addresses can be used in documentation and network examples.

What is a router's default behavior toward test-net and link-local address?

Note: Although the test-net addresses are set aside for teaching and learning purposes, we also make use of the private address space (in addition to the Cisco-owned public addresses) for examples in this book.

Lab - Identifying IPv4 Addresses (ITN 8.1.4.8/NB 7.1.4.8)

IPv6 Network Addresses

As you surely know by now, IPv6 was designed to be the successor to IPv4 with its much larger 128-bit address space, providing for 340 undecillion addresses. The sensor-equipped, Internet-ready devices of tomorrow will include everything from automobiles and biomedical devices, to household appliances and natural ecosystems—an Internet of Things. With an increasing Internet population, limited IPv4 address space, issues with NAT, and an Internet of Things, the time has come to begin the transition to IPv6.

There are basically three migration techniques to move from IPv4 to IPv6:

- _____: Allows IPv4 and IPv6 to coexist on the same network

- _____: Transporting an IPv6 packet over an IPv4 network

- _____: Allows IPv6-enabled devices to communicate with IPv4-enabled devices using a technique similar to NAT for IPv4

Representing IPv6 Addresses

IPv6 addresses are 128 bits in length and written as a string of hexadecimal values. Every 4 bits is represented by a single hexadecimal digit, for a total of 32 hexadecimal values.

The preferred format for writing an IPv6 address is x:x:x:x:x:x:x:x, with each x consisting of four hexadecimal values. A *hextet* is the unofficial term used to refer to a segment of 16 bits or four hexadecimal values. Each x is a single hextet, 16 bits or four hexadecimal digits.

Preferred format means the IPv6 address is written using all 32 hexadecimal digits. It does not necessarily mean it is the ideal method for representing the IPv6 address.

What are the two rules used to reduce the number of digits required to represent an IPv6 address?

Table 8-5 provides a listing of ten fictitious IPv6 addresses. Use the two rules to practice compressing the IPv6 addresses into a shorter form.

Table 8-5   IPv6 Address Representations

Full IPv6 Address	Compressed IPv6 Address
2013:0000:0123:4567:89AB:CDEF:0020:0001	
AB1E:2B00:0000:1234:5678:9101:1112:1113	
BB2B:EF12:BFF3:9125:1111:0101:1111:0101	
2001:0000:0DB8:1111:0000:0000:0000:0200	
0000:0000:0000:1234:6678:9101:0000:34AB	
1129:1984:2233:4455:6677:0000:0000:0101	
1031:1976:0001:0002:0003:0004:0000:0101	
0000:0000:0000:0000:0000:0000:0000:0001	
1111:0000:0000:0000:0000:0000:0101:1111	
2012:ABCD:EF01:2345:0678:0910:AAAA:BBBB	

Identify IPv6 Address Types

Match the description on the left with the type of IPv6 address on the right. This exercise is a one-to-one matching.

Descriptions

a. Typical IPv6 prefix used to indicate the network portion of the address

b. IPv6 address represented as :: (compressed format) (cannot be assigned to an interface)

c. Unique, Internet-routable IPv6 address (dynamic or static)

d. Used to communicate with other devices on the same IPv6 subnet

e. IPv6 address represented as ::1 (compressed format)

IPv6 Address Types

_____ unspecified

_____ /64

_____ loopback

_____ link local

_____ global unicast

In Table 8-6, fill in the value range for the first hextet based on the type of IPv6 address.

Table 8-6   First Hextet Determines the Type of IPv6 Address

First Hextet (0000 to FFFF)	Type of IPv6 Address
to	Loopback address, any address, unspecified address, or IPv4 compatible
to	Global unicast address (a routable address in a range of addresses that is currently being handed out by the Internet Assigned Numbers Authority [IANA])
to	Link local (a unicast address which identifies the host computer on the local network)
to	Unique local (a unicast address which can be assigned to a host to identify it as being part of a specific subnet on the local network)
to	Multicast address

Match the IPv6 address type on the left with the IPv6 address on the right. Some answers may be used more than once.

IPv6 Address Type

- **a.** loopback address
- **b.** global unicast address
- **c.** link-local address
- **d.** unique-local address
- **e.** multicast address

IPv6 Address

____ 2001:0DB8:1:ACAD::FE55:6789:B210

____ ::1

____ FC00:22:A:2::CD4:23E4:76FA

____ FF00::

____ FF02::2

____ 2033:DB8:1:1:22:A33D:259A:21FE

____ FE80::3201:CC01:65B1

____ FF00::DB7:4322:A231:67C

IPv6 Unicast Addresses

IPv6 global unicast addresses are globally unique and routable on the IPv6 Internet. Currently, only global unicast addresses with the first 3 bits of 001 or 2000::/3 are being assigned.

Note: The 2001:0DB8::/32 address has been reserved for documentation purposes, including use in examples. So, it will be used throughout this book.

Figure 8-2 shows the structure and range of a global unicast address. Fill in the blanks to indicate how many bits are used by each of the three parts.

Figure 8-2   IPv6 Global Unicast Address Structure

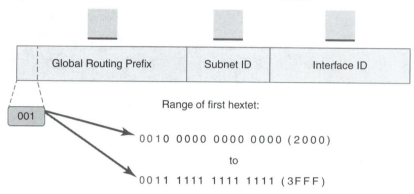

Currently, regional Internet registries (RIRs) assign a /48 global routing prefix to customers. This includes everyone from enterprise business networks to individual households. This is more than enough address space for most customers.

The 3-1-4 Rule

The IPv6 global unicast address can look complicated. Rick Graziani, in his book *IPv6 Fundamentals*, explains his 3-1-4 rule for breaking down a global unicast address into its three parts. Each number in the 3-1-4 rule refers to the number of hextets, as follows:

- 3: Indicates the three hextets, or 48 bits, of the global routing prefix.

- 1: Indicates the one hextet, or 16 bits, of the subnet ID.

- 4: Indicates the four hextets, or 64 bits, of the interface ID.

Using the 3-1-4 rule, complete Table 8-7 indicating which portion of the IPv6 global unicast address is the global routing prefix, the subnet ID, and the interface ID.

Table 8-7   Examples of /48 Global Unicast Addresses

Global Unicast Address	Global Routing Prefix (3)	Subnet ID (1)	Interface ID (4)
2001:0DB8:AAAA:1234:1111:2222:3333:4444			
2001:0DB8:BBBB:4321:AAAA:BBBB:CCCC:DDDD			
2001:0DB8:AAAA:0001:0000:0000:0000:0100			
2001:0DB8:AAAA:9:0:0:0:A			
2001:0DB8:AAAA:0001::0200			
2001:DB8:AAAA::200			
2001:DB8::ABC:0			
2001:DB8:ABC::			
2001:DB8:ABC::FFFF:FFFF:FFFF:FFFF			
2001:DB8::FFFF:FFFF:FFFF:FFFF:FFFF			

Static Configuration of Global Unicast Addressing

To configure a router interface with an IPv6 global unicast address, use the command **ipv6 address** *ipv6-address/prefix-length*. Given the topology shown in Figure 8-3, finish the router script for configuring the R1 interfaces with IPv6 addressing.

Figure 8-3   IPv6 Addressing Topology

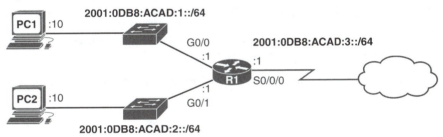

Script for R1

```
R1(config)# interface gigabitethernet 0/0
R1(config-if)#
R1(config-if)# no shutdown
R1(config-if)# interface gigabitethernet 0/1
R1(config-if)#
R1(config-if)# no shutdown
R1(config-if)# interface serial 0/0/0
R1(config-if)#
R1(config-if)# no shutdown
```

Dynamic Configuration of Global Unicast Addressing

Define and briefly explain SLAAC.

IPv6 routers periodically send out ICMPv6 _____ (RA) messages to all IPv6-enabled devices on the network. By default, Cisco routers send out RA messages every ____ seconds. An IPv6 device on the network does not have to wait for these periodic RA messages. A device can send a _____ (RS) message to the router, to which the router will respond with an RA.

However, before a router can send RA messages, it must first be enabled as an IPv6 router with the _____ command.

RA messages contain the prefix, prefix length, and other information for the device. In addition, the RA message can contain one of three options for the device to use to obtain its addressing information. Explain each option.

- Option 1: SLAAC Only:

- Option 2: SLAAC and DHCPv6:

- Option 3: DHCPv6 Only:

IPv6 Multicast Addresses

IPv6 multicast addresses have the prefix FF00::/8. There are two types of IPv6 multicast addresses: assigned multicast and solicited node multicast.

Explain the difference between assigned multicast and solicited node multicast.

Lab - Identifying IPv6 Addresses (ITN 8.2.5.4/NB 7.2.5.4)

Lab - Configuring IPv6 Addresses on Network Devices (ITN 8.2.5.5/VNB 7.2.5.5)

Packet Tracer - Configuring IPv6 Addressing (ITN 8.2.5.3/NB 7.2.5.3)

Connectivity Verification

Verifying end-to-end connectivity is important when first implementing a network. But it is also an important troubleshooting tool. Using connectivity tools, the network administrator can track the source of a connectivity issue.

ICMP Message Types

Internet Control Message Protocol (ICMP) messages common to both ICMPv4 and ICMPv6 include the following:

- Host Confirmation: The local host sends an ICMP _____ _____ to a destination host. If available, the destination host responds with an _____ _____. The ____ command can be used by an administrator to generate this verification test.

- Destination or Service Unreachable: This message is used when a host or gateway receives a packet that it cannot deliver. The message will include a code that indicates why the packet could not be delivered. What is the meaning of each of the following Destination Unreachable codes for ICMPv4:

  - 0 -

  - 1 -

  - 2 -

  - 3 -

- Time Exceeded: If a router receives a packet and decrements the ____(____-__-___) field in the IPv4 packet to ____, it discards the packet and sends a Time Exceeded message to the source host. Instead of the ____ field, ICMPv6 uses the ____ _____ field.

- Route Redirection: Explain this message type.

Testing the Path

To test the path from end to end and locate the place in the path where connectivity fails, use the _____ utility. The command for this test is _____ in Cisco IOS and _____ in Windows.

Explain how this testing utility works.

Lab - Testing Network Connectivity with Ping and Traceroute (ITN 8.3.2.7/NB 7.3.2.7)

Packet Tracer - Verifying IPv4 and IPv6 Addressing (ITN 8.3.2.5/NB 7.3.2.5)

Packet Tracer - Pinging and Tracing to Test the Path (ITN 8.3.2.6/NB 7.3.2.6)

Packet Tracer - Troubleshooting IPv4 and IPv6 Addressing (ITN 8.3.2.8/NB 7.3.2.8)

Packet Tracer – Skills Integration Challenge (ITN 8.4.1.2/NB 7.4.1.2)

CHAPTER 9

Subnetting IP Networks

Understanding the hierarchical structure of the IP address and how to modify that hierarchy in order to more efficiently meet routing requirements is an important part of planning an IP addressing scheme. This chapter reviews the process of subnetting IP networks. First, we review a process for subnetting IPv4 networks. Then, you practice subnetting skills, including several scenarios. Then, we briefly review subnetting IPv6 networks.

Subnetting an IPv4 Network

The process of segmenting a network, by dividing it into multiple smaller network spaces, is called *subnetting*. These subnetworks are called *subnets*. Although subnetting calculators are plentiful and freely accessible on the Internet, you must know how to subnet without using a calculator when you sit for the CCENT exam. Furthermore, subnetting skill will serve you well when troubleshooting common IP addressing issues.

Subnetting in Four Steps

Everyone has a preferred method of subnetting. Each teacher will use a slightly different strategy to help students master this crucial skill. The method I prefer can be broken down into four steps:

Step 1.   Determine how many bits to borrow based on the network requirements.

Step 2.   Determine the new subnet mask.

Step 3.   Determine the subnet multiplier.

Step 4.   List the subnets, including subnetwork address, host range, and broadcast address.

Subnetting Example

The best way to demonstrate the four steps of subnetting is to use an example. Let's assume that you are given the network address 192.168.1.0/24, you need 30 hosts per network, and want to create as many subnets as possible.

Determine How Many Bits to Borrow

Because our requirement specifies 30 host addresses per subnet, we need to first determine the minimum number of host bits to leave. The remaining bits can be borrowed:

Host Bits = Bits Borrowed + Bits Left

To provide enough address space for 30 hosts, we need to leave 5 bits. Use the following formula:

$2^{BL} - 2$ = number of host addresses

where the exponent *BL* is bits left in the host portion.

Remember, the "minus 2" is to account for the network and broadcast addresses that cannot be assigned to hosts.

In this example, leaving 5 bits in the host portion will provide the right number of host address:

$2^5 - 2 = 30$

Because we have 3 bits remaining in the original host portion, we borrow all these bits to satisfy the requirement to "create as many subnets as possible." To determine how many subnets we can create, use the following formula:

2^{BB} = Number of subnets

where the exponent *BB* is bits borrowed from the host portion.

In this example, borrowing 3 bits from the host portion will create 8 subnets: $2^3 = 8$.

As shown in Table 9-1, the 3 bits are borrowed from the far-left bits in the host portion. The highlighted bits in the table show all possible combinations of manipulating the 8 bits borrowed to create the subnets.

Table 9-1   Binary and Decimal Value of the Subnetted Octet

Subnet Number	Last Octet Binary Value	Last Octet Decimal Value
0	00000000	.0
1	00100000	.32
2	01000000	.64
3	01100000	.96
4	10000000	.128
5	10100000	.160
6	11000000	.192
7	11100000	.224

Determine the New Subnet Mask

Notice in Table 9-1 that the network bits now include the 3 borrowed host bits in the last octet. Add these 3 bits to the 24 bits in the original subnet mask and you have a new subnet mask, /27. In decimal format, you turn on the 128, 64, and 32 bits in the last octet for a value of 224. So, the new subnet mask is 255.255.255.224.

Determine the Subnet Multiplier

Notice in Table 9-1 that the last octet decimal value increments by 32 with each subnet number. The number 32 is the subnet multiplier. You can quickly find the subnet multiplier using one of two methods:

- Method 1: Subtract the last nonzero octet of the subnet mask from 256. In this example, the last nonzero octet is 224. So, the subnet multiplier is 256 − 224 = 32.

- Method 2: The decimal value of the last bit borrowed is the subnet multiplier. In this example, we borrowed the 128 bit, the 64 bit, and the 32 bit. The 32 bit is the last bit we borrowed and is, therefore, the subnet multiplier.

By using the subnet multiplier, you no longer have to convert binary subnet bits to decimal.

List the Subnets, Host Ranges, and Broadcast Addresses

Listing the subnets, host ranges, and broadcast addresses helps you see the flow of addresses within one address space. Table 9-2 documents our subnet addressing scheme for the 192.168.1.0/24 address space. Fill in any missing information.

Table 9-2   Subnet Addressing Scheme for 192.168.1.0/24: 30 Hosts Per Subnet

Subnet Number	Subnet Address	Host Range	Broadcast Address
0	192.168.1.0	192.168.1.1–192.168.1.30	192.168.1.31
1	192.168.1.32	192.168.1.33–192.168.1.62	
2		192.168.1.65–192.168.1.94	192.168.1.95
3	192.168.1.96		
4	192.168.1.128	192.168.1.129–192.168.1.158	192.168.1.159
5		192.168.1.161–192.168.1.190	192.168.1.191
6	192.168.1.192		
7			

Use the four subnetting steps to complete the following scenarios.

Subnetting Scenario 1

Subnet the address space 10.10.0.0/16 to provide at least 100 host addresses per subnet while creating as many subnets as possible.

1. How many bits should your borrow?

2. What is the new subnet mask in dotted-decimal and prefix notation?

3. What is the subnet multiplier?

In Table 9-3, list the first three subnets, host ranges, and broadcast addresses.

Table 9-3   Subnet Addressing Scheme for Scenario 1

Subnet Number	Subnet Address	Host Range	Broadcast Address
0			
1			
2			

Subnetting Scenario 2

Subnet the address space 10.10.0.0/16 to provide at least 500 subnet addresses.

1. How many bits should your borrow?

2. What is the new subnet mask in dotted-decimal and prefix notation?

3. What is the subnet multiplier?

In Table 9-4, list the first three subnets, host ranges, and broadcast addresses.

Table 9-4   Subnet Addressing Scheme for Scenario 2

Subnet Number	Subnet Address	Host Range	Broadcast Address
0			
1			
2			

Subnetting Scenario 3

Subnet the address space 10.10.10.0/23 to provide at least 60 host addresses per subnet while creating as many subnets as possible.

1. How many bits should your borrow?

2. What is the new subnet mask in dotted-decimal and prefix notation?

3. What is the subnet multiplier?

In Table 9-5, list the first three subnets, host ranges, and broadcast addresses.

Table 9-5   Subnet Addressing Scheme for Example 3

Subnet Number	Subnet Address	Host Range	Broadcast Address
0			
1			
2			

Lab - Calculating IPv4 Subnets (ITN 9.1.4.8/NB 8.1.3.8)

Lab - Subnetting Network Topologies (ITN 9.1.4.9/NB 8.1.3.9)

Lab - Researching Subnet Calculators (ITN 9.1.4.10/NB 8.1.3.10)

Packet Tracer - Subnetting Scenario 1 (ITN 9.1.4.6/NB 8.1.3.6)

Packet Tracer - Subnetting Scenario 2 (ITN 9.1.4.7/NB 8.1.3.7)

VLSM Addressing Schemes

Variable-length subnet masking (VLSM) subnetting is similar to traditional subnetting in that bits are borrowed to create subnets. The formulas to calculate the number of hosts per subnet, and the number of subnets created still apply. The difference is that subnetting is not a single-pass activity.

VLSM Review

You probably noticed that the starting address space in Subnetting Scenario 3 is not an entire classful address. In fact, it is subnet 5 from Subnetting Scenario 2. So in Subnetting Scenario 3, you "subnetted a subnet." That is what VLSM is in a nutshell: subnetting a subnet.

Let's use a small example. Given the address space 172.30.4.0/22 and the network requirements shown in Figure 9-1, apply an addressing scheme that conserves the most amount of addresses for future growth.

Figure 9-1   VLSM Example Topology

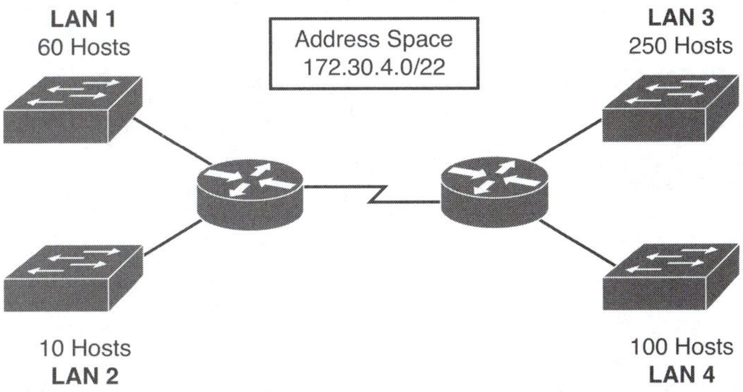

We need five subnets: four LAN subnets and one WAN subnet. Starting with the largest host requirement on LAN 3, begin subnetting the address space.

To satisfy the 250 hosts requirement, we leave 8 hosts bits ($2^8 - 2 = 254$ hosts per subnet). Because we have 10 host bits total, we borrow 2 bits to create the first round of subnets ($2^2 = 4$ subnets). The starting subnet mask is /22 or 255.255.252.0. We turn on the next two bits in the subnet mask to get /24 or 255.255.255.0. The multiplier is 1. The four subnets are as follows:

- Subnet 0: 172.30.4.0/24

- Subnet 1: 172.30.5.0/24

- Subnet 2: 172.30.6.0/24

- Subnet 3: 172.30.7.0/24

Assigning Subnet 0 to LAN 3, we are left with three /24 subnets. Continuing on to the next largest host requirement on LAN 4, we take Subnet 1, 172.30.5.0/24, and subnet it further.

To satisfy the 100 hosts requirement, we leave 7 bits ($2^7 - 2 = 128$ hosts per subnet). Because we have 8 host bits total, we can borrow only 1 bit to create the subnets ($2^1 = 2$ subnets). The starting subnet mask is /24 or 255.255.255.0. We turn on the next bit in the subnet mask to get /25 or 255.255.255.128. The multiplier is 128. The two subnets are as follows:

- Subnet 0: 172.30.5.0/25

- Subnet 1: 172.30.5.128/25

Assigning Subnet 0 to LAN 4, we are left with one /25 subnet and two /24 subnets. Continuing on to the next largest host requirement on LAN 1, we take Subnet 1, 172.30.5.128/25, and subnet it further.

To satisfy the 60 hosts requirement, we leave 6 bits ($2^6 - 2 = 62$ hosts per subnet). Because we have 7 host bits total, we borrow 1 bit to create the subnets ($2^1 = 2$ subnets). The starting subnet mask is /25 or 255.255.255.128. We turn on the next bit in the subnet mask to get /26 or 255.255.255.192. The multiplier is 64. The two subnets are as follows:

- Subnet 0: 172.30.5.128/26

- Subnet 1: 172.30.5.192/26

Assigning Subnet 0 to LAN 1, we are left with one /26 subnet and two /24 subnets. Finishing our LAN subnetting with LAN 2, we take Subnet 1, 172.30.5.192/26, and subnet it further.

To satisfy the 10 hosts requirement, we leave 4 bits ($2^4 - 2 = 14$ hosts per subnet). Because we have 6 host bits total, we borrow 2 bits to create the subnets ($2^2 = 4$ subnets). The starting subnet mask is /26 or 255.255.255.192. We turn on the next two bits in the subnet mask to get /28 or 255.255.255.240. The multiplier is 16. The four subnets are as follows:

- Subnet 0: 172.30.5.192/28

- Subnet 1: 172.30.5.208/28

- Subnet 2: 172.30.5.224/28

- Subnet 3: 172.30.5.240/28

Assigning Subnet 0 to LAN 2, we are left with three /28 subnets and two /24 subnets. To finalize our addressing scheme, we need to create a subnet only for the WAN link, which needs only two host addresses. We take Subnet 1, 172.30.5.208/28, and subnet it further.

To satisfy the two hosts requirement, we leave 2 bits ($2^2 - 2 = 2$ hosts per subnet). Because we have 4 host bits total, we borrow 2 bits to create the subnets ($2^2 = 4$ subnets). The starting subnet mask is /28 or 255.255.255.240. We turn on the next 2 bits in the subnet mask to get /30 or 255.255.255.252. The multiplier is 4. The four subnets are as follows:

- Subnet 0: 172.30.5.208/30

- Subnet 1: 172.30.5.212/30

- Subnet 2: 172.30.5.216/30

- Subnet 3: 172.30.5.220/30

We assign Subnet 0 to the WAN link. We are left with three /30 subnets, two /28 subnets, and two /24 subnets.

VLSM Addressing Design Exercises

In the following VLSM addressing design exercises, you apply your VLSM addressing skills to a three router topology. Each exercise is progressively more difficult than the last. There may be more than one correct answer in some situations. However, you should always practice good addressing design by assigning your subnets contiguously.

Exercise 1

Assume that 4 bits were borrowed from the host portion of 192.168.1.0/24. You are *not* using VLSM. Starting with Subnet 0, label Figure 9-2 contiguously with subnets. Start with the LAN on RTA and proceed clockwise.

Figure 9-2   Addressing Design Exercise 1 Topology: Subnets

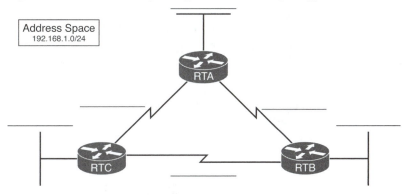

How many *total* valid host addresses will be wasted on the WAN links?

Now come up with a better addressing scheme using VLSM. Start with the same 4 bits borrowed from the host portion of 192.168.1.0/24. Label each of the LANs with a subnet. Then subnet the next available subnet to provide WAN subnets without wasting any host addresses. Label Figure 9-3 with the subnets.

Figure 9-3   Addressing Design Exercise 1 Topology: VLSM Subnets

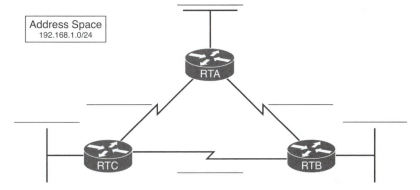

List the address space that is still available for future expansion.

The topology shown in Figure 9-4 has LAN subnets already assigned out of the 192.168.1.0/24 address space. Using VLSM, create and label the WANs with subnets from the remaining address space.

Figure 9-4   Addressing Design Exercise 1 Topology: WAN Subnets

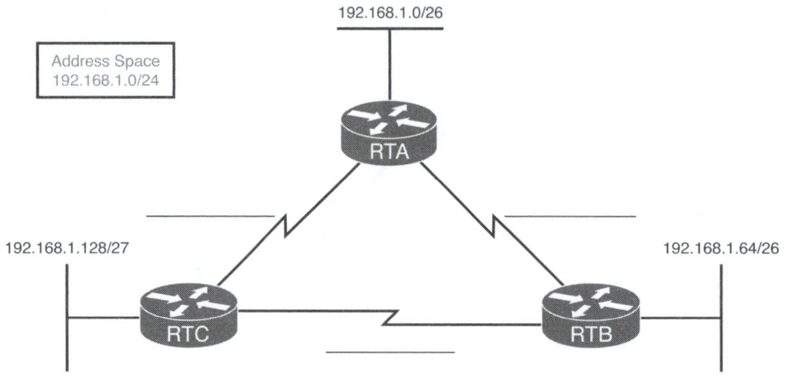

192.168.1.0/26

Address Space
192.168.1.0/24

RTA

192.168.1.128/27   192.168.1.64/26

RTC   RTB

List the address space that is still available for future expansion.

Exercise 2

Your address space is 192.168.1.192/26. Each LAN needs to support ten hosts. Use VLSM to create a contiguous IP addressing scheme. Label Figure 9-5 with your addressing scheme. Don't forget the WAN links.

Figure 9-5   Addressing Design Exercise 2 Topology

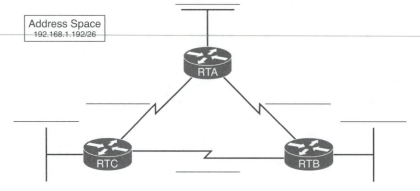

Address Space
192.168.1.192/26

RTA

RTC   RTB

List the address space that is still available for future expansion.

Exercise 3

Your address space is 192.168.6.0/23. The number of hosts needed for each LAN is shown in Figure 9-6. Use VLSM to create a contiguous IP addressing scheme. Label Figure 9-6 with your addressing scheme. Don't forget the WAN links.

Figure 9-6   Addressing Design Exercise 3 Topology

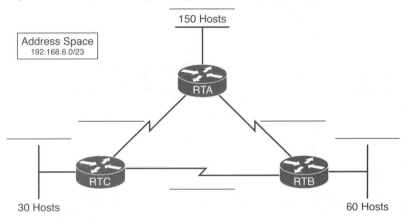

List the address space that is still available for future expansion.

Exercise 4

Your address space is 10.10.96.0/21. The number of hosts needed for each LAN is shown in Figure 9-7. Use VLSM to create a contiguous IP addressing scheme. Label Figure 9-7 with your addressing scheme. Don't forget the WAN links.

Figure 9-7   Addressing Design Exercise 4 Topology

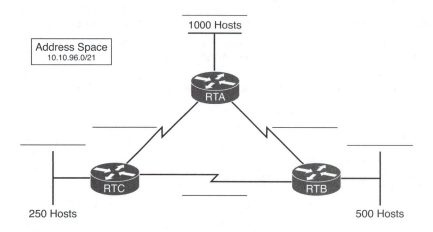

List the address space that is still available for future expansion.

 Lab - Designing and Implementing a Subnetted IPv4 Addressing Scheme (ITN 9.2.1.3/NB 8.2.1.3)

Lab - Designing and Implementing a VLSM Addressing Scheme (ITN 9.2.1.4/NB 8.2.1.4)

 Packet Tracer - Designing and Implementing a VLSM Addressing Scheme (ITN 9.2.1.5/NB 8.2.1.5)

Design Considerations for IPv6

An IPv6 address space is not subnetted to conserve addresses; rather, it is subnetted to support hierarchical, logical design of the network. Whereas IPv4 subnetting is about managing address conservation, IPv6 subnetting is about building an addressing hierarchy based on the number of routers and the networks they support.

Subnetting an IPv6 Network

The subnet ID of an IPv6 address provides 16 bits for subnetting. That's a total of 2^{16} or 65,536 subnets—plenty of subnets for small to medium-sized businesses. In addition, each subnet has 64 bits for the interface ID. That's roughly 18 quintillion addresses, obviously more than will ever be needed in one IP network segment.

Subnets created from the subnet ID are easy to represent because there is no conversion to binary required. To determine the next available subnet, just count up in hexadecimal, as shown in Figure 9-8.

Figure 9-8   Subnetting an IPv6 Address by Incrementing the Subnet ID

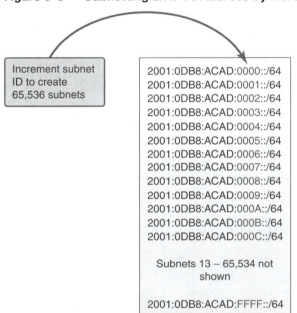

IPv6 Subnetting Practice

In practice, subnetting IPv6 is straightforward. The only possible difficulty is counting in hexadecimal as you increment the subnet ID.

IPv6 Subnetting Scenario 1

Assume that the network administrator allotted your section of the network four /64 IPv6 subnets starting with the subnet address space 2001:DB8:CAFE:F00D::/64. What would be the next three /64 subnets?

IPv6 Subnetting Scenario 2

Assume that the network administrator allotted your section of the network four /64 IPv6 subnets starting with the subnet address space 2001:DB8:CAFE:AA9F::/64. What would be the next three /64 subnets?

IPv6 Subnetting Scenario 3

Assume that the network administrator allotted your section of the network four /64 IPv6 subnets starting with the subnet address space 2001:DB8:CAFE:9EFD::/64. What would be the next three /64 subnets?

Packet Tracer - Implementing a Subnetted IPv6 Addressing Scheme (ITN 9.3.1.4/NB 8.3.1.4)

Packet Tracer - Skills Integration Challenge (ITN 9.4.1.2/NB 8.4.1.2)

CHAPTER 10

Application Layer

Applications, such as HTTP, video streaming, online gaming, and chat, provide the human interface to the underlying network. They enable us to send and receive data with relative ease. In this chapter, we review the role of the application layer.

Application Layer Protocols

By now, you should be familiar with both the OSI and TCP/IP models. The TCP/IP application layer includes a number of protocols that provide specific functionality to a variety of end-user applications.

OSI and TCP/IP Model Comparison

To review the structure of the OSI and TCP/IP models, label Figure 10-1 with the layers for each model.

Figure 10-1   The OSI and TCP/IP Models

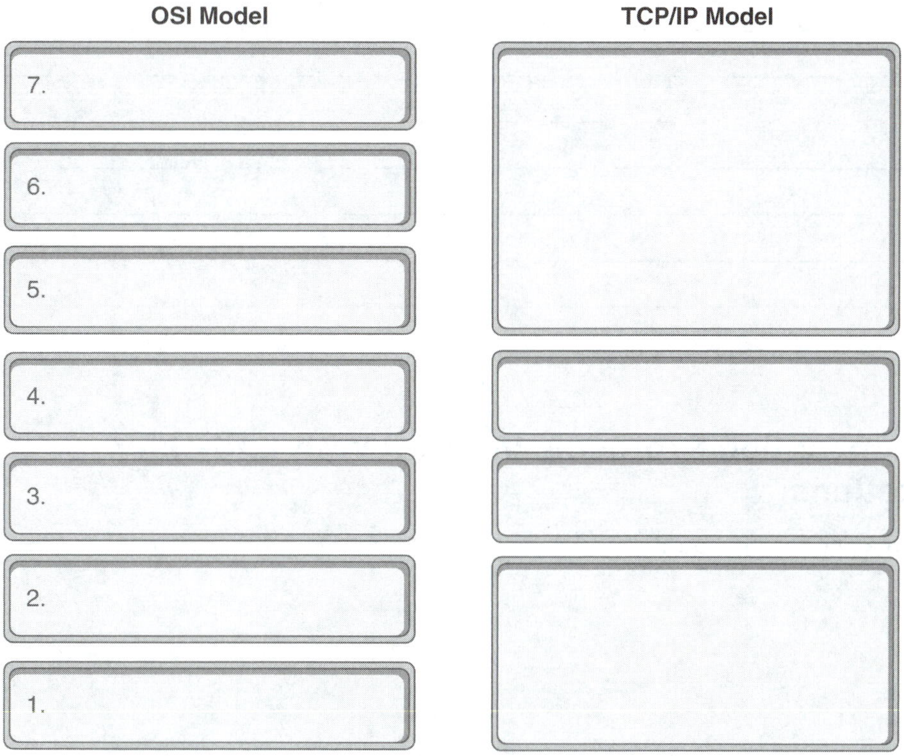

Application and Presentation Protocols and Standards

Provide the missing information in Table 10-1. Write in the full name for each acronym and indicate whether the protocol or standard belongs to the application layer or the presentation layer. You may not have seen some of these acronyms. If so, search the Internet for answers.

Table 10-1 Application and Presentation Protocols and Standards

Acronym	Full Name	OSI Application Layer	OSI Presentation Layer
IMAP			
MPEG			
TFTP			
ASCII			
PNG			
XML			
POP			
FTP			
SMTP			
HTML			
GIF			
HTTP			
SSH			
DHCP			
SNMP			
DNS			
JPEG			

How Application Protocols Interact with End-User Applications

Describe the peer-to-peer model.

List at least four common peer-to-peer applications.

Describe the client/server model.

Well-Known Application Layer Protocols and Services

There are dozens of well-known application layer protocols and services. In this section, we review the more important ones to your CCENT studies.

Web and Mail Services

Web Services

A web address or _____ (URL), such as http://www.cisco.com/index.html, can be broken down into three basic parts:

- http://:

- www.cisco.com:

- index.html:

Briefly explain how HTTP works.

What is the difference between HTTP and HTTPS?

Email Services

Email supports three separate protocols for operation:

- _____ (_____)

- _____ (_____)

- _____ (_____)

The application layer process that sends mail uses _____. When a client sends email, the client process connects with a server process on well-known port ___. A client retrieves email, however, using one of two application layer protocols: ____ or _____. With ____, mail is downloaded from the server to the client and then deleted on the server. The server starts the ____ service by passively listening on TCP port ___ for client connection requests. However, when a client connects to server running _____, copies of the messages are downloaded to the client application. The original messages are kept on the server until manually deleted.

IP Addressing Services

Domain Names

The _____ _____ _____ (DNS) was created for _____ _____ to _____ resolution. DNS uses a distributed set of servers to resolve the names associated with _____.

The DNS server stores different types of resource records used to resolve names. These records contain the name, address, and type of record.

Some of these record types are as follows:

- A:

- NS:

- CNAME:

- MX:

Briefly explain how a DNS server or end system can reduce bandwidth and upstream server processing required for DNS queries.

What is the command to display all the cached DNS entries on a Windows PC?

Briefly explain the DNS hierarchical system.

Computer operating systems have a utility called _____ that allows the user to manually query the name servers to resolve a given hostname. This utility can also be used to troubleshoot name resolution issues and to verify the current status of the name servers.

DHCP

The _____ (DHCP) automates the assignment of

-
-
-
- Other IP networking parameters (such as a domain name and DNS server)

What is the alternative to using DHCP?

What are some common situations where you would use DHCP and where you would use static addressing?

Label Figure 10-2 with the four DHCP messages.

Figure 10-2   DHCP Messages

Figure 10-2a DHCP Messages

When a DHCP-configured device boots or connects to the network, the client broadcasts a _____ message to identify any available DHCP servers on the network. A DHCP server replies with a _____ message, which offers a lease to the client. The message contains the IP address and subnet mask to be assigned, the IP address of the DNS server, and the IP address of the default gateway. The lease offer also includes the duration of the lease. The client may receive multiple _____ messages if there is more than one DHCP server on the local network; therefore, it must choose between them, and sends a _____ message that identifies the explicit server and lease offer that the client is accepting. Assuming that the IP address requested by the client, or offered by the server, is still available, the server returns a _____ message that acknowledges to the client that the lease is finalized. If the offer is no longer valid, perhaps because of a timeout or another client taking the lease, the selected server responds with a _____ message. If a DHCPNAK message is returned, the selection process must begin again with a new DHCPDISCOVER message being transmitted.

File Sharing Services

The ___ _____ _____ (FTP) was developed to allow for data transfers between a client and a server. An FTP client is an application that runs on a computer that is used to push and pull data from a server running an ___ _____ (FTPd).

In Figure 10-3, label and describe the two connections required between the client and server.

Figure 10-3 FTP Connection Process

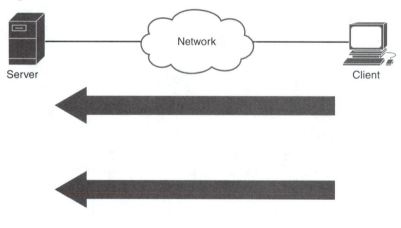

Get Data

Lab - Observing DNS Resolution (ITN 10.2.2.9/NB 4.2.2.9)

Lab - Exploring FTP (ITN 10.2.3.3/NB 4.2.3.3)

Packet Tracer - Web and Email (ITN 10.2.1.8/NB 4.2.1.8)

Packet Tracer - DNS and DHCP (ITN 10.2.2.8/NB 4.2.2.8)

Packet Tracer - FTP (ITN 10.2.3.2/NB 4.2.3.2)

The Message Heard Around the World

An entertaining resource to help you visualize networking concepts is the animated movie *Warriors of the Net*, by TNG Media Lab. Although the animations often have simplifications in them, there is one outright error in the video. About 5 minutes in, this statement is made: "What happens when Mr. IP doesn't receive an acknowledgment? He simply sends a replacement packet." This is not a function of the Layer 3 Internet Protocol, which is an "unreliable," best-effort delivery protocol, but rather a function of the transport layer TCP protocol.

Download the movie from http://www.warriorsofthe.net.

CHAPTER 11

It's a Network

So far, you have learned about the services that a data network can provide to the human network, examined the features of each layer of the OSI model and the operations of TCP/IP protocols, and looked in detail at Ethernet. In this chapter, we step back and see how to assemble these elements together in a functioning network that can be maintained.

Create and Grow

Growth is a natural process for many small businesses, and their networks must grow accordingly. Ideally, the network administrator has enough lead time to make intelligent decisions about growing the network in line with the growth of the company.

Devices in a Small Network

In Table 11-1, indicate the major design area for each of the design focuses.

Table 11-1   Identify Areas of Design Focus

Design Focus	Design Area				
	Ports	Speed	Expandable	Manageable	Cost
IP addressing scheme					
NIC capacity of devices					
Types of interfaces required					
Types of cable runs					
Prioritization of data traffic					
Number of interfaces needed					
Bandwidth required					
Upgrades to network devices					
Initial, basic cost of network devices					
Varying cable connection types					

Protocols in a Small Network

Match the services or protocols on the left with a server on the right.

Services and Protocols

    a. Uses SMTP, POP3, and/or IMAP

    b. Service that provides the IP address of a website or domain name so a host can connect to it

    c. Service that allows administrators to log in to a host from a remote location and control the host as though they were logged in locally

    d. Uses HTTP

    e. Service that allows for the download and upload of files between a client and server

    f. Service that assigns the IP address, subnet mask, default gateway, and other information to clients

Servers

_____ web server

_____ Telnet Server

_____ FTP server

_____ DNS server

_____ email server

_____ DHCP server

Growing to Larger Networks

List and briefly describe four elements require to scale a network.

Keeping the Network Safe

Attacks to a network can be devastating and can result in a loss of time and money due to damage or theft of important information or assets. Even in small networks, it is necessary to consider security threats and vulnerabilities when planning a network implementation.

Network Device Security Measures

In Table 11-2, indicate which security threat applies to each scenario.

Table 11-2   Identify the Type of Security Threat

Scenario	Information Theft	Identity Theft	Data Loss/ Manipulation	Disruption of Service
Preventing legal users from accessing data services				
Making illegal online purchases				
Sending a virus to reformat a hard drive				
Stealing a company's user database				
Overloading a network to keep users out				
Impersonating someone to obtain credit				
Altering data records				
Accessing scientific research reports				

In Table 11-3, match the security best practice to the appropriate security management type.

Table 11-3   Indentify the Type of Security Best Practice

Security Practice	Hardware	Environmental	Electrical	Maintenance
Control access to console ports				
Lock up devices to prevent unauthorized access				
Install UPS systems				
Create positive air flow				
Label critical cables and components				
Install redundant power supplies				
Use security cameras				
Control temperature and humidity				

Vulnerabilities and Network Attacks

Match the scenario on the left with the type of security attack on the right.

Scenario

a. Sharon works for the finance department in her company. Her network administrator has given the finance department employees public IP addresses to access the Internet bank account. After an hour of work, the finance department members are told that the company bank account has been compromised.

b. Jeremiah downloaded some software from the Internet. He opened the file and his hard drive crashed immediately. He lost all information on his computer.

c. Angela receives an email with a link to her favorite online store, which is having a sale. She uses the link provided and is directed to a site that looks like her favorite online store. She orders from the web page using her credit card. Later, Angela discovers that her credit card has been used to pay for additional merchandise that she did not order.

d. Eli opened an email sent to him by a friend. Later in the day, Eli received telephone calls from his friends saying they received emails from him that he did not knowingly send.

e. George is ordering a pair of shoes from a bidding site. There are 20 seconds left in the bidding cycle. George decides to ping the bidding site, over and over again, to stop anyone else from bidding on his shoes. The 20 seconds pass, and George wins the bid.

f. Arianna was working on the Internet. A pop-up appeared stating that she needed to update her operating system by clicking the link. When she clicked the link, a program was installed on her computer (unknown to Arianna).

Type of Security Attack

____ Trojan horse

____ Denial of Service

____ Access

____ Worm

____ Reconnaissance

____ Virus

 Lab - Researching Network Security Threats (ITN/NB 11.2.2.6)

Mitigating Network Attacks

Match the step description on the left to the four steps in worm attack mitigation listed on the right.

Step Description

    a. Start patching all systems and, if possible, scanning for vulnerable systems.

    b. Some worms may require complete core system reinstallations to clean the system.

    c. Compartmentalize uninfected parts of the network.

    d. Disconnect, remove, or block infected machines from the network.

Four Steps in Worm Attack Treatment

____ Step 1: Containment

____ Step 2: Inoculation

____ Step 3: Quarantine

____ Step 4: Treatment

Briefly explain each of the *A*'s in the acronym AAA.

Securing Devices

In the space provided, record the commands to implement the following security policy on a router or switch:

- Encrypt all plain-text passwords.

- Enforce minimum password length of ten characters.

- Allow up to five attempts within 1 minute, after which additional attempts are blocked for 5 minutes.

- Enforce a 20-minute timeout on Telnet lines.

- Allow only Secure Shell (SSH) access that uses a 1024-bit key and enforces local logins.

Script (include prompt)

 Lab - Accessing Network Devices with SSH (ITN/NB 11.2.4.5)

Lab - Securing Network Devices (ITN/NB 11.2.4.6)

Basic Network Performance

After the network has been implemented, a network administrator must be able to test the network connectivity to ensure that it is operating appropriately. In addition, it is a good idea for the network administrator to document the network.

Using the ping Command

In Table 11-4, match the symbol with the correct ping reply message description.

Table 11-4   Identify the Meaning of a Cisco Router Ping Message

Description	!	.	U
An ICMP unreachable message was received.			
Indicates receipt of an ICMP echo reply message.			
Indicates a time expired while waiting for an ICMP echo reply message.			

Refer to Figure 11-1. You need to test routing to make sure that R2 can route to end devices attached to the R1 LAN. In the command output that follows the figure, complete the commands to do an extended ping, testing connectivity to the R2 LAN interface.

Figure 11-1   Extended ping Topology

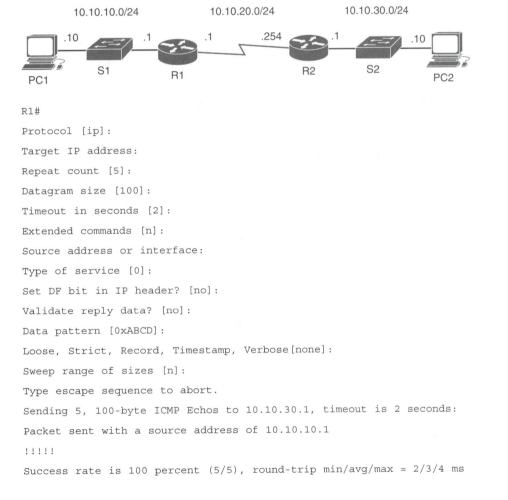

```
R1#
Protocol [ip]:
Target IP address:
Repeat count [5]:
Datagram size [100]:
Timeout in seconds [2]:
Extended commands [n]:
Source address or interface:
Type of service [0]:
Set DF bit in IP header? [no]:
Validate reply data? [no]:
Data pattern [0xABCD]:
Loose, Strict, Record, Timestamp, Verbose[none]:
Sweep range of sizes [n]:
Type escape sequence to abort.
Sending 5, 100-byte ICMP Echos to 10.10.30.1, timeout is 2 seconds:
Packet sent with a source address of 10.10.10.1
!!!!!
Success rate is 100 percent (5/5), round-trip min/avg/max = 2/3/4 ms
```

Tracing a Route

Refer to Figure 11-1. What command would you use, including prompt, to trace a route from PC1 to PC2?

What command would you use to trace a route from R1 to PC2?

Packet Tracer - Test Connectivity with Traceroute (ITN/NB 11.3.2.2)

Lab - Testing Network Latency with Ping and Traceroute (ITN/NB 11.3.2.3)

show Commands

Network technicians use **show** commands extensively for viewing configuration files, checking the status of device interfaces and processes, and verifying the device operational status. Answer the following questions related to **show** commands.

1. Which commands would provide the IP address, network prefix, and interface?

2. Which commands provide the IP address and interface assignment, but not the network prefix?

3. Which commands provide the status of the interfaces?

4. Which commands provide information about the IOS loaded on the router?

5. Which commands provide information about the addresses of the router interfaces?

6. Which commands provide information about the amount of and Flash memory available?

7. Which commands provide information about the lines being used for configuration or device monitoring?

8. Which commands provide traffic statistics of router interfaces?

9. Which commands provide information about paths available for network traffic?

Match the **show** command description on the left with the **show** command on the right.

show Command Description

a. You are on a call with the Cisco Technical Assistance personnel. They ask you for the switch IOS name, RAM, NVRAM, and flash available. They also ask for the hexadecimal boot location.

b. You suspect there is a problem with the current switch configuration. You want to see the saved configuration so that you can compare it to what is currently running.

c. Your network documentation really needs to be updated. A quick listing of the IP addresses of your routers in relation to their MAC addresses would help finish the task for recording purposes.

d. You are running the EIGRP routing protocol and need to know the update intervals and what active interfaces and networks are being advertised by your router.

e. You cannot get to the Internet. You need to find out whether your router has a path to the Internet and which protocols are being used to provide the paths.

f. A switch is the closest intermediary device to you. It has 24 ports. You want to see a simple list of the ports being used, their status, and the VLAN IP address of the switch.

show Command

_____ show ip protocol

_____ show arp

_____ show ip route

_____ show version

_____ show ip interface brief

_____ show startup-config

Lab - Using the CLI to Gather Network Device Information.pdf (ITN/NB 11.3.4.6)

Packet Tracer
☐ Activity

Packet Tracer - Using show Commands (ITN/NB 11.3.3.4)

Managing IOS Configuration Files

In addition to implementing and securing a small network, it is also the job of the network administrator to manage configuration files. Managing the configuration files is important for purposes of backup and retrieval in the event of a device failure. This section includes a Packet Tracer activity and several important labs you should complete.

Indicate the commands used to generate the output in Example 11-1.

Example 11-1   Cisco IOS File System Commands

```
Router#

File Systems:


        Size        Free      Type   Flags   Prefixes
           -           -      opaque    rw     archive:
           -           -      opaque    rw     system:
           -           -      opaque    rw     tmpsys:
           -           -      opaque    rw     null:
           -           -      network   rw     tftp:
*    256487424   182394880     disk    rw     flash0: flash:#
           -           -        disk    rw      flash1:
      262136      245440      nvram    rw      nvram:
           -           -      opaque    wo     syslog:
           -           -      opaque    rw     xmodem:
           -           -      opaque    rw     ymodem:
           -           -      network   rw     rcp:
           -           -      network   rw     http:
           -           -      network   rw     ftp:
           -           -      network   rw     scp:
           -           -      opaque    ro     tar:
           -           -      network   rw     https:
           -           -      opaque    ro     cns:


Router#
Directory of flash0:/


    1   -rw-     68831808    Apr 3 2013 21:53:06 +00:00   c1900-universalk9-mz.
SPA.152-4.M3.bin
    2   -rw-         2903    Aug 9 2012 16:12:34 +00:00   cpconfig-19xx.cfg
    3   -rw-      3000320    Aug 9 2012 16:12:46 +00:00   cpexpress.tar
    4   -rw-         1038    Aug 9 2012 16:12:56 +00:00   home.shtml
```

```
    5   -rw-       122880    Aug 9 2012 16:13:04 +00:00   home.tar
    6   -rw-      1697952    Aug 9 2012 16:13:18 +00:00   securedesktop-ios-
3.1.1.45-k9.pkg
    7   -rw-       415956    Aug 9 2012 16:13:30 +00:00   sslclient-win-1.1.4.176.pkg
    8   -rw-         1389    Feb 6 2013 17:40:08 +00:00   my-running-config


256487424 bytes total (182394880 bytes free)


Router#
Router#
Directory of nvram:/


  253   -rw-         1279                    <no date>   startup-config
  254   ----            5                    <no date>   private-config
  255   -rw-         1279                    <no date>   underlying-config
    1   -rw-         2945                    <no date>   cwmp_inventory
    4   ----            0                    <no date>   rf_cold_starts
    5   ----           92                    <no date>   persistent-data
    6   -rw-           17                    <no date>   ecfm_ieee_mib
    7   -rw-          559                    <no date>   IOS-Self-Sig#1.cer
    8   -rw-          559                    <no date>   IOS-Self-Sig#2.cer
    9   -rw-          559                    <no date>   IOS-Self-Sig#3.cer
   10   -rw-          559                    <no date>   IOS-Self-Sig#4.cer
   11   -rw-          559                    <no date>   IOS-Self-Sig#5.cer
   12   -rw-          559                    <no date>   IOS-Self-Sig#6.cer
   13   -rw-          559                    <no date>   IOS-Self-Sig#7.cer
   14   -rw-          559                    <no date>   IOS-Self-Sig#8.cer
   15   -rw-            0                    <no date>   ifIndex-table
Router#
Router# pwd
flash0:/
```

Lab - Managing Router Configuration Files with Tera Term (ITN/NB 11.4.2.6)

Lab - Managing Device Configuration Files Using TFTP, Flash, and USB (ITN/NB 11.4.2.7)

Lab - Researching Password Recovery Procedures (ITN/NB 11.4.2.8)

Packet Tracer - Backing up Configuration Files (ITN/NB 11.4.2.5)

Integrated Routing Services

An integrated router is like having several different devices connected together. For example, the connection between the switch and the router still occurs, but it occurs internally. When a packet is forwarded from one device to another on the same local network, the integrated switch will automatically forward the packet to the destination device. If a packet is forwarded to a device on a remote network, however, the integrated switch will then forward the packet to the internal router connection. The internal router will then determine the best path and forward the packet out accordingly. Although a device can be connected to one of the switch ports, it is increasingly common for devices in the home to connect wirelessly. This section focuses on wireless technology and security.

List at least three benefits of wireless LAN technology.

List and briefly describe three limitations of wireless LAN technology.

List three wireless security steps you should take when installing a new home wireless router.

Capstone Project - Design and Build a Small Business Network (ITN 11.6.1.1)

Packet Tracer - Configuring a Linksys Router (ITN 11.5.2.4)

Packet Tracer - Skills Integration Challenge (ITN 11.6.1.2/NB 11.5.1.2)

CHAPTER 12

Introduction to Switched Networks

Modern networks continue to evolve to keep pace with the changing way organizations carry out their daily business. Different devices must seamlessly work together to provide a fast, secure, and reliable connection between hosts. LAN switches provide the connection point for end users into the enterprise network and are also primarily responsible for the control of information within the LAN environment. In this chapter, we review current network design models and the way LAN switches build forwarding tables to switch data efficiently.

LAN Design

In today's globalized workplace, employees can access resources from anywhere in the world and information must be available at any time, and on any device. To encourage collaboration, business networks not only support traditional data access, but employ converged solutions to support voice and video as well. In this section, we review some basic design principles relating to LANs.

LAN Design Principles

Watch this Cisco video on YouTube:

http://youtu.be/lCg2HctgvJE or search YouTube for "Evolution of Borderless Networks"

Then briefly describe the Cisco Borderless Network.

Indicate which borderless switched network design principles is best described by the characteristic in Table 12-1.

Table 12-1   Identify the Borderless Switched Network Design Principle

Characteristic	Hierarchical	Modularity	Resiliency	Flexibility
Allows networks to grow and provide on-demand services				
Uses all network resources available to provide data traffic load sharing				
Helps every device on every tier to employ a specific role				
Provides a way for the network to always be accessible				

In Table 12-2, identify which layer for each of the switch functions is described.

Table 12-2   Indentify the Hierarchical Layer

Switch Function	Core	Distribution	Access
Can be combined with the Distribution Layer to provide for a collapsed design			
Allows data to flow on equal-cost switching paths to the backbone			
Supports Layer 2 broadcast domains and Layer 3 routing boundaries			
The network backbone area for switching			
Includes redundancy as an important feature for switched network access			
Helps applications to operate on the switched network more safely and securely			
Provides direct, switched network connectivity to the user			
Interfaces with the backbone and users to provide intelligent switching, routing, and security			
Provides fault isolation and high-speed backbone switch connectivity			

Selecting Switch Hardware

Match the switch selection criteria on the left with the switch category names on the right.

Switch Selection Criteria

a. How fast the interfaces will process network data

b. Ability to adjust to growth of network users

c. Switches with preset features or options

d. Continuous access to the network

e. Availability through PoE

f. Daisy-chain switches with high-bandwidth throughput

g. Includes number/speed of interfaces, features, and expandability

h. The capacity to store frames in the cache

i. Affected by the number of network devices to support

j. Switches with insertable switching line/port cards

Switch Category Name

_____ cost

_____ modular

_____ frame buffers

_____ scalability

_____ port speed

_____ stackable

_____ power

_____ fixed configuration

_____ port density

_____ reliability

The Switched Environment

In a LAN switch, a master switching table describes a strict association between addresses and ports. Cisco LAN switches use this table to forward traffic based on the ingress port and the destination MAC address. LAN switches also segment collision domains so that devices that share the same logical network do not have to share bandwidth (as with hubs). In this section, we look at frame forwarding methods and how switches alleviate congestion on the network.

Frame Forwarding Methods and Terminology

Switches use basically two methods to forward frames: store-and-forward and cut-through. In store-and-forward switching, when the switch receives the frame, it stores the data in _____ _____ until the complete frame has been received. During the storage process, the switch performs an error check using the _____ trailer portion of the Ethernet frame. After confirming the integrity of the frame, the frame is _____. If an error is detected, the frame is _____.

In cut-through switching, the switch buffers just enough of the frame to read the _____ MAC address so that it can determine to which port to forward the data.

In Table 12-3, indicate which method matches the descriptions.

Table 12-3   Identify the Frame Forwarding Method

Description	Store-and-Forward	Cut-Through
Checks the frame for errors before releasing it out of its switch ports. If the full frame was not received, the switch discards it.		
Low-latency switch method used by high-performance computing (HPC) applications requiring process-to-process latencies of 10 microseconds or less.		
No error checking on frames is performed by the switch before releasing the frame out of its ports.		
Buffers frames until the full frame has been received by the switch.		
ASICs-capable switch function; allows frames to be filtered and forwarded after the first 14 bytes and an additional 40 bytes in the frame header have been received.		

Building the MAC Address Table

Assume that the switch in Figure 12-1 was just installed and powered on. The MAC address table is empty. Answer the following questions and complete Table 12-4 as the switch would build it.

Figure 12-1   Building the MAC Address Table

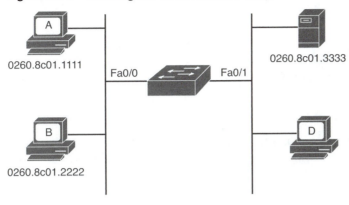

Table 12-4   MAC Address Table

Port	MAC Address

1. Host A sends a unicast frame to Host B. What entry, if any, will the switch enter in its MAC address table?

    What will the switch do with the frame?

2. Host B responds to Host A with a unicast frame. What entry, if any, will the switch enter in its MAC address table?

    What will the switch do with the frame?

3. Host D attempts to log in to Server C. What entry, if any, will the switch enter in its MAC address table?

    What will the switch do with the frame?

4. Server C responds to the login attempt by Host D. What entry, if any, will the switch enter in its MAC address table?

What will the switch do with the frame?

5. Server C sends out a broadcast frame announcing its services to all potential clients. What entry, if any, will the switch enter in its MAC address table?

What will the switch do with the frame?

Collision and Broadcast Domains

Using Figure 12-2, circle all the collision domains with a solid line and all the broadcast domains with a dashed line.

Figure 12-2   Collision and Broadcast Domains: Topology 1

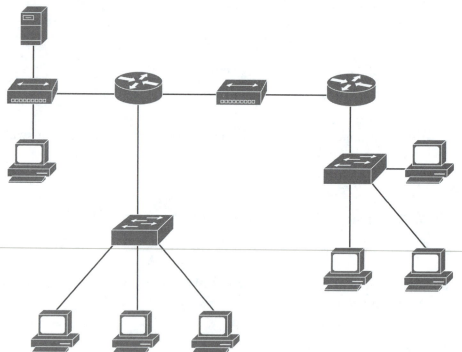

Using Figure 12-3, circle all the collision domains with a solid line and all the broadcast domains with a dashed line.

Figure 12-3   Collision and Broadcast Domains: Topology 2

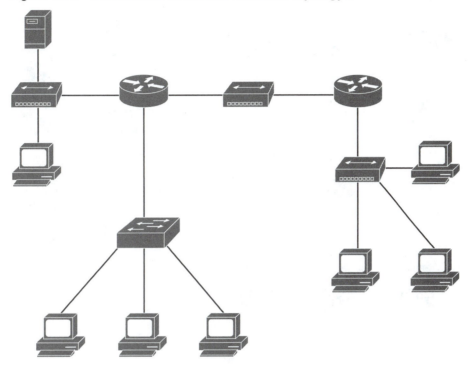

Using Figure 12-4, circle all the collision domains with a solid line and all the broadcast domains with a dashed line.

Figure 12-4   Collision and Broadcast Domains: Topology 3

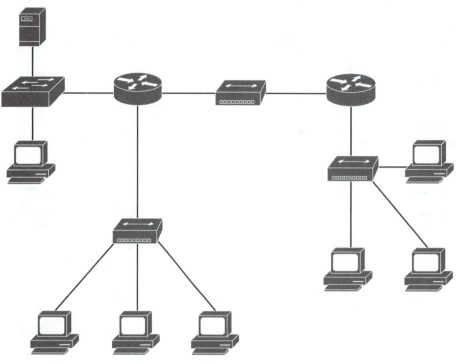

Packet Tracer - Skills Integration Challenge (RSE 1.3.1.2/SwN 1.3.1.3)

Packet Tracer
☐ Activity

CHAPTER 13

Basic Switching Concepts and Configuration

Although Cisco LAN switches are ready to go "out of the box," they also require certain configurations for them to boot and carry out their functionality in a reliable, secure manner. Although they normally operate at the network access layer of the TCP/IP model and base their forwarding decisions on MAC addresses, they are routinely configured with an IP address to allow remote management. This chapter reviews some of the basic switch configuration settings required to maintain a secure, available, switched LAN environment.

Basic Switch Configuration

After the switch is powered on and goes through its boot sequence, it is ready to be configured. To prepare a switch for remote management access, the switch must be configured with an IP address, a subnet mask, and a default gateway. In this section, we review the boot sequence and configuring a switch's initial settings.

Switch Boot Sequence

Briefly explain the steps in the switch boot sequence.

After a Cisco switch is powered on, it goes through the following boot sequence:

Step 1.

Step 2.

Step 3.

Step 4.

Step 5.

Half-Duplex, Full-Duplex, and Auto-MDIX

_____ communication relies on unidirectional data flow, where sending and receiving data are not performed at the same time. This is similar to how walkie-talkies or two-way radios communicate.

_____ communication is the most common today. Data flow is bidirectional, so data can be sent and received at the same time. The collision detect circuit is _____.

The Cisco Catalyst switches have three settings:

- The ____ option sets autonegotiation of duplex mode. With autonegotiation enabled, the two ports communicate to decide the best mode of operation.

- The ___ option sets full-duplex mode.

- The ___ option sets half-duplex mode.

For Fast Ethernet and 10/100/1000 ports, the default is ____. For 100BASE-FX ports, the default is ____.

In addition, you can now use the _____ interface configuration command in the CLI to enable the automatic medium-dependent interface crossover (auto-MDIX) feature, which detects the required cable type for copper Ethernet connections and configures the interfaces accordingly.

Configure a Switch with Initial Settings

In this exercise, use Figure 13-1 and Table 13-1 to answer the following questions. Some of these questions are review from previous chapters.

Figure 13-1   Basic Switch Configuration Topology

10.1.1.0/24

Table 13-1   Addressing Table for Chapter 2 Topology

Device	Interface	IP Address	Subnet Mask	Default Gateway
R1	G0/0	10.1.1.1	255.255.255.0	N/A
S1	VLAN 99	10.1.1.11	255.255.255.0	10.1.1.1
PC1	NIC	10.1.1.21	255.255.255.0	10.1.1.1

When configuring a switch, certain basic tasks are performed, including the following:

- Naming the switch

- Setting passwords

- Configuring a banner

- Configuring the VLAN interface

- Saving changes on a switch

- Verifying basic configuration

The first prompt is at ____ EXEC mode and allows you to view the state of the switch. What major limitation does this mode have?

What is the switch prompt for this mode?

The _____ command is used to enter _____ EXEC mode. What is the major difference between this mode and the previous mode?

What is the switch prompt for this mode?

Basic Configuration Tasks

Table 13-2 lists the basic switch configuration tasks in the left column. Fill in the right column with the correct command syntax for each of the tasks. Do not enter the actual values for command parameters at this point. Only record the syntax. The first one is done for you as an example.

Table 13-2   Basic Switch Configuration Command Syntax

Configuration Task	Command Syntax
Naming the switch	
Setting the privileged mode encrypted password	
Encrypting all clear-text passwords	
Entering console line configuration	
Setting the console password	
Requiring users to log in	
Entering vty line configuration mode	
Setting the vty passwords	
Requiring users to log in	
Configuring a message-of-the-day banner	
Configuring the VLAN interface	
Configuring addressing on an interface	
Activating an interface	
Configuring the default gateway	
Setting the port speed to 100 Mbps	
Setting the duplex mode to full	
Setting the port speed to autoconfigure	
Setting the duplex mode to autoconfigure	
Setting the port to automatically detect the cable connection type	
Saving changes on a router	

Applying a Basic Configuration

The following exercise walks you through a basic configuration.

First, enter global configuration mode for the switch:

```
Switch#
```

Next, apply a unique hostname to the switch. Use S1 for this example:

```
Switch(config)#
```

Now, configure the password that is to be used to enter privileged EXEC mode. Use **class** as the password:

```
S1 (config)#
```

Next, configure the console and Telnet lines with the password cisco. The console commands follow:

```
S1(config)#
S1(config-line)#
S1(config-line)#
```

The Telnet lines use similar commands:

```
S1(config-line)#
S1(config-line)#
S1(config-line)#
```

Return to global configuration mode:

```
S1(config-line)#
```

From global configuration mode, configure the message-of-the-day banner. Use the following text: Authorized Access Only. A delimiting character such as a # is used at the beginning and at the end of the message.

```
S1(config)#
```

Refer to Table 13-1 for the VLAN interface configuration information. What is the command to enter VLAN interface configuration mode for S1?

```
S1(config)#
```

Enter the command to configure the IP address using the address specified in Table 13-1.

```
S1(config-if)#
```

VLAN interfaces on the 2960 switch do not need to be manually activated. However, if you are using a 2950 switch or if the interface is manually down, you need to activate the interface. Enter the command to activate the VLAN interface:

```
S1(config-if)#
```

Enter interface configuration mode for the Fa0/5 interface connected to PC1:

```
S1(config)#
```

Enter the command to set the interface to 100 Mbps:

```
S1(config-if)#
```

Enter the command to force full-duplex operation:

```
S1(config-if)#
```

Enter the command to activate the interface:

```
S1(config-if)#
```

Return to global configuration mode:

```
S1(config-if)#
```

Use the address in Table 13-1 to configure S1 with a default gateway:

```
S1(config)#
```

Return to the privileged EXEC prompt:

`S1(config)#`

What command will save the current configuration?

`S1#`

Verifying Basic Switch Configuration

You can verify basic configurations using the four basic **show** commands in Table 13-3. The second four basic **show** commands in the table do not necessarily verify the configuration but might also be helpful. List the command in the left column that fits the description in the right column.

Table 13-3   Basic Router Configuration Verification Commands

Command	Description
	Displays interface status and configuration for a single interface or all interfaces available on the switch
	Displays the startup configuration file stored in NVRAM
	Displays the current running configuration that is stored in RAM
	Displays abbreviated interface configuration information, including IP address and interface status
	Displays information about the flash file system
	Displays system hardware and software status
	Displays the session command history
	Displays the MAC forwarding table

 Lab - Basic Switch Configuration (RSE 2.1.1.6/SwN 2.2.1.6)

Switch Security: Management and Implementation

In modern networks, security is integral to implementing any device, protocol, or technology. You should already have strong skills in configuring passwords on a switch. The exercises in this section review configuring Secure Shell (SSH), common security attacks, and configuring port security.

Configuring SSH

Older switches may not support secure communication with _____ (SSH). However, Packet Tracer and the more recent 2960 IOS images do support SSH. Why is Telnet an unsecure way of accessing a network device?

To implement SSH, you need to generate RSA keys. RSA involves a public key, kept on a public RSA server, and a private key, kept only by the sender and receiver.

To configure a Catalyst 2960 switch as an SSH server, fill in the blanks in the following steps:

Step 1.   Configure a host domain for S1. Use the domain mydomain.com.

```
S1(config)#
```

Step 2.   Enter the command to generate an encrypted RSA key pair. Use 1024 as the modulus size.

```
S1(config)#
The name for the keys will be: S1.mydomain.com
Choose the size of the key modulus in the range of 360 to 2048 for your
   General Purpose Keys. Choosing a key modulus greater than 512 may take
   a few minutes.

How many bits in the modulus [512]:
% Generating 1024 bit RSA keys, keys will be non-exportable...[OK]
      %SSH-5-ENABLED: SSH 1.99 has been enabled
```

Step 3.   Enter the command to verify the current SSH configuration:

```
S1#
SSH Enabled - version 1.99
      Authentication timeout: 120 secs; Authentication retries: 3
```

Step 4.   Enter the commands to configure SSH version 2, change the timeout to 30 seconds, and change the authentication retries to 5:

```
S1(config)#
S1(config)#
S1(config)#
```

Step 5.   Enter the command to configure all vty lines to allow only SSH access:

```
S1(config)#
S1(config-line)#
```

Packet Tracer - Configuring SSH (RSE 2.2.1.4/SwN 2.3.1.4)

Common Security Attacks

Match the security attack description on the left with the security attack type on the right.

Security Attack Description

a. Floods the DHCP server with DHCP requests to use all the available addresses (simulates a denial-of-service [DoS] attack on the switch)

b. Uses fake MAC addresses to overflow the MAC address table

c. Allows an attacker to configure a fake DHCP server on the network to issue DHCP addresses to clients

d. Allows the attacker to see surrounding IP addresses, software versions, and native VLAN information to enact a DoS attack

e. Uses a "dictionary" to find common passwords (tries to initiate a Telnet session using what the "dictionary" suggests for the passwords)

Security Attack Type

____ brute force

____ CDP

____ MAC flooding

____ DHCP starvation

____ DHCP snooping

Configuring Port Security

A switch that does not provide port security allows an attacker to attach a system to an unused, enabled port and to perform information gathering or to launch attacks.

All switch ports or interfaces should be secured before the switch is deployed. Port security can limit the number of valid MAC addresses allowed on a port to one and automatically shut down a port if a security violation occurs. In addition, all unused ports should be administratively shut down.

List the three ways a switch can learn the MAC addresses allowed on a port.

  ■

  ■

  ■

List and explain the three violation modes you can configure.

  ■

  ■

  ■

In Table 13-4, list the violation mode and answer yes or no to each of the different effects listed.

Table 13-4   Port Security Violation Modes

Violation Mode	Forwards Traffic	Sends SNMP Trap	Sends Syslog Message	Displays Error Message	Increases Violation Counter	Shuts Down Port

In Table 13-5, list the default security settings for ports.

Table 13-5   Port Security Default Settings

Feature	Default Setting
Port security	
Maximum number of secure MAC addresses	
Violation mode	
Sticky address learning	

Reference Figure 13-2 when answering the port security questions that follow.

Figure 13-2   Configuring Port Security Topology

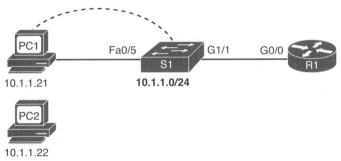

Enter the commands to enable port security on interface FastEthernet 0/5:

```
S1(config)#
S1(config-if)#
```

Although 1 is the default setting, enter the command to explicitly configure the maximum number of secure MAC addresses to 1:

```
S1(config-if)#
```

Enter the command to enable dynamically learned MAC addresses to be added to the running configuration:

```
S1(config-if)#
```

Enter the command to set the violation mode to shutdown:

```
S1(config-if)#
```

What command can you use to verify port security on the entire switch?

What command do you use to verify port security on interface FastEthernet 0/5?

Assume PC2 in Figure 13-2 is attached to FastEthernet 0/5 after the MAC address for PC1 has already been learned. Port security disables the interface. Further assume that PC2 is replacing PC1. What steps must you take to enable PC2 to gain access to the network?

1. Remove the "stuck" MAC address from the running configuration using the no switchport port-security mac-address sticky mac_address command.

2. Reactivate the shutdown interface with the no shutdown command. On some switches, you must administratively shut down the interface before entering the no shutdown command. However, on 2960 switches this is not necessary.

Configuring NTP

The _____ (NTP) allows network devices to synchronize their time settings with an NTP server. NTP can get the correct time from an internal or external time source including the following:

-

-

-

NTP Commands

A network device can be configured as either an NTP server or an NTP client. To allow the software clock to be synchronized by an NTP time server, use the _____ command in global configuration mode.

To configure a device as having an NTP master clock to which peers can synchronize themselves, use the _____ command in global configuration mode.

To display the status of NTP associations, use the _____ command in privileged EXEC mode. This command will indicate the IP address of any peer devices that are synchronized to this peer, statically configured peers, and stratum number.

The _____ user EXEC command can be used to display such information as the NTP synchronization status, the peer that the device is synchronized to, and in which NTP strata the device is functioning.

Lab - Configuring Switch Security Measures Security (RSE 2.2.4.10/SwN 2.3.4.10)

Packet Tracer - Configuring Switch Port Security (RSE 2.2.4.8/SwN 2.3.4.8)

Packet Tracer - Troubleshooting Switch Port Security Security (RSE 2.2.4.9/SwN 2.3.4.9)

Packet Tracer - Skills Integration Challenge (RSE 2.3.1.3/SwN 2.4.1.2)

CHAPTER 14

VLANs

One of the contributing technologies to excellent network performance is the separation of large broadcast domains into smaller ones with virtual local-area networks (VLANs). Smaller broadcast domains limit the number of devices participating in broadcasts and allow devices to be separated into functional groups. This chapter offers exercises to help you review how to configure, manage, and troubleshoot VLANs and Ethernet trunk links. It also reviews security considerations and strategies relating to VLANs and trunks and best practices for VLAN design.

VLAN Segmentation

VLANs give network administrators flexibility in LAN design. VLANs extend the traditional router-bounded broadcast domain to a VLAN-bounded broadcast domain; VLANs make it possible to sculpt a broadcast domain into any shape that can be defined and bounded by the switches within the network.

Overview of VLANs

A VLAN creates a _____ broadcast domain that can span multiple physical LAN segments. VLANs enable the implementation of access and security policies according to specific groupings of users. Each switch port can be assigned to only one VLAN. What are two exceptions to this rule?

Briefly describe each of the following primary benefits of using VLANs:

- Security:

- Cost reduction:

- Better performance:

- Shrink broadcast domains:

- Improved IT staff efficiency:

- Simpler project and application management:

How does a VLAN implementation affect your addressing scheme?

There are a number of distinct types of VLANs used in modern networks. Some VLAN types are defined by traffic classes. Other types of VLANs are defined by the specific function that they serve.

_____ VLAN

A _____ VLAN is a VLAN that is configured to carry user-generated traffic. A VLAN carrying voice or management traffic would not be part of a _____ VLAN. It is common practice to separate voice and management traffic from _____ traffic.

_____ VLAN

All switch ports become a part of the _____ VLAN after the initial boot of a switch loading the default configuration. The _____ VLAN for Cisco switches is VLAN _.

What is the primary reason for having this VLAN?

What are three unique features about VLAN 1?

Native VLAN

Briefly explain the purpose for the native VLAN.

Management VLAN

Briefly explain the purpose for the management VLAN.

Voice VLAN

A separate VLAN is needed to support Voice over IP (VoIP). List four requirements of VoIP traffic:

Packet Tracer - Who Hears the Broadcast? (RSE/SwN 3.1.1.5)

VLANs in a Multiswitched Environment

Briefly define a VLAN trunk.

Explain what a switch does with a frame received on an access port assigned to one VLAN before placing the frame on a trunk link for all VLANs:

The VLAN tag field consists of the following fields:

- _____: A 2-byte value called the tag protocol ID (TPID) value. For Ethernet, it is set to hexadecimal _____.

- _____: A 3-bit value that supports level or service implementation.

- _____ (CFI): A 1-bit identifier that enables Token Ring frames to be carried across Ethernet links.

- _____ (VID): A 12-bit VLAN identification number that supports up to _____ ___.

What does the switch do after tagging the frame, but before it switches it to the outbound port?

The native VLAN is used for control traffic, which is not tagged. What does an 802.1Q trunk do if it receives a frame tagged with the native VLAN ID?

Packet Tracer - Investigating a VLAN Implementation (RSE/SwN 3.1.2.7)

VLAN Implementations

In this section, we review VLAN implementations, including configuring and verifying VLANs, trunking VLANS, and troubleshooting VLAN and trunking issues.

VLAN Configuration Exercise

Use the information in Figure 14-1 and Table 14-1 to answer the following questions related to configuring VLANs and trunks.

Figure 14-1   VLAN Configuration Topology

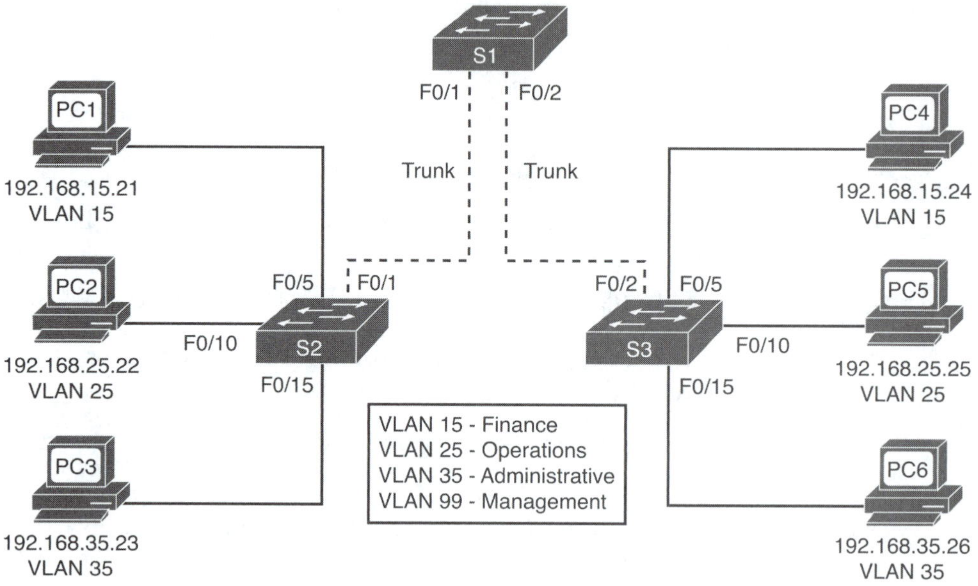

Table 14-1   VLAN Configuration Addressing Table

Device	Interface	IP Address	Subnet Mask	Default Gateway
S1	VLAN 99	192.168.99.11	255.255.255.0	N/A
S2	VLAN 99	192.168.99.12	255.255.255.0	N/A
S3	VLAN 99	192.168.99.13	255.255.255.0	N/A
PC1	NIC	192.168.15.21	255.255.255.0	192.168.15.1
PC2	NIC	192.168.25.22	255.255.255.0	192.168.25.1
PC3	NIC	192.168.35.23	255.255.255.0	192.168.35.1
PC4	NIC	192.168.15.24	255.255.255.0	192.168.15.1
PC5	NIC	192.168.25.25	255.255.255.0	192.168.25.1
PC6	NIC	192.168.35.26	255.255.255.0	192.168.35.1

Enter the commands, including the switch prompts, to configure the management interface on each switch.

Enter the commands, including the switch prompts, to configure the VLANs on each switch. (The commands are the same on each switch, so you only need to enter the commands for S1 here.)

Enter the commands, including the switch prompts, to configure access ports and assign VLANs for the PCs that are attached to S2 and S3. (Because the commands are the same on both switches, you only need to record them once.)

After you configure a VLAN, you can validate the VLAN configurations using Cisco IOS **show** commands. Enter the command used to display the following output:

```
S1#


VLAN Name                             Status    Ports
---- -------------------------------- --------- -------------------------------
1    default                          active    Fa0/3, Fa0/4, Fa0/5, Fa0/6
                                                Fa0/7, Fa0/8, Fa0/9, Fa0/10
                                                Fa0/11, Fa0/12, Fa0/13, Fa0/14
                                                Fa0/15, Fa0/16, Fa0/17, Fa0/18
                                                Fa0/19, Fa0/20, Fa0/21, Fa0/22
                                                Fa0/23, Fa0/24, Gig1/1, Gig1/2
15   Finance                          active
25   Operations                       active
35   Administrative                   active
99   Management                       active
1002 fddi-default                     active
1003 token-ring-default               active
1004 fddinet-default                  active
1005 trnet-default                    active
S1#
```

Enter the command used to display the information for only one VLAN, specifying the VLAN number:

```
S1#

VLAN Name                             Status    Ports
---- -------------------------------- --------- -------------------------------
15   Finance                          active

VLAN Type  SAID       MTU   Parent RingNo BridgeNo Stp  BrdgMode Trans1 Trans2
---- ----- ---------- ----- ------ ------ -------- ---- -------- ------ ------
15   enet  100015     1500  -      -      -        -    -        0      0

S1#
```

Enter the command used to display the information for only one VLAN, specifying the VLAN name:

```
S1#

VLAN Name                             Status    Ports
---- -------------------------------- --------- -------------------------------
25   Operations                       active

VLAN Type  SAID       MTU   Parent RingNo BridgeNo Stp  BrdgMode Trans1 Trans2
---- ----- ---------- ----- ------ ------ -------- ---- -------- ------ ------
25   enet  100025     1500  -      -      -        -    -        0      0

S1#
```

Enter the command that will display the following output:

```
S1#
Number of existing VLANs          : 9
Number of existing VTP VLANs      : 9
Number of existing extended VLANs : 0
```

Enter the command that will display the following output:

```
S2#
Name: Fa0/5
Switchport: Enabled
Administrative Mode: static access
Operational Mode: static access
Administrative Trunking Encapsulation: dot1q
Operational Trunking Encapsulation: native
Negotiation of Trunking: On
Access Mode VLAN: 15 (Finance)
Trunking Native Mode VLAN: 1 (default)
```

```
Voice VLAN: none

Administrative private-vlan host-association: none

Administrative private-vlan mapping: none

Administrative private-vlan trunk native VLAN: none

Administrative private-vlan trunk encapsulation: dot1q

Administrative private-vlan trunk normal VLANs: none

Administrative private-vlan trunk private VLANs: none

Operational private-vlan: none

Trunking VLANs Enabled: ALL

Pruning VLANs Enabled: 2-1001

Capture Mode Disabled

Capture VLANs Allowed: ALL

Protected: false

Appliance trust: none
```

Practice VLAN Configuration

Now you are ready to use Packet Tracer, another simulator, or lab equipment to apply your VLAN configurations.

Packet Tracer - Configuring VLANs (RSE/SwN 3.2.1.7)

VLAN Trunk Configuration Exercise

In Table 14-2, enter the syntax for each of the trunk configuration commands.

Table 14-2   Trunk Configuration Commands

Description	Syntax
Force the link to be a trunk link.	`S1(config-if)#`
Specify a native VLAN for untagged 802.1Q trunks.	`S1(config-if)#`
Specify the list of VLANs to be allowed on the trunk link.	`S1(config-if)#`

On S1, enter the commands to configure Fast Ethernet 0/1 to be an 802.1Q trunk. Use VLAN 99 as the native VLAN.

```
S1(config)#
S1(config-if)#
S1(config-if)#
```

What command will display the switch port status of the new trunk port shown in Example 14-1?

Example 14-1   Verifying a Trunk Configuration

```
S1#
Name: Fa0/1
Switchport: Enabled
Administrative Mode: trunk
Operational Mode: trunk
Administrative Trunking Encapsulation: dot1q
Operational Trunking Encapsulation: dot1q
Negotiation of Trunking: On
Access Mode VLAN: 1 (default)
Trunking Native Mode VLAN: 99 (VLAN0099)
Administrative Native VLAN tagging: enabled
Voice VLAN: none
Administrative private-vlan host-association: none
Administrative private-vlan mapping: none
Administrative private-vlan trunk native VLAN: none
Administrative private-vlan trunk Native VLAN tagging: enabled
Administrative private-vlan trunk encapsulation: dot1q
Administrative private-vlan trunk normal VLANs: none
Administrative private-vlan trunk associations: none
Administrative private-vlan trunk mappings: none
Operational private-vlan: none
Trunking VLANs Enabled: ALL
Pruning VLANs Enabled: 2-1001
Capture Mode Disabled
Capture VLANs Allowed: ALL

Protected: false
Unknown unicast blocked: disabled
Unknown multicast blocked: disabled
Appliance trust: none
S1#
```

Practice Trunk Configuration

Now you are ready to use Packet Tracer, another simulator, or lab equipment to add trunking to your VLAN configuration exercise. PCs in the same VLAN but attached to a different switch should now be able to ping each other.

Lab - Configuring VLANs and Trunking (RSE/SwN 3.2.2.5)

Packet Tracer - Configuring Trunks (RSE/SwN 3.2.2.4)

Dynamic Trunking Protocol

Dynamic Trunking Protocol (DTP) is a Cisco proprietary protocol that negotiates both the status of trunk ports and the trunk encapsulation of trunk ports. To enable trunking from a Cisco switch to a device that does not support DTP, use the _____ and _____ interface configuration mode commands. This causes the interface to become a trunk, but not generate DTP frames.

A switch port on a Cisco Catalyst switch supports a number of trunking modes. Identify the commands used to configure the trunking mode:

- _____: Puts the interface into permanent nontrunking mode and negotiates to convert the link into a nontrunk link.

- _____: Puts the interface into permanent trunking mode and negotiates to convert the neighboring link into a trunk link. The interface becomes a trunk interface even if the neighboring interface is not a trunk interface.

- _____: Makes the interface actively attempt to convert the link to a trunk link. The interface becomes a trunk interface if the neighboring interface is set to _____, _____, or _____ mode. This is the default switchport mode on older switches, such as the Catalyst 2950 and 3550 series switches.

- _____: Prevents the interface from generating DTP frames. You can use this command only when the interface switchport mode is **access** or **trunk**. You must manually configure the neighboring interface as a trunk interface to establish a trunk link.

- _____: Enables the interface to convert the link to a trunk link. The interface becomes a trunk interface if the neighboring interface is set to _____ or _____. This is the default switchport mode for all Ethernet interfaces.

In Table 14-3, the arguments for the **switchport mode** command are listed for the local side of the link down the first column and for the remote side of the link across the first row. Indicate whether the link will transition to access mode or trunk mode after the two switches have sent DTP messages.

Table 14-3   Trunk Negotiation Combinations

	Dynamic Auto	Dynamic Desirable	Trunk	Access
Dynamic auto				
Dynamic desirable				
Trunk				Limited Connectivity
Access			Limited Connectivity	

In Figure 14-2, indicate which DTP combinations between two switches will become trunk links and which will become access links.

Figure 14-2 Predict DTP Behavior

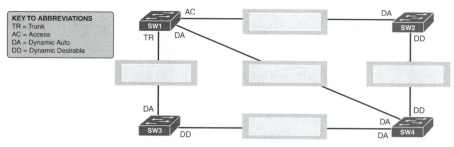

Troubleshoot VLANs and Trunks

Given the information shown in Figure 14-3 and assuming all subnets are /24, locate and explain the issue.

Figure 14-3 Troubleshooting VLANs and Trunks: IP Addressing

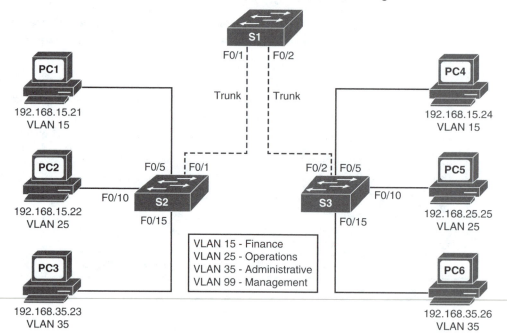

Each VLAN must correspond to a unique IP subnet. If two devices in the same VLAN have different subnet addresses, they cannot communicate. PC2 cannot communicate with P5 because, even though they are in the same VLAN, they are on different subnets.

If IP addressing issues are resolved but there is still no connection between the devices, you will need to troubleshoot VLAN configurations and assignments. Complete the flowchart in Figure 14-4, which can be used to resolve a VLAN configuration issue.

Figure 14-4   Troubleshooting VLANs and Trunks: Missing VLAN

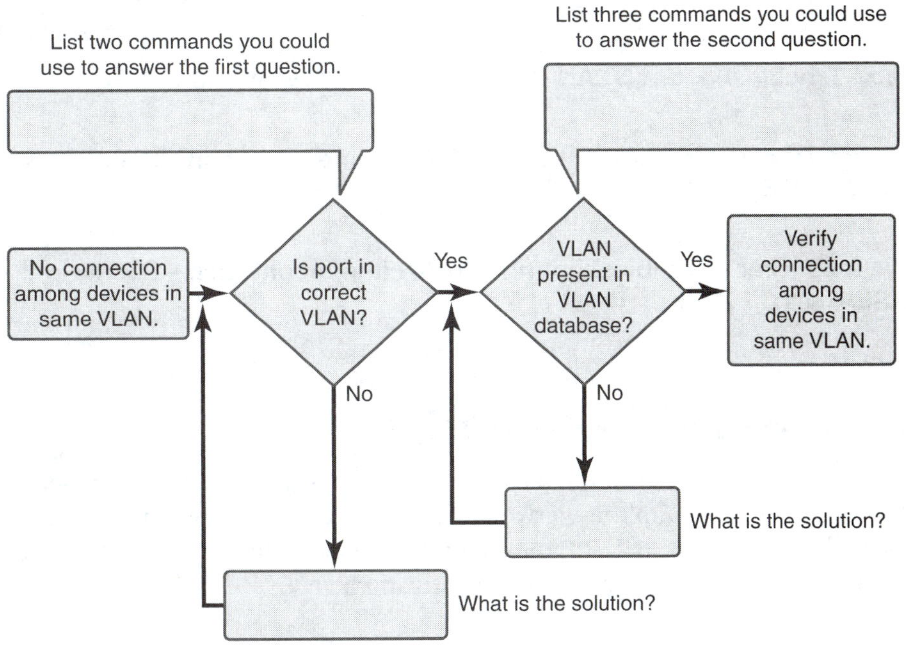

Sometimes a switch port may behave like a trunk port even if it is not configured as a trunk port. For example, an access port might accept frames from VLANs different from the VLAN to which it is assigned. This is called VLAN _____.

In Table 14-4, indicate which trunking problem is associated with each example.

Table 14-4   Troubleshooting VLANs and Trunks: Trunk Issues

Problem	Result	Example
	Causes unexpected traffic or no traffic to be sent over the trunk	List of VLANs is incomplete.
	Poses a security risk and creates unintended results	One port is in VLAN 99; the other is in VLAN 1.
	Causes loss of network connectivity	One port is configured as access mode, and the other is configured as trunk mode.

What command can you use to quickly check on the status of all the trunk ports on the switch?

What commands can you use to correct the list of VLANs for a trunk?

Lab - Troubleshooting VLAN Configurations (RSE/SwN 3.2.4.9)

Packet Tracer - Troubleshooting a VLAN Implementation - Scenario 1 (RSE/SwN 3.2.4.7)

Packet Tracer - Troubleshooting a VLAN Implementation - Scenario 2 (RSE/SwN 3.2.4.8)

VLAN Security and Design

There are a number of different types of VLAN attacks in modern switched networks. The VLAN architecture simplifies network maintenance and improves performance, but it also opens the door to abuse. It is important to understand the general methodology behind these attacks and the primary approaches to mitigate them.

Switch Spoofing Attack

Switch spoofing is a type of VLAN _____ attack that works by taking advantage of an incorrectly configured trunk port. In a basic switch spoofing attack, the attacker takes advantage of the fact that the default configuration of the switch port is _____. The network attacker configures a system to spoof itself as a switch. Describe this spoof.

What is the best way to prevent switch spoofing?

How would you disable DTP?

Double-Tagging Attack

Briefly explain a double-tagging VLAN hopping attack.

What is the best way to prevent a double-tagging VLAN hopping attack?

PVLAN Edge

The use of the private VLAN edge feature ensures that no exchange of unicast, broadcast, or multicast traffic occurs between protected ports on the local switch.

In Figure 14-5, PC1 and PC2 should not be able to see each other's Layer 2 traffic.

Figure 14-5   PVLAN Edge Configuration Scenario

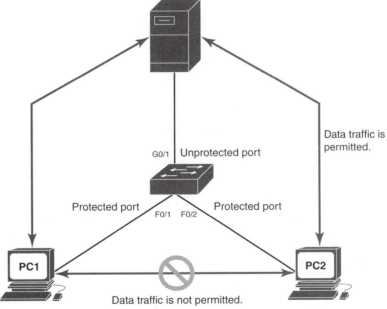

Record the commands to configure the switch so that PC1 and PC2 can communicate with the server but not with each other.

 Lab - Implementing VLAN Security (RSE/SwN 3.3.2.4)

 Packet Tracer - Skills Integration Challenge (RSE/SwN 3.4.1.2)

CHAPTER 15

Routing Concepts

The router uses its routing table to determine the best path to use to forward a packet. It is the responsibility of the routers to deliver those packets in a timely manner. The effectiveness of internetwork communications depends, to a large degree, on the ability of routers to forward packets in the most efficient way possible. This chapter reviews router configurations, path determination, and routing table analysis.

Initial Configuration of a Router

Although there are many devices and technologies collaboratively working together to enable data transfer across networks, the primary device is the router. Stated simply, a router connects one network to another network.

Functions of a Router

A router is essentially a specialized computer. It requires a CPU and memory to temporarily and permanently store data to execute operating system instructions, such as system initialization, routing functions, and switching functions.

Routers store data using a variety of memory structures:

- _____ (_____): Provides temporary storage for various applications and processes, including the running IOS. Contents are lost when powered off.

- _____ (_____): Provides permanent storage for boot instructions, basic diagnostic software, and a limited IOS in case the router cannot load the full-featured IOS.

- _____ (_____): Provides permanent storage for the startup configuration file.

- _____: Provides permanent storage for the IOS and other system-related files.

In Table 15-1, indicate the memory type in the first column and whether the memory is volatile or nonvolatile in the second column.

Table 15-1   Types of Router Memory

Memory	Volatile or Nonvolatile?	Stores
		Startup configuration file
		Boot instructions Basic diagnostic software Limited IOS
		IOS Other system files
		Running IOS Running configuration file IP routing and ARP table Packet buffer

Each _____ that a router connects to usually requires a separate interface. These interfaces are used to connect a combination of both _____ (_____) and _____ _____ (_____). _____ are commonly _____ networks that contain devices such as PCs, printers, and servers. _____ are used to connect networks over a large _____ area and are commonly used to connect a LAN to the _____ (_____) network.

What are the two primary functions of a router?

The router uses its _____ to determine the best path to forward the packet. When a match is found, the router _____ the IP packet into the data link frame of the outgoing or exit interface, and the packet is then forwarded toward its destination.

It is possible for a router to receive a packet _____ in one type of data link frame, such as an Ethernet frame, and to forward the packet out an interface that uses a different type of data link frame.

Routers use _____ routes and _____ protocols to learn about remote networks and build their routing tables.

Briefly compare process switching, fast switching, and Cisco Express Forwarding (CEF).

In Figure 15-1, draw the path that each packet will take through a router that is using process switching.

Figure 15-1   Process Switching Diagram

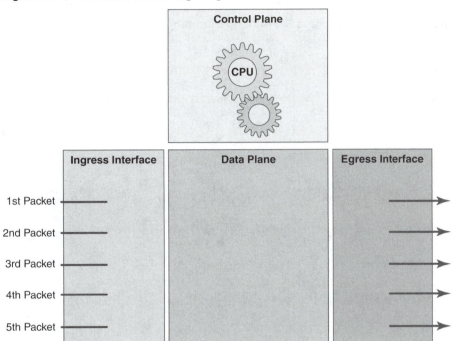

In Figure 15-2, draw the path that each packet will take through a router that is using fast switching.

Figure 15-2   Fast Switching Diagram

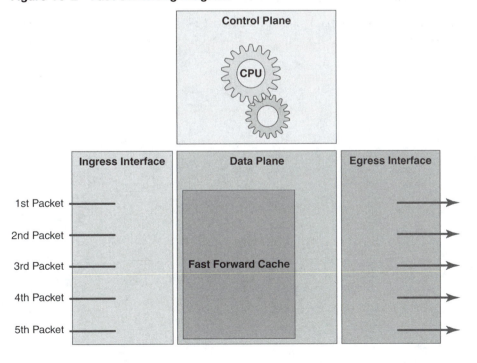

In Figure 15-3, draw the path that each packet will take through a router that is using CEF.

Figure 15-3 Cisco Express Forwarding Diagram

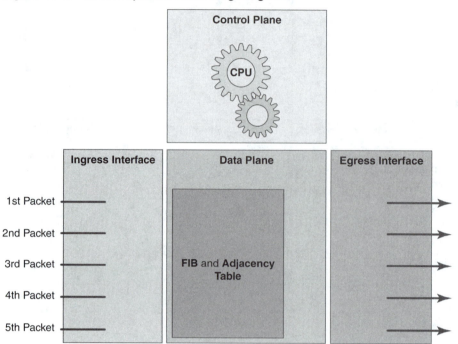

External Router Features

Figure 15-4 shows the backplane of a Cisco 1941 router. Match the letter in the figure with the backplane port or slot name.

Figure 15-4 Identify Router Components

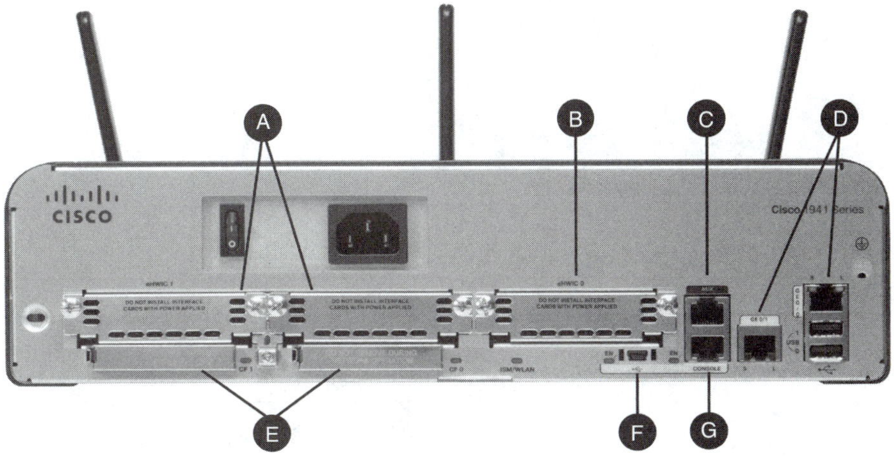

_ 4-GB flash card slots

_ Console RJ-45 port

_ eWHIC 0 slot

_ Console USB mini-B port

_ LAN interfaces

_ Double-wide eHWIC slots

_ AUX port

Lab - Mapping the Internet (RSE 4.1.1.9/RP 1.1.1.9)

Packet Tracer
☐ Activity

Packet Tracer - Using Traceroute to Discover the Network (RSE 4.1.1.8/RP 1.1.1.8)

In Figure 15-5, the LED lights are marked for each port type on the 1941 router. Complete Table 15-2 describing the meaning of each of the LED lights.

Figure 15-5   Zoom in View of Cisco 1941 LED Lights

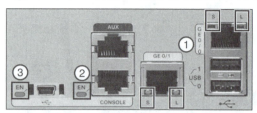

Table 15-2   LED Light Codes and Descriptions

No.	Port	LED	Code/Color	Description
1	GE0/0 and GE0/1	S (Speed)	1 blink + pause	
			2 blink + pause	
			3 blink + pause	
		L (Link)	Green	
			Off	
2	Console	EN	Green	
			Off	
3	USB	EN	Green	
			Off	

Topology and Addressing Documentation

What three pieces of addressing information does a device need to access the network?

- _____: Identifies a unique host on a local network

- _____: Identifies with which network subnet the host can communicate

- _____: Identifies the router to send a packet to when the destination is not on the same local network subnet

The topology in Figure 15-6 is properly labeled with device names, connections, and addressing. Document the addressing scheme for Figure 15-6 in Table 15-3.

Figure 15-6   Topology Diagram

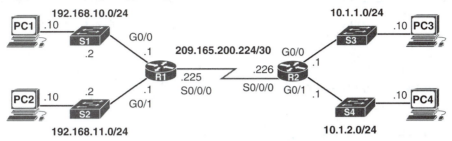

Table 15-3   Addressing Table for Figure 15-6

Device	Interface	IP Address	Subnet Mask	Default Gateway
R1	G0/0			N/A
	G0/1			N/A
	S0/0/0			N/A
R2	G0/0			N/A
	G0/1			N/A
	S0/0/0			N/A
S1	VLAN 1			
S2	VLAN 1			
S4	VLAN 1			
S4	VLAN 1			
PC1	NIC			
PC2	NIC			
PC3	NIC			
PC4	NIC			

Record the commands necessary to configure S1 with appropriate IP addressing according to your documentation in Table 15-3.

Packet Tracer - Documenting the Network (RSE 4.1.2.9/RP 1.1.2.9)

Configure and Verify Dual-Stack IPv4 and IPv6 Addressing

In this activity, you document the configuration for a router that is running both IPv4 and IPv6 (dual stack). The topology is shown in Figure 15-7, and the addressing scheme is documented in Table 15-4.

Figure 15-7   Dual-Stack Topology

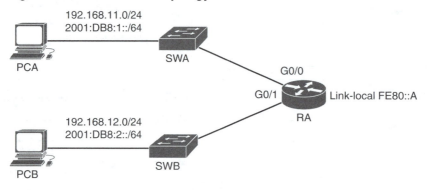

Table 15-4   Addressing Table for Figure 15-7

Device	Interface	IPv6 Address/Prefix IP Address	Subnet Mask	Default Gateway
RA	G0/0	192.168.11.1	255.255.255.0	N/A
		2001:DB8:1::1/64		N/A
	G0/1	192.168.12.1	255.255.255.0	N/A
		2001:DB8:2::1/64		N/A
	Link local	FE80::A		N/A
PCA	NIC	192.168.11.10	255.255.255.0	192.168.11.1
		2001:DB8:1::3/64		FE80::A
PCA	NIC	192.168.12.10	255.255.255.0	192.168.12.1
		2001:DB8:2::3/64		FE80::A

In the space provided, document the script for configuring RA, including the following:

- Hostname
- Passwords
- Banner
- Interface addressing and descriptions

To verify your script is accurate, you will need to apply it to a router, either in a simulator or on real equipment. After you have done so, verify the configuration with a number of commands.

Record the command that generated the following output:

```
RA#

Interface                IP-Address      OK? Method Status                Protocol

GigabitEthernet0/0       192.168.11.1    YES manual up                    up

GigabitEthernet0/1       192.168.12.1    YES manual up                    up

Serial0/0/0              unassigned      YES unset  administratively down down

Serial0/0/1              unassigned      YES unset  administratively down down

Vlan1                    unassigned      YES unset  administratively down down
```

```
RA#

Codes: L - local, C - connected, S - static, R - RIP, M - mobile, B - BGP
       D - EIGRP, EX - EIGRP external, O - OSPF, IA - OSPF inter area
       N1 - OSPF NSSA external type 1, N2 - OSPF NSSA external type 2
       E1 - OSPF external type 1, E2 - OSPF external type 2, E - EGP
       i - IS-IS, L1 - IS-IS level-1, L2 - IS-IS level-2, ia - IS-IS inter area
       * - candidate default, U - per-user static route, o - ODR
       P - periodic downloaded static route


Gateway of last resort is not set


      192.168.11.0/24 is variably subnetted, 2 subnets, 2 masks
C        192.168.11.0/24 is directly connected, GigabitEthernet0/0
L        192.168.11.1/32 is directly connected, GigabitEthernet0/0
      192.168.12.0/24 is variably subnetted, 2 subnets, 2 masks
C        192.168.12.0/24 is directly connected, GigabitEthernet0/1
L        192.168.12.1/32 is directly connected, GigabitEthernet0/1
```

```
RA#

GigabitEthernet0/0 is up, line protocol is up (connected)
  Hardware is CN Gigabit Ethernet, address is 0006.2a7b.b501 (bia 0006.2a7b.b501)
  Internet address is 192.168.11.1/24
  MTU 1500 bytes, BW 1000000 Kbit, DLY 10 usec,
     reliability 255/255, txload 1/255, rxload 1/255
  Encapsulation ARPA, loopback not set
  Keepalive set (10 sec)
  Full-duplex, 100Mbps, media type is RJ45
  output flow-control is unsupported, input flow-control is unsupported
  ARP type: ARPA, ARP Timeout 04:00:00,
  Last input 00:00:08, output 00:00:05, output hang never
  Last clearing of "show interface" counters never
  Input queue: 0/75/0 (size/max/drops); Total output drops: 0
  Queueing strategy: fifo
  Output queue :0/40 (size/max)
```

```
    5 minute input rate 0 bits/sec, 0 packets/sec
    5 minute output rate 0 bits/sec, 0 packets/sec
        10 packets input, 1184 bytes, 0 no buffer
        Received 0 broadcasts, 0 runts, 0 giants, 0 throttles
        0 input errors, 0 CRC, 0 frame, 0 overrun, 0 ignored, 0 abort
        0 watchdog, 1017 multicast, 0 pause input
        0 input packets with dribble condition detected
        10 packets output, 1184 bytes, 0 underruns
        0 output errors, 0 collisions, 1 interface resets
        0 unknown protocol drops
        0 babbles, 0 late collision, 0 deferred
        0 lost carrier, 0 no carrier
        0 output buffer failures, 0 output buffers swapped out
```

```
RA#
GigabitEthernet0/0 is up, line protocol is up (connected)
  Internet address is 192.168.11.1/24
  Broadcast address is 255.255.255.255
  Address determined by setup command
  MTU is 1500 bytes
  Helper address is not set
  Directed broadcast forwarding is disabled
  Outgoing access list is not set
  Inbound  access list is not set
  Proxy ARP is enabled
  Security level is default
  Split horizon is enabled
  ICMP redirects are always sent
  ICMP unreachables are always sent
  ICMP mask replies are never sent
  IP fast switching is disabled
  IP fast switching on the same interface is disabled
  IP Flow switching is disabled
  IP Fast switching turbo vector
  IP multicast fast switching is disabled
  IP multicast distributed fast switching is disabled
  Router Discovery is disabled
  IP output packet accounting is disabled
  IP access violation accounting is disabled
  TCP/IP header compression is disabled
  RTP/IP header compression is disabled
  Probe proxy name replies are disabled
  Policy routing is disabled
  Network address translation is disabled
```

```
        BGP Policy Mapping is disabled

        Input features: MCI Check

        WCCP Redirect outbound is disabled

        WCCP Redirect inbound is disabled

        WCCP Redirect exclude is disabled
```

```
RA#

GigabitEthernet0/0              [up/up]

    FE80::A

    2001:DB8:1::1

GigabitEthernet0/1              [up/up]

    FE80::A

    2001:DB8:2::1

Serial0/0/0                     [administratively down/down]

Serial0/0/1                     [administratively down/down]

Vlan1                           [administratively down/down]
```

```
RA#

GigabitEthernet0/0 is up, line protocol is up

  IPv6 is enabled, link-local address is FE80::A

  No Virtual link-local address(es):

  Global unicast address(es):

    2001:DB8:1::1, subnet is 2001:DB8:1::/64

  Joined group address(es):

    FF02::1

    FF02::2

    FF02::1:FF00:1

    FF02::1:FF00:A

  MTU is 1500 bytes

  ICMP error messages limited to one every 100 milliseconds

  ICMP redirects are enabled

  ICMP unreachables are sent

  ND DAD is enabled, number of DAD attempts: 1

  ND reachable time is 30000 milliseconds

  ND advertised reachable time is 0 milliseconds

  ND advertised retransmit interval is 0 milliseconds

  ND router advertisements are sent every 200 seconds

  ND router advertisements live for 1800 seconds

  ND advertised default router preference is Medium

  Hosts use stateless autoconfig for addresses.
```

```
RA#
IPv6 Routing Table - 5 entries
Codes: C - Connected, L - Local, S - Static, R - RIP, B - BGP
       U - Per-user Static route, M - MIPv6
       I1 - ISIS L1, I2 - ISIS L2, IA - ISIS interarea, IS - ISIS summary
       O - OSPF intra, OI - OSPF inter, OE1 - OSPF ext 1, OE2 - OSPF ext 2
       ON1 - OSPF NSSA ext 1, ON2 - OSPF NSSA ext 2
       D - EIGRP, EX - EIGRP external
C   2001:DB8:1::/64 [0/0]
     via ::, GigabitEthernet0/0
L   2001:DB8:1::1/128 [0/0]
     via ::, GigabitEthernet0/0
C   2001:DB8:2::/64 [0/0]
     via ::, GigabitEthernet0/1
L   2001:DB8:2::1/128 [0/0]
     via ::, GigabitEthernet0/1
L   FF00::/8 [0/0]
     via ::, Null0
RA#
```

Lab - Configuring Basic Router Settings with IOS CLI (RSE 4.1.4.6/RP 1.1.4.6)

Lab - Configuring Basic Router Settings with CCP (RSE 4.1.4.7/RP 1.1.4.7)

Packet Tracer - Configuring IPv4 and IPv6 Interfaces (RSE 4.1.3.5/RP 1.1.3.5)

Packet Tracer - Configuring and Verifying a Small Network (RSE 4.1.4.5/RP 1.1.4.5)

Routing Decisions

The activities in this section review the specifics of the two primary functions of a router: path determination and switching packets.

Path Determination

Complete the flowchart in Figure 15-9 to indicate the path determination decisions that a router makes based on the destination address and the information in the routing table.

Figure 15-8   Path Determination Flowchart

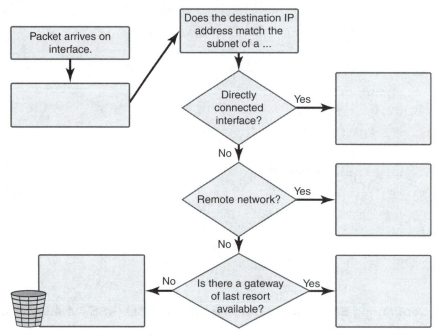

Match the path determination decision on the left with the scenario on the right. Some decisions may be used more than once.

Decision

    a. Drop the packet and send an ICMP message back to the source IP address.

    b. Encapsulate the frame and forward it out of the exit interface to the next hop.

    c. Check the ARP cache and forward to the host on the local subnet.

Scenario

_____ Your router has received a packet destined for an IP address of a local subnet. Your router has a recorded routing table entry for this subnet, and it is on a directly connected interface.

_____ Your router received a packet destined for an IP address on a remote network. Your router has a routing table entry for the remote network.

_____ Your router received a packet destined for an IP address on another network. The destination IP address is not on a local network and does not match anything in your routing table. There is no gateway of last resort available.

_____ Your router received a packet destined for an IP address on another network. The destination IP address is not on a local network and does not match anything in your routing table, but there is a gateway of last resort.

Concept of Administrative Distance Exercise

A router can learn about a route from multiple sources. If the type of source for two or more routes is different, the router must use administrative distance to help make the path determination decision.

Complete Table 15-5 for the default administrative distances used by a Cisco router.

Table 15-5   Default Administrative Distances

Route Source	AD
Connected	
EIGRP summary route	5
External BGP	20
Internal EIGRP	
IGRP	100
	110
IS-IS	115
	120
External EIGRP	170
Internal BGP	200
Unknown	255

Switching Packets Between Networks

Refer to Figure 15-9 to answer the following questions.

Figure 15-9   Mapping Layer 2 and Layer 3 Addresses

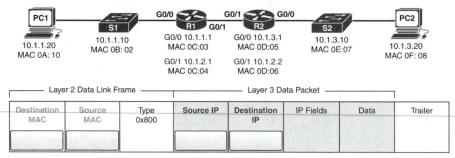

PC1 sends a ping to PC2. What are the Layer 2 and Layer 3 addresses that PC1 will use to encapsulate the packet and frame before sending it to R1?

- Destination MAC:

- Source MAC:

- Source IP:

- Destination IP:

R1 receives the ping from PC1. What are the Layer 2 and Layer 3 addresses that R1 will use to encapsulate the packet and frame before sending it to R2?

- Destination MAC:

- Source MAC:

- Source IP:

- Destination IP:

R2 receives the ping from R1. What are the Layer 2 and Layer 3 addresses that R2 will use to encapsulate the packet and frame before sending it to PC2?

- Destination MAC:

- Source MAC:

- Source IP:

- Destination IP:

PC2 receives the ping from R2. What are the Layer 2 and Layer 3 addresses that PC2 will use to encapsulate the reply packet and frame before sending it to R2?

- Destination MAC:

- Source MAC:

- Source IP:

- Destination IP:

What role do the switches have in relation to addressing in this scenario?

What do you notice about the Layer 2 addressing?

What do you notice about the Layer 3 addressing?

Router Operation

The routing table of a router stores information about directly connected routes learned when an interface is configured with an IP address and is activated. The routing table also stores information about remote networks connected to other routers. These routes are learned either from static configurations or dynamically through a configured routing protocol.

Analyze the Routing Table

Use the **show ip route** command to display the routing table for IPv4 routes, as shown in Example 15-1.

Example 15-1   IPv4 Routing Table

```
R1# show ip route
<output omitted>
Gateway of last resort is not set
      10.0.0.0/8 is variably subnetted, 2 subnets, 2 masks
D        10.1.1.0/24 [90/2170112] via 209.165.200.226, 00:00:05, Serial0/0/0
D        10.1.2.0/24 [90/2170112] via 209.165.200.226, 00:00:05, Serial0/0/0
      192.168.10.0/24 is variably subnetted, 2 subnets, 3 masks
C        192.168.10.0/24 is directly connected, GigabitEthernet0/0
L        192.168.10.1/32 is directly connected, GigabitEthernet0/0
      192.168.11.0/24 is variably subnetted, 2 subnets, 3 masks
C        192.168.11.0/24 is directly connected, GigabitEthernet0/1
L        192.168.11.1/32 is directly connected, GigabitEthernet0/1
      209.165.200.0/24 is variably subnetted, 2 subnets, 3 masks
C        209.165.200.224/30 is directly connected, Serial0/0/0
L        209.165.200.225/32 is directly connected, Serial0/0/0
R1#
```

The sources of the routing table entries are identified by a code. The code identifies how the route was learned. What does each of the following codes mean?

- L:

- C:
- S:
- D:
- O:

Refer to the topology in Figure 15-10. R1 has learned the route shown in the route entry below the topology. Label each part of the route entry with the letter shown in the legend.

Figure 15-10 Identify Parts of a Route Table Entry

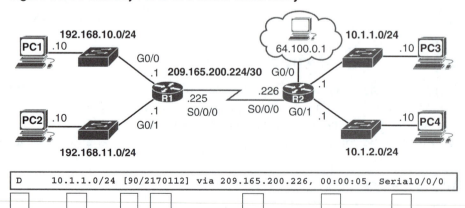

Legend

A	Identifies the destination network
B	Identifies the amount of elapsed time since the network was discovered
C	Identifies the outgoing interface on the router to reach the destination network
D	Identifies the next hop IP address to reach the remote network
E	Identifies how the network was learned by the router
F	Identifies the administrative distance (trustworthiness) of the route source
G	Identifies the metric to reach the remote network

Directly Connected, Static, and Dynamic Routes

What three things must happen before the interface state on a router is considered up/up and added to the IPv4 routing table?

-
-
-

In the following exercise, you configure three directly connected routers.

Enter the router prompt and commands to configure the GigabitEthernet 0/0 interface on R2 with the IP address 10.1.1.1 and subnet mask 255.255.255.0. Describe the link as Link to LAN 3 and activate the interface.

```
*Aug 11 15:08:34.139: %LINK-3-UPDOWN: Interface GigabitEthernet0/0, changed state to
down

*Aug 11 15:08:36.951: %LINK-3-UPDOWN: Interface GigabitEthernet0/0, changed state to
up

*Aug 11 15:08:37.951: %LINEPROTO-5-UPDOWN: Line protocol on Interface
GigabitEthernet0/0, changed state to up
```

Enter the router prompt and commands to configure the GigabitEthernet 0/1 interface on R2 with the IP address 10.1.2.1 and subnet mask 255.255.255.0. Describe the link as Link to LAN 4 and activate the interface.

```
*Aug 11 15:09:56.915: %LINK-3-UPDOWN: Interface GigabitEthernet0/1, changed state to
down

*Aug 11 15:09:59.951: %LINK-3-UPDOWN: Interface GigabitEthernet0/1, changed state to
up

*Aug 11 15:10:00.951: %LINEPROTO-5-UPDOWN: Line protocol on Interface
GigabitEthernet0/1, changed state to up
```

Enter the router prompt and commands to configure the Serial 0/0/0 interface with the IP address 209.165.200.226 and subnet mask 255.255.255.252. Describe the link as Link to R1 and activate the interface.

```
*Aug 11 15:11:18.451: %LINK-3-UPDOWN: Interface Serial0/0/0, changed state to up

*Aug 11 15:11:19.451: %LINEPROTO-5-UPDOWN: Line protocol on Interface Serial0/0/0,
changed state to up
```

What are the two common types of static routes?

-

-

What is the command syntax to configure the two types of IPv4 static routes?

Enter the router prompt and commands to configure R2 with an IPv4 static route to the 192.168.10.0/24 network using the Serial 0/0/0 exit interface.

Enter the router prompt and commands to configure R2 with an IPv4 default route using the Serial 0/0/0 exit interface.

What is the command syntax to configure the two types of IPv6 static routes?

Enter the router prompt and commands to configure R2 with an IPv6 static route to the 2001:DB8:1:1::/64 network using the Serial 0/0/0 exit interface.

Enter the router prompt and commands to configure R2 with an IPv6 default route using the Serial 0/0/0 exit interface.

What are the four main routing protocols that are the focus of the CCENT and CCNA certifications?

Packet Tracer - Investigating Directly Connected Routes (RSE 4.3.2.5/RP 1.3.2.5)

CHAPTER 16

Inter-VLAN Routing

VLANs segment a switched network to provide improved performance, manageability, and security. Trunks are used to carry information from multiple VLANs between devices. However, because these VLANs have segmented the network, a Layer 3 process is required to allow traffic to move from one network segment to another. In this chapter, we look at the implementation of inter-VLAN routing.

Inter-VLAN Routing Configuration

Remember that a VLAN is a broadcast domain, so computers on separate VLANs are unable to communicate without the intervention of a routing device. Any device that supports Layer 3 routing, such as a router or a multilayer switch, can be used to perform the necessary routing functionality.

Types of Inter-VLAN Routing

Briefly describe each of the types of inter-VLAN routing.

In Figure 16-1, identify the type of inter-VLAN routing shown in each of the topologies.

Figure 16-1   Topology Examples of Types of Inter-VLAN Routing

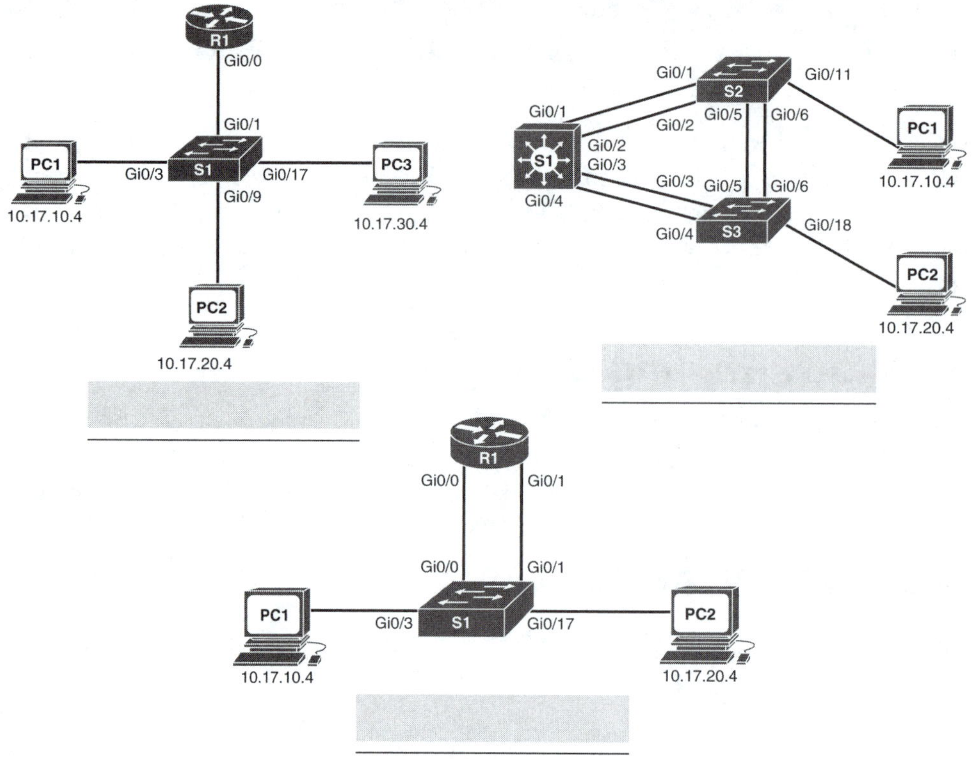

Configuring Inter-VLAN Routing

Legacy inter-VLAN routing (or per-interface inter-VLAN routing) requires multiple physical interfaces between the router and the switch. The switch interfaces are set to access mode and assigned one VLAN. The router needs nothing special to route the VLAN traffic other than addressing for the VLAN's subnet. Because this is legacy inter-VLAN routing, we will not review it any further. You just need to be aware of what it is and how it is configured.

An alternative in larger networks is to use VLAN trunking and subinterfaces. VLAN trunking allows a single physical router interface to route traffic for multiple VLANs. This technique is termed router on a stick and uses virtual subinterfaces on the router to overcome the hardware limitations based on physical router interfaces.

List the commands including command syntax and prompt to configure a router for router-on-a-stick inter-VLAN routing:

List the commands including syntax and prompt to configure a switch to support inter-VLAN routing.

What commands cannot be used on the router? Why?

Refer to Figure 16-2 and enter the commands for both R1 and S1 to enable inter-VLAN routing.

Figure 16-2   Inter-VLAN Routing Topology

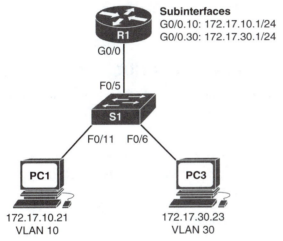

```
R1(config)#
```

```
S1(config)#
```

Lab - Configuring Per-Interface Inter-VLAN Routing (RSE 5.1.2.4/SwN 6.1.2.4)

Lab - Configuring 801.2Q Trunk-Based Inter-VLAN Routing (RSE 5.1.3.7/SwN 6.1.3.7)

Packet Tracer - Configuring Router-on-a-Stick Inter-VLAN Routing (RSE 5.1.3.6/SwN 6.1.3.6)

Troubleshoot Inter-VLAN Routing

Several common switch misconfigurations can arise when configuring routing between multiple VLANs. One of the best ways to practice troubleshooting is to team up with a partner. Using an existing configuration that is fully operational, each of you takes a turn introducing a few errors so that the other team member has a chance to use troublehooting skills to locate and solve the problem. However, it helps to know which commands are most useful in troubleshooting inter-VLAN routing issues.

Inter-VLAN Troubleshooting Scenarios

As you know, the **ping** and **tracert/traceroute** can be helpful in isolating the general location of a connectivity problem. But to further isolate an inter-VLAN routing issue, you might need several additional commands.

In Examples 16-1 and 16-2, fill in the command used to generate the output. Highlight relevant parts of the output that would help in isolating inter-VLAN routing issues. Then document the error and possible solution.

Example 16-1   Inter-VLAN Troubleshooting Scenario 1

```
Switch#
Name: Gi0/23
Switchport: Enabled
Administrative Mode: dynamic auto
Operational Mode: static access
Administrative Trunking Encapsulation: dot1q
Operational Trunking Encapsulation: native
Negotiation of Trunking: On
Access Mode VLAN: 1 (default)
Trunking Native Mode VLAN: 1 (default)
(output omitted)
```

What error or errors do you see in Example 16-1?

What solution would you recommend?

Example 16-2   Inter-VLAN Troubleshooting Scenario 2

```
Interface                      IP-Address      OK? Method Status
Protocol
Embedded-Service-Engine0/0 unassigned    YES unset  administratively down down
GigabitEthernet0/0             unassigned      YES unset  administratively down down
GigabitEthernet0/0.10          172.17.10.1     YES manual up                    up
GigabitEthernet0/0.30          172.17.30.1     YES manual up                    up
GigabitEthernet0/1             unassigned      YES unset  administratively down down
Serial0/0/0                    unassigned      YES unset  administratively down down
Serial0/0/1                    unassigned      YES unset  administratively down down
```

What error or errors do you see in Example 16-2?

What solution would you recommend?

Refer to the topology in Figure 16-3.

Figure 16-3   Inter-VLAN Troubleshooting Scenario 3

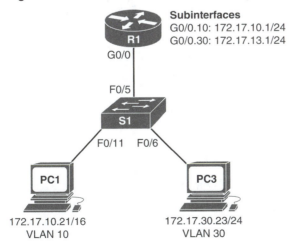

Subinterfaces
G0/0.10: 172.17.10.1/24
G0/0.30: 172.17.13.1/24

R1

G0/0

F0/5

S1

F0/11   F0/6

PC1
172.17.10.21/16
VLAN 10

PC3
172.17.30.23/24
VLAN 30

What error or errors do you see?

What solution would you recommend?

 Packet Tracer - Troubleshooting Inter-VLAN Routing (RSE 5.2.2.4/SwN 6.2.2.4)

Layer 3 Switching

Router on a stick is simple to implement because routers are usually available in every network. But most enterprise networks use multilayer switches to achieve high-packet processing rates using hardware-based switching.

Layer 3 Switching Operation

All Catalyst multilayer switches support the following types of Layer 3 interfaces:

- _____: A pure Layer 3 interface similar to a physical interface on a Cisco IOS router.

- _____ (SVI): A virtual VLAN interface for inter-VLAN routing. In other words, SVIs are the virtual-routed VLAN interfaces.

What kind of switch forwarding do high-performance Catalyst switches use?

What are some reasons and advantages for configuring SVIs?

-

-

-

-

-

-

-

What is the purpose of the **no switchport** command?

What are two advantages of using a multilayer switch port?

- ▪
- ▪

Configuring Static Routes on a Catalyst 2960

By using the **sdm lanbase-routing** template, a Catalyst 2960 switch can function as a Layer 3 device and route between VLANs and a limited number of static routes.

Record the command to display the current Switch Database Manager (SDM) template.

```
S1#
 The current template is "default" template.
 The selected template optimizes the resources in
 the switch to support this level of features for
 0 routed interfaces and 255 VLANs.

   number of unicast mac addresses:              8K
   number of IPv4 IGMP groups:                   0.25K
   number of IPv4/MAC qos aces:                  0.125k
   number of IPv4/MAC security aces:             0.375k
```

Record the command that will display the options shown in the following output:

```
S1# configure terminal
Enter configuration commands, one per line.  End with CNTL/Z.
S1(config)#
   default                Default bias
   dual-ipv4-and-ipv6  Support both IPv4 and IPv6
   lanbase-routing        Supports both IPv4 and IPv6 Static Routing
   qos                    QoS bias
```

Record the command to configure the switch to support routing.

```
S1(config)#
Changes to the running SDM preferences have been stored, but cannot take effect
until the next reload.
Use 'show sdm prefer' to see what SDM preference is currently active.
```

Record the command to reload the switch at the current prompt.

```
Switch(config)#

System configuration has been modified. Save? [yes/no]: yes

Building configuration...

[OK]

Proceed with reload? [confirm]

*Mar 20 00:10:24.557: %SYS-5-RELOAD: Reload requested by console. Reload Reason:
Reload command.
```

The switch is now in user EXEC mode. Record the commands to enter privileged EXEC mode and display the current SDM template.

```
S1>

S1#

 The current template is "lanbase-routing" template.

 The selected template optimizes the resources in

 the switch to support this level of features for

 0 routed interfaces and 255 VLANs.


  number of unicast mac addresses:                    4K

  number of IPv4 IGMP groups + multicast routes:    0.25K

  number of IPv4 unicast routes:                      0.75K

     number of directly-connected IPv4 hosts:         0.75K

     number of indirect IPv4 routes:                  16

  number of IPv6 multicast groups:                    0.375k

  number of directly-connected IPv6 addresses:       0.75K

     number of indirect IPv6 unicast routes:          16

  number of IPv4 policy based routing aces:          0

  number of IPv4/MAC qos aces:                        0.125k

  number of IPv4/MAC security aces:                   0.375k

  number of IPv6 policy based routing aces:          0

  number of IPv6 qos aces:                            0.375k

  number of IPv6 security aces:                       127

S1#
```

Record the commands necessary to configure S1 with a default route to the next-hop IP address 192.168.1.10.

```
S1# configure terminal

Enter configuration commands, one per line.  End with CNTL/Z.

S1(config)#

S1(config)#
```

What command displays the following output at the current prompt?

```
S1(config)#
Codes: L - local, C - connected, S - static, R - RIP, M - mobile, B - BGP
       D - EIGRP, EX - EIGRP external, O - OSPF, IA - OSPF inter area
       N1 - OSPF NSSA external type 1, N2 - OSPF NSSA external type 2
       E1 - OSPF external type 1, E2 - OSPF external type 2
       i - IS-IS, su - IS-IS summary, L1 - IS-IS level-1, L2 - IS-IS level-2
       ia - IS-IS inter area, * - candidate default, U - per-user static route
       o - ODR, P - periodic downloaded static route, H - NHRP, l - LISP
       + - replicated route, % - next hop override


Gateway of last resort is 192.168.1.10 to network 0.0.0.0


S*     0.0.0.0/0 [1/0] via 192.168.1.10
       192.168.1.0/24 is variably subnetted, 2 subnets, 2 masks
C          192.168.1.0/24 is directly connected, Vlan1
L          192.168.1.1/32 is directly connected, Vlan1
       192.168.2.0/24 is variably subnetted, 2 subnets, 2 masks
C          192.168.2.0/24 is directly connected, Vlan2
L          192.168.2.1/32 is directly connected, Vlan2
```

Layer 3 Switching Troubleshooting Scenarios

Use Figure 16-4 for each of the following Layer 3 switching troubleshooting scenarios.

Figure 16-4   Layer 3 Switching Troubleshooting Topology

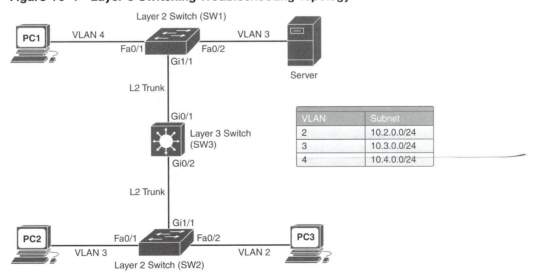

PC2 is unable to communicate with PC3 but can communicate with all other devices. Refer to the command output in Example 16-3. Then select the most likely causes for this issue. More than one answer choice may be selected.

Example 16-3   Layer 3 Switching Troubleshooting Scenario 1

```
SW3# show ip route
<output omitted>
Gateway of last resort is not set
     10.0.0.0/8 is variably subnetted, 3 subnets, 3 masks
C       10.2.0.0/24 is directly connected, Vlan5
C       10.3.0.0/24 is directly connected, Vlan3
C       10.4.0.0/24 is directly connected, Vlan4
```

VLAN 5 IP address is not correct.

VLAN 4 has no IP address.

VLAN 3 IP address is not correct.

VLAN 2 is not configured.

VLAN 3 and 4 are shut down.

PC3 is unable to communicate with any of the other devices, including its own gateway. Refer to the command output in Example 16-4. Then select the most likely causes for this issue. More than one answer choice may be selected.

Example 16-4   Layer 3 Switching Troubleshooting Scenario 2

```
SW3# show ip route
<output omitted>
Gateway of last resort is not set
     10.0.0.0/8 is variably subnetted, 3 subnets, 3 masks
C        10.2.0.0/30 is directly connected, Vlan2
C        10.3.0.0/24 is directly connected, Vlan3
C        10.4.0.0/24 is directly connected, Vlan4
```

VLAN 4 subnet mask is not correct.

VLAN 4 IP address is not correct.

VLAN 2 subnet mask is not correct.

VLAN 2 is not configured.

VLAN 3 IP address is not correct.

PC1 is unable to communicate with PC2 or PC3 but can communicate with the server. Refer to the command output in Example 16-4. Then select the most likely causes for this issue. More than one answer choice may be selected.

Example 16-5   Layer 3 Switching Troubleshooting Scenario 3

```
SW3# show interface trunk
Port          Mode          Encapsulation   Status          Native vlan
Gig0/1        auto          n-802.1q                trunking    1
```

VLAN 2 and 3 are being pruned from the trunk links.

SW2 is shut down.

The trunk encapsulation is not correct.

The gigabit 0/2 port is not configured as a trunk.

The gigabit 0/1 port is not configured as a trunk.

VLAN 2 is not configured.

 Lab - Troubleshooting Inter-VLAN Routing (RSE 5.3.2.4/SwN 6.3.2.4)

 Packet Tracer - Skills Integration Challenge (RSE 5.4.1.2/SwN 6.4.1.2)

Packet Tracer
☐ **Activity**

CHAPTER 17

Static Routing

Routers learn about remote networks using one of the following methods:

- Dynamically, using routing protocols
- Manually, using static routes

This chapter covers static routing, including default routes and summary routes, for both IPv4 and IPv6 networks.

Static Routing Implementation

Unlike a dynamic routing protocol, static routes are not automatically updated and must be manually reconfigured any time the network topology changes. A static route does not change until the administrator manually reconfigures it.

Static Routing Overview

In Table 17-1, indicate the type of routing for each characteristic.

Table 17-1   Dynamic vs. Static Routing

Characteristic	Dynamic Routing	Static Routing
This type of routing is more secure.		
The route to the destination depends on the current topology.		
Administrator intervention is required when there is a topology change.		
Uses no extra router resources.		
Suitable for simple and complex topologies.		
This type of routing is less secure.		
Configuration complexity increases with network size.		
Configuration complexity is generally independent of the network size.		
Uses more CPU, memory, and link bandwidth.		
The route to the destination is always the same.		
Suitable for simple topologies.		
Automatically adapts to topology changes.		

Briefly describe three reasons to use static routing.

■

■

■

Identify Types of Static Routes

Briefly describe each of the following types of static routes:

■ Standard static route:

■ Default static route:

■ Summary static route:

■ Floating static route:

In Table 17-2, indicate what type of route is described.

Table 17-2   Identify Types of Static Routes

Static Routing Descriptor	Standard	Default	Summary	Floating
Uses a single network address to send multiple static routes to one destination address				
Backs up a route already discovered by a dynamic routing protocol				
Configured with a higher administrative distance than the original dynamic routing protocol				
Useful when connecting to stub networks				
Matches all packets and sends them to a specific default gateway				
Commonly used with edge routers to connect to the ISP network				

Configure Static and Default Routes

We briefly covered static and default route configurations in Chapter 15, "Routing Concepts." In this chapter, we use a master topology to guide your configuration of both IPv4 and IPv6 static routes.

Configuring IPv4 Static and Default Routes

Figure 17-1 shows the topology for IPv4 routes, and Table 17-3 shows the addressing scheme.

Note: The topology uses loopback interfaces to simulate directly connected LANs. By using loopback interfaces, you can build rather complex scenarios without the need for a physical interface for every network.

Figure 17-1   Topology for IPv4 Static Routes

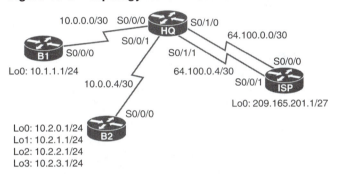

Table 17-3   Addressing Table for IPv4 Static Routes Topology

Device	Interface	IP Address	Subnet Mask
ISP	S0/0/0	64.100.0.1	255.255.255.252
	S0/0/1	64.100.0.5	255.255.255.252
HQ	S0/0/0	10.0.0.1	255.255.255.252
	S0/0/1	10.0.0.5	255.255.255.252
	S0/1/0	64.100.0.2	255.255.255.252
	S0/1/1	64.100.0.6	255.255.255.252
B1	S0/0/0	10.0.0.2	255.255.255.252
	Lo0	10.1.1.1	255.255.255.0
B2	S0/0/0	10.0.0.6	255.255.255.252
	Lo0	10.2.0.1	255.255.255.0
	Lo1	10.2.1.1	255.255.255.0
	Lo2	10.2.2.1	255.255.255.0
	Lo3	10.2.3.1	255.255.255.0

For now, we focus only on standard static routes and default routes. But you should already be able to see how summary routes and floating static routes would be helpful in this topology.

B1 and B2 Routing Strategy

Because B1 and B2 are both stub routers, what type of static route would you configure on these routers?

Record the commands to configure the appropriate type of static route on B1 using the next-hop IP address argument.

B1#

Record the commands to configure the appropriate type of static route on B2 using the exit interface argument.

B2#

HQ Routing Strategy

HQ operates as a hub router for B1 and B2 and provides access to the Internet through ISP. What type of static routes would you configure on HQ?

Record the commands to configure the appropriate type of static routes on HQ. Assume that HQ will use both links to ISP. Configure the routes to B1 and B2 with the next-hop IP address argument. Configure the routes to ISP with the exit interface argument.

Briefly explain a fully specified static route and when it might be used.

Lab - Configuring IPv4 Static and Default Routes (RSE 6.2.2.5/RP 2.2.2.5)

Packet Tracer
☐ Activity

Packet Tracer - Configuring IPv4 Static and Default Routes (RSE 6.2.2.4/RP 2.2.2.4)

Configuring IPv6 Static and Default Routes

Figure 17-2 shows the topology for IPv6 routes and Table 17-4 shows the addressing scheme.

Figure 17-2   Topology for IPv6 Static Routes

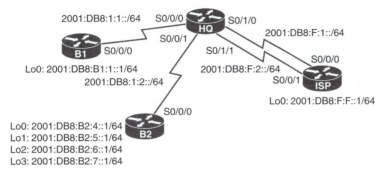

Table 17-4   Addressing Table for IPv6 Static Routes Topology

Device	Interface	IPv6 Address/Prefix
ISP	S0/0/0	2001:DB8:F:1::1/64
	S0/0/1	2001:DB8:F:2::1/64
	Link local	FE80::F
HQ	S0/0/0	2001:DB8:1:1::1/64
	S0/0/1	2001:DB8:1:2::1/64
	S0/1/0	2001:DB8:F:1::2/64
	S0/1/1	2001:DB8:F:2::2/64
	Link local	FE80::A
B1	S0/0/0	2001:DB8:1:1::2/64
	Lo0	2001:DB8:B1:1::1/64
	Link local	FE80::1
B2	S0/0/0	2001:DB8:1:2::2/64
	Lo0	2001:DB8:B2:4::1/64
	Lo1	2001:DB8:B2:5::1/64
	Lo2	2001:DB8:B2:6::1/64
	Lo3	2001:DB8:B2:7::1/64
	Link local	FE80::2

For now, we focus only on standard static routes and default routes.

B1 and B2 Routing Strategy

Because B1 and B2 are both stub routers, what type of static route would you configure on these routers?

Record the commands to configure the appropriate type of static route on B1 using the next-hop IP address argument.

```
B1#
```

Record the commands to configure the appropriate type of static route on B2 using the exit interface argument.

```
B2#
```

HQ Routing Strategy

HQ operates as a hub router for B1 and B2 and provides access to the Internet through an ISP. What type of static routes would you configure on HQ?

Record the commands to configure the appropriate type of static routes on HQ. Assume that HQ will use both links to ISP. Configure the routes to B1 and B2 with the next-hop IP address argument. Configure the routes to ISP with the exit interface argument.

In what situation must you use a fully specified IPv6 static route?

Record the commands to configure a fully specified IPv6 default route from B1 to HQ using the link-local address.

```
B1#
```

Lab - Configuring IPv6 Static and Default Routes (RSE 6.2.4.5/RP 2.2.4.5)

Packet Tracer
☐ Activity

Packet Tracer - Configuring IPv6 Static and Default Routes (RSE 6.2.4.4/RP 2.2.4.4)

Review of CIDR and VLSM

This section includes a discussion of classful addressing, CIDR, and how to calculate a summary route. We covered VLSM in detailed in Chapter 9, "Subnetting IP Networks"; refer back to that material if you need a refresher.

Classful Addressing

In the original specification of IPv4 described in RFCs 790 and 791, the authors established classes to provide three different address spaces for small, medium, and large networks.

Fill in the empty cells in Table 17-3 to complete the IPv4 address classes.

Table 17-3   IPv4 Class Structure

Class	High-order Bits	Start	End	Subnet Mask	# of Networks	# of Hosts/ Network
A	0xxxxxxx	0.0.0.0	127.255.255.255	255.0.0.0	126	~16.7 million
B						
C						
D				N/A	N/A	N/A
E				N/A	N/A	N/A

CIDR and Route Summarization

The classful addressing specified in RFCs 790 and 791 resulted in a tremendous waste of address space. For this reason, classless interdomain routing (CIDR) was introduced in 1993. CIDR replaced the classful network assignments, and address classes (A, B, and C) became obsolete. Using CIDR, the network address is no longer determined by the value of the first octet. Instead, the network portion of the address is determined by the subnet mask, also known as the network prefix, or prefix length (that is, /8, /19, and so on).

Briefly describe how CIDR reduces the size of routing tables and manages the IPv4 address space more efficiently using

- Route summarization:

- Supernetting:

The mechanics for calculating a summary route are rather straightforward and required before you can configure a summary route. Determining the summary route and subnet mask for a group of networks can be done in the following three steps:

Step 1.   List the networks in binary format.

Step 2.   Count the number of far-left matching bits. This identifies the prefix length or subnet mask for the summarized route.

Step 3.   Copy the matching bits, and then add 0 bits to the rest of the address to determine the summarized network address.

Let's walk through the steps with an example. Figure 17-3 shows a hub-and-spoke topology with three branch routers. B1 has a supernet assigned to its LAN. B2 and B3 each have regular Class C networks assigned to their LANs. Note that the network addresses are contiguous and can be easily summarized into one network/prefix combination, as shown in Example 17-1.

Figure 17-3   Hub-and-Spoke Topology with Contiguous LANs

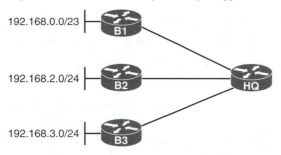

192.168.0.0/23 — B1

192.168.2.0/24 — B2 — HQ

192.168.3.0/24 — B3

Example 17-1   Summary Route Calculation

```
Network            3rd Octet

192.168.0.0        00000000

192.168.2.0        00000010

192.168.3.0        00000011

----------------------

192.168.0.0        00000000
```

The highlighted matching bits shown in the example become part of the summarized network address. The remaining 2 bits plus the 8 bits in the fourth octet are now the host portion. Subtract the 10 host bits from the 32 bits to get the summary prefix 22. Therefore, 192.168.0.0/22 is the summary address of the contiguous networks 192.168.0.0/23, 192.168.2.0/24, and 192.168.3.0/24.

Practice calculating summary routes in the next three scenarios.

Summary Route Calculation Scenario 1

Summarize the networks 10.10.8.0/24, 10.10.9.0/24, 10.10.10.0/24, and 10.10.11.0/24.

Summary Route Calculation Scenario 2

Summarize the networks 192.168.0.0/24, 192.168.1.0/25, 192.168.1.128/26, 192.168.1.192/27, and 192.168.1.224/27.

Summary Route Calculation Scenario 3

Summarize the networks 172.16.0.0/14, 172.20.0.0/15, 172.22.0.0/15, and 172.24.0.0/13.

Lab - Designing and Implementing Addressing with VLSM (RSE 6.3.3.7/RP 2.3.3.7)

Packet Tracer - Designing and Implementing a VLSM Addressing Scheme (RSE 6.3.3.6/RP 2.3.3.6)

Configure Summary and Floating Static Routes

There is not a lot more to say about summary routes, although we will practice calculating a few IPv6 summary routes. Now that you know how to calculate an IPv4 summary, configuring the IPv4 summary static route is the same as configuring an IPv4 standard static route. Floating static routes use an additional argument in the static route command so that you can manually set the administrative distance. In this section, you will configure summary and floating static routes for both IPv4 and IPv6 networks.

Configure IPv4 Summary Routes

Refer back to the IPv4 topology in Figure 17-1. Calculate the summary for the four simulated LANs on B2.

Record the command to configure an IPv4 summary static route on HQ using the exit interface argument.

```
HQ(config)#
```

Refer back to the three summary route calculation scenarios in the Section Review of CIDR and VLSM. Record the command to configure a summary static route for each scenario. Use Serial 0/0/0 as the exit interface.

Summary Route Configuration Scenario 1

```
Router(config)#
```

Summary Route Configuration Scenario 2

```
Router(config)#
```

Summary Route Configuration Scenario 3

```
Router(config)#
```

Which of the three scenario summary routes are considered supernets? Why?

Packet Tracer - Configuring IPv4 Route Summarization - Scenario 1 (RSE 6.4.1.5/RP 2.4.1.5)

Packet Tracer - Configuring IPv4 Route Summarization - Scenario 2 (RSE 6.4.1.6/RP 2.4.1.6)

Configure IPv6 Summary Routes

Aside from the fact that IPv6 addresses are 128 bits long and written in hexadecimal, summarizing IPv6 addresses is actually similar to the summarization of IPv4 addresses. It just requires a few extra steps due to the abbreviated IPv6 addresses and hex conversion.

Summarizing IPv6 networks into a single IPv6 prefix and prefix length can be done in seven steps. For example, let's use the topology shown in Figure 17-4.

Step 1.   List the network addresses (prefixes) and identify the part where the addresses differ.

```
2001:DB8:1:8::/64
2001:DB8:1:A::/64
2001:DB8:1:C::/64
2001:DB8:1:E::/64
```

Step 2.   Expand the hextets if they are abbreviated. Here, we didn't expand the last four hextets because we know that they are all 0s.

```
2001:0DB8:0001:0008::/64
2001:0DB8:0001:000A::/64
2001:0DB8:0001:000C::/64
2001:0DB8:0001:000E::/64
```

Step 3.   Convert the hextet that is different to binary.

```
2001:0DB8:0001:0000000000001000::/64
2001:0DB8:0001:0000000000001010::/64
2001:0DB8:0001:0000000000001100::/64
2001:0DB8:0001:0000000000001110::/64
```

Step 4.   Count the number of far-left matching bits to determine the prefix length for the summary route. In this example, the prefix length will be /61.

```
2001:0DB8:0001:0000000000001000::/64
2001:0DB8:0001:0000000000001010::/64
2001:0DB8:0001:0000000000001100::/64
2001:0DB8:0001:0000000000001110::/64
   16 + 16 + 16 +       13       = /61
```

Step 5.   Copy the matching bits, and then add 0 bits to determine the summarized network address (prefix).

```
2001:0DB8:0001:0000000000001000::/64
2001:0DB8:0001:0000000000001000::/64
2001:0DB8:0001:0000000000001000::/64
2001:0DB8:0001:0000000000001000::/64
```

Step 6.   Convert the binary section back to hex.

```
2001:0DB8:0001:0000000000001000::/64
2001:0DB8:0001:0000000000001000::/64
2001:0DB8:0001:0000000000001000::/64
2001:0DB8:0001:0000000000001000::/64
          2001:DB8:1:8::
```

Step 7.   Append the prefix of the summary route (result of Step 4).

```
2001:0DB8:0001:0000000000001000::/64
2001:0DB8:0001:0000000000001000::/64
2001:0DB8:0001:0000000000001000::/64
2001:0DB8:0001:0000000000001000::/64
          2001:DB8:1:8::/61
```

Refer back to the IPv6 topology in Figure 17-2. Calculate the summary for the four simulated LANs on B2.

Record the command to configure an IPv6 summary static route on HQ using the exit interface argument.

```
HQ(config)#
```

Lab - Calculating Summary Routes with IPv4 and IPv6 (RSE 6.4.2.5/RP 6.4.2.5)

Packet Tracer - Configuring IPv6 Route Summarization (RSE 6.4.2.4/RP 2.4.2.4)

Configure Floating Static Routes

As you recall from Chapter 15, administrative distance is used by the router to choose a route when more than one route exists for a given destination. We can leverage this route decision process to create a floating static route that will not be installed in the routing table unless the primary static route fails.

For example, refer back to the topologies in Figures 17-1 and 17-2. HQ has two connections to ISP. Let's assume that the link attached to Serial 0/1/0 is a high-speed primary route that HQ uses as the primary route to send traffic to ISP. The other link attached to Serial 0/1/1 is a much slower connection and is used only as a backup route in case the primary route fails.

To configure this backup route as a floating static route, we must manually set the administrative distance to be higher than the default administrative distance of a static route. Because a static route's default administrative distance is 1, anything higher than 1 will suffice to create the floating static route. The command syntax for both IPv4 and IPv6 static and default routes with the administrative distance option follows:

```
ip route network mask {next-hop-ip | exit-intf} [admin-dist]

ip route 0.0.0.0 0.0.0.0 {exit-intf | next-hop-ip} [admin-dist]

ipv6 route ::/0 {ipv6-address | interface-type interface-number} [admin-dist]

ipv6 route ipv6-prefix/prefix-length {ipv6-address|interface-type interface-number}
[admin-dist]
```

Refer to Figure 17-1. Record the command to configure HQ with an IPv4 floating static default route to ISP.

```
HQ(config)#
```

Assume that ISP is also configured with static routes. Record the commands to configure ISP with an IPv4 summary static route to the 10.0.0.0/14 address space using Serial 0/0/0 as the exit interface.

```
ISP(config)#
```

Record the command to configure ISP with an IPv4 floating static route to the 10.0.0.0/14 address space using Serial 0/0/1 as the exit interface.

```
ISP(config)#
```

Refer to Figure 17-2. Record the command to configure HQ with an IPv6 floating static default route to ISP.

```
HQ(config)#
```

ISP would need at least four IPv6 static routes to the networks accessible through HQ. Record the commands to configure a floating static summary route to the four simulated B2 LANs. Use Serial 0/0/1 as the exit interface.

```
ISP(config)#
```

Packet Tracer - Configuring a Floating Static Route (RSE 6.4.3.4/RP 2.4.3.4)

Troubleshoot Static and Default Route Issues

When there is a change in the network, connectivity may be lost. Network administrators are responsible for pinpointing and solving the problem. To find and solve these issues, a network administrator must be familiar with the tools to help isolate routing problems quickly.

Common IOS troubleshooting commands include the following:

```
ping
traceroute
show ip route
show ip interface brief
show cdp neighbors detail
```

IPv4 Static and Default Route Implementation

One of the best ways to learn how to troubleshoot a given technology is to practice. Implement the IPv4 scenario in Figure 17-1 and Table 17-3 in a simulator or lab equipment. Verify your configurations by testing for full connectivity. From B1 and B2, you should be able to ping the loopback interface on ISP. After you have a complete implementation, ask a fellow student or lab partner to break your configuration. Use your troubleshooting skills to locate and solve the problem.

IPv6 Static and Default Route Implementation

Now practice implementing IPv6 static and default routes. For an extra challenge, implement IPv6 in a dual-stack configuration with your IPv4 implementation. Verify connectivity, and then have your lab partner break your configuration. Use your troubleshooting skills to locate and solve the problem.

Lab - Troubleshooting Static Routes (RSE 6.5.2.5/RP 2.5.2.5)

Packet Tracer - Troubleshooting Static Routes (RSE 6.5.2.3/RP 2.5.2.3)

Packet Tracer - Troubleshooting VLSM and Route Summarization (RSE 6.5.2.4/RP 2.5.2.3)

Packet Tracer Skills Integration Challenge (RSE 6.6.1.2/RP 2.6.1.2)

CHAPTER 18

Routing Dynamically

Routers forward packets by using information in the routing table. Routes to remote networks can be learned by the router in two ways: static routes and dynamic routes. In a large network with numerous networks and subnets, configuring and maintaining static routes between these networks requires a great deal of administrative and operational overhead. Implementing dynamic routing protocols can ease the burden of configuration and maintenance tasks and give the network scalability.

Dynamic Routing Protocols

Dynamic routing protocols have been used in networks since the late 1980s. As networks evolved and became more complex, new routing protocols emerged. To support the communication based on IPv6, newer versions of the IP routing protocols have been developed.

Dynamic Routing Protocol Operation

List at least three purposes of a dynamic routing protocol.

-
-
-
-

Briefly describe the three main components of dynamic routing protocols.

- Data structures:

- Routing protocol messages:

- Algorithm:

Compare Static and Dynamic Routing

In Table 18-1, indicate whether the characteristic applies to static routing or dynamic routing.

Table 18-1   Static and Dynamic Routing Characteristics

Characteristic	Static Routing	Dynamic Routing
Suitable for multiple router topologies.		
If possible, adapts topology to reroute traffic.		
Easy to implement in a small network.		
Requires more CPU, RAM, and link bandwidth.		
Route to the destination is always the same.		
More secure because route information is not advertised.		

From Cold Start to Convergence

Cold Start

What does a router know when it first boots?

After it boots, what does the router know about the network topology?

In Figure 18-1, the routers have booted. However, they have not yet discovered any neighbors. In the tables below each router, fill in the networks, interfaces, and hop counts that each router has installed in its routing table.

Figure 18-1   Network Discovery: Cold Start

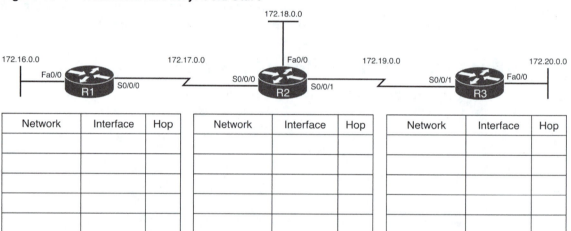

Network	Interface	Hop

Network	Interface	Hop

Network	Interface	Hop

Exchanging the Routing Information

What is required before the routers will start sending each other updates?

For the first round of updates after a cold start, what information will the updates include?

In Figure 18-2, the routers have completed their initial exchange of routing updates. In the tables that follow each router, fill in the networks, interfaces, and hop counts that each router now has installed in its routing table.

Figure 18-2   Network Discovery: Initial Exchange

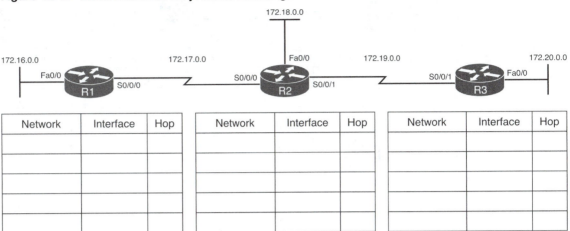

At this point in the network discovery process, the routing tables are incomplete. In other words, the network has not yet converged.

Which routing tables and which networks still need to be discovered?

Next Update

Continuing the journey toward convergence, the routers exchange the next round of periodic updates.

In Figure 18-3, the routers have completed their next round of updates. In the tables after each router, fill in the networks, interfaces, and hop counts that each router now has installed in its routing table.

Figure 18-3   Network Discovery: Next Update

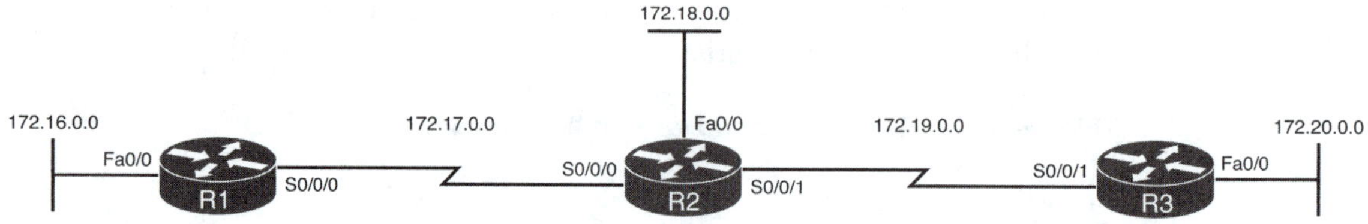

172.18.0.0

172.16.0.0   172.17.0.0   Fa0/0   172.19.0.0   172.20.0.0
Fa0/0   S0/0/0   S0/0/1   Fa0/0
        S0/0/0   S0/0/1
R1   R2   S0/0/1   R3

Network	Interface	Hop		Network	Interface	Hop		Network	Interface	Hop

Convergence

The network has converged when all routers have complete and accurate information about the entire network, as should be shown in Figure 18-3. Convergence time is the time it takes routers to share information, calculate best paths, and update their routing tables. A network is not completely operable until the network has converged; therefore, most networks require short convergence times.

Convergence is both collaborative and independent. Explain what this means.

Packet Tracer - Investigating Convergence (RSE 7.1.3.6/RP 3.1.3.6)

Dynamic Routing Protocols Classification Chart

The chart in Figure 18-4 is a succinct way to represent the major classifications of dynamic routing protocols. For each of the empty boxes, write in the missing protocol.

Figure 18-4   Classifying Dynamic Routing Protocols

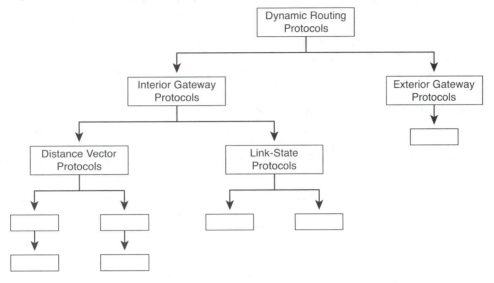

Routing Protocols Characteristics

Briefly explain each of the following routing protocol characteristics.

Time to Convergence

Scalability

Classless (Use of VLSM) or Classful

Resource Usage

Implementation and Maintenance

Comparing Routing Protocol Characteristics

In Table 18-2, routing protocols are compared based on the characteristics you briefly described in the previous exercise. For each characteristic, circle the description that applies to each routing protocol. For example, RIP is slow to converge. So, you would circle Slow in the Speed of Convergence row under both RIPv1 and RIPv2.

Table 18-2   Routing Protocol Characteristics

	Distance Vector				Link-State	
	RIPv1	RIPv2	IGRP	EIGRP	OSPF	IS-IS
Speed of Convergence	Slow Fast	Slow Fast	Slow Fast	Slow Fast	Slow Fast	Slow Fast
Scalability (Size of Network)	Small Large	Small Large	Small Large	Small Large	Small Large	Small Large
Use of VLSM	Yes No	Yes No	Yes No	Yes No	Yes No	Yes No
Resource Usage	Low Medium High	Low Medium High	Low Medium High	Low Medium High	Low Medium High	Low Medium High
Implementation and Maintenance	Simple Complex	Simple Complex	Simple Complex	Simple Complex	Simple Complex	Simple Complex

Distance Vector Dynamic Routing

Distance vector routing protocols share updates between neighbors. Each router is only aware of the network addresses of its own interfaces and the remote network addresses it can reach through its neighbors. Routers using distance vector routing are not aware of the network topology.

Distance Vector Operation and Terminology

At the core of the distance vector protocol is the routing algorithm. The algorithm is used to calculate the best paths and then send that information to the neighbors. The algorithm is responsible for what three processes?

- ▪
- ▪
- ▪

Match the distance vector term on the left with the description on the right. This exercise is a one-to-one matching. Each term has exactly one matching description.

Term

   a. algorithm

   b. Bellman-Ford

   c. broadcast updates

   d. DUAL

   e. neighbors

   f. periodic updates

Description

____ A timed process, with updates sent to neighboring routers at regular intervals.

____ A process where neighbor routers receive network updates at a specific network address.

____ EIGRP uses this algorithm process as developed by Cisco.

____ RIP uses this algorithm process.

____ Process that calculates the best paths to networks.

____ Describes routers that share a link and the same routing protocol.

Comparing RIP and EIGRP

In Table 18-3, indicate the routing protocol for each characteristic or features.

Table 18-3   RIP and EIGRP Comparison

Characteristic or Feature	RIP	EIGRP
Multicasts bounded, triggered updates to 224.0.0.10.		
Broadcasts routing updates to 255.255.255.255.		
Version 2 supports VLSM and classless routing.		
Forms neighbor adjacencies table.		
Uses administrative distance of 120.		
Fastest converging routing protocol.		
Uses DUAL algorithm.		
Maximum limit of 255 hops.		
Routing updates sent every 30 seconds.		
Maximum limit of 15 hops.		
Sends hello packets.		
Version 2 multicasts updates to 224.0.0.9.		
Uses administrative distance of 90 for internal routes.		

Packet Tracer - Comparing RIP and EIGRP Path Selection (RSE 7.2.2.4/RP 3.2.2.4)

RIP and RIPng Routing

Although RIP is rarely used in modern networks, it is useful as a foundation for understanding basic network routing. For this reason, this section provides practice for configuring RIPv2 and RIPng.

Configuring RIPv2

Refer to the topology in Figure 18-5 and the addressing scheme in Table 18-4. Label the topology with interface designations and network addresses.

Figure 18-5   RIPv2 Topology

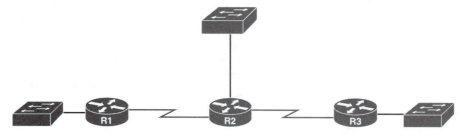

Table 18-4   RIPv2 Addressing Scheme

Device	Interface	IPv4 Address	Subnet Mask
R1	G0/0	172.16.1.1	255.255.255.0
	S0/0/0	172.16.2.1	255.255.255.0
R2	G0/0	172.16.3.1	255.255.255.0
	S0/0/0	172.16.2.2	255.255.255.0
	S0/0/1	172.16.4.2	255.255.255.0
R3	G0/0	172.16.5.1	255.255.255.0
	S0/0/1	172.16.4.1	255.255.255.0

Record the commands to configure each router with RIPv2, disable automatic summarization, and stop routing updates from propagating out unnecessary interfaces.

```
R1#
```

```
R2#
```

```
R3#
```

What is the effect of disabling automatic summarization?

List three reasons for disabling routing updates out unnecessary interfaces.

Assume that R1 is connected to the Internet out of Serial 0/0/1. Record the commands to configure a default route and advertise the default route to R2.

```
R1(config)#
```

Configuring RIPng

Refer to the topology in Figure 18-6 and the addressing scheme in Table 18-5. Label the topology with interface designations and network addresses.

Figure 18-6   RIPng Topology

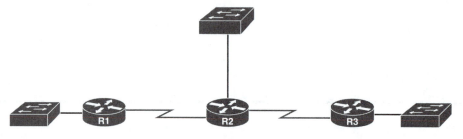

Table 18-5   RIPng Addressing Scheme

Device	Interface	IPv6 Address/Prefix
R1	G0/0	2001:DB8:1:1::1/64
	S0/0/0	2001:DB8:1:2::1/64
R2	G0/0	2001:DB8:1:3::1/64
	S0/0/0	2001:DB8:1:2::2/64
	S0/0/1	2001:DB8:1:4::2/64
R3	G0/0	2001:DB8:1:5::1/64
	S0/0/1	2001:DB8:1:4::1/64

Record the commands to configure each router with RIPng. Use a name of your choice.

```
R1#
```

```
R2#
```

```
R3#
```

Lab - Configuring RIPv2 (RSE 7.3.2.4/RP 3.3.2.4)

Packet Tracer - Configuring RIPv2 (RSE 7.3.1.8/RP 3.3.1.8)

Packet Tracer - Configuring RIPng (RSE 7.3.2.3/RP 3.3.2.3)

Link-State Dynamic Routing

Distance vector routing protocols are like road signs; routers must make preferred path decisions based on a distance or metric to a network. Just as travelers trust a road sign to accurately state the distance to the next town, a distance vector router trusts that another router is advertising the true distance to the destination network.

Link-state routing protocols take a different approach. Link-state routing protocols are more like a road map because they create a topological map of the network and each router uses this map to determine the shortest path to each network. Just as you refer to a map to find the route to another town, link-state routers use a map to determine the preferred path to reach another destination.

Link-State Routing Protocol Operation

Link-state routing protocols are also known as _____ (SPF) protocols and are built around Edsger _____'s SPF algorithm.

The IPv4 link-state routing protocols include

- _____ (_____)
- _____ (_____)

Just like RIP and EIGRP, basic OSPF operations can be configured using the

- _____ global configuration command
- _____ command to advertise networks

The SPF algorithm accumulates _____ along each path, from source to destination. Each router calculates the SPF algorithm and determines the _____ from its own perspective.

Using Figure 18-7, complete the following tables filling in the appropriate information for each router. As an example, Table 18-6 for R1 is partially complete.

Figure 18-7   Topology of Link-State Routers

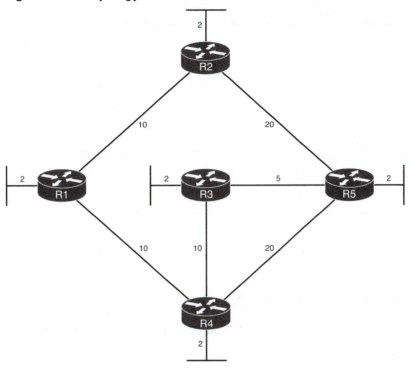

Table 18-6   SPF Tree for R1

Destination	Shortest Path	Cost
R2 LAN	R1 to R2	12
R3 LAN	R1 to R4 to R3	22
R4 LAN		
R5 LAN		

Table 18-7   SPF Tree for R2

Destination	Shortest Path	Cost
R1 LAN		
R3 LAN		
R4 LAN		
R5 LAN		

Table 18-8   SPF Tree for R3

Destination	Shortest Path	Cost
R1 LAN		
R2 LAN		
R4 LAN		
R5 LAN		

Table 18-9 SPF Tree for R4

Destination	Shortest Path	Cost
R1 LAN		
R2 LAN		
R3 LAN		
R5 LAN		

Table 18-10 SPF Tree for R5

Destination	Shortest Path	Cost
R1 LAN		
R2 LAN		
R3 LAN		
R4 LAN		

Building the Link-State Database

All routers in the area will complete the following generic link-state routing process to reach a state of convergence:

1. Each router learns about its own links and its own directly connected networks. This is done by detecting that an interface is in the __ state.

2. Each router is responsible for meeting its neighbors on directly connected networks. Link state routers do this by exchanging _____ packets with other link-state routers on _____ networks.

3. Each router builds a link-state packet (LSP) containing the state of each _____ _____ link. This is done by recording all the pertinent information about each neighbor, including _____, _____, and _____.

4. Each router floods the LSP to all neighbors, who then store all LSPs received in a _____ ____. Neighbors then flood the LSPs to their neighbors until all routers in the area have received the LSPs. Each router stores a copy of each LSP received from its neighbors in a local _____.

5. Each router uses the _____ to construct a complete map of the _____ and computes the best path to each destination network.

The topology in Figure 18-8 now shows the network addresses and interfaces for R5.

Figure 18-8   Topology the Perspective of R5

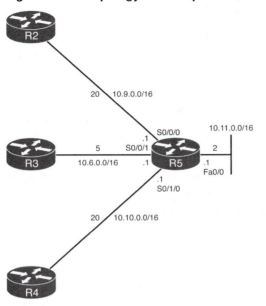

The first step in the link-state routing process is that each router learns about its own links and its own directly connected networks. This occurs when you correctly configure and activate the interfaces.

In Table 18-11, list the link-state information for R5, including the network address, type of interface, the address, cost, and neighbor.

Table 18-11   Link-State Information for R5

Network Address	Interface	IP Address	Cost	Neighbor

The second step in the link-state routing process is that each router is responsible for meeting its neighbors on directly connected networks.

Routers with link-state routing protocols use a _____ protocol to discover any neighbors on its links. In relation to link state routing, what is a neighbor?

Small hello packets are periodically exchanged between two adjacent neighbors and serve as a _____ function to monitor the state of the neighbor. If a router stops receiving hello packets from a neighbor, that neighbor is considered _____ and the adjacency is broken.

The third step in the link-state routing process is that each router builds a link-state packet (LSP) containing the state of each directly connected link.

Once a router has established its adjacencies, it can build its LSPs that contain the link-state information about its links. Table 18-9 you filled out previously should contain all of the information for R5's LSP.

The fourth step in the link-state routing process is that each router floods the LSP to all neighbors, who then store all LSPs received in a database.

What happens when a router receives an LSP from a neighbor?

The final step in the link-state routing process is for a router to use its own database to construct a complete map of the topology and compute the best path to each destination network.

After each router has propagated its own LSPs using the link-state flooding process, each router will then have an LSP from every link-state router in the routing area. These LSPs are stored in the link-state database. Each router in the routing area can now use the SPF algorithm to construct the SPF trees that you saw earlier.

Figure 18-9 shows the entire topology with network addresses.

Figure 18-9   Topology of Link-State Routers with Network Address

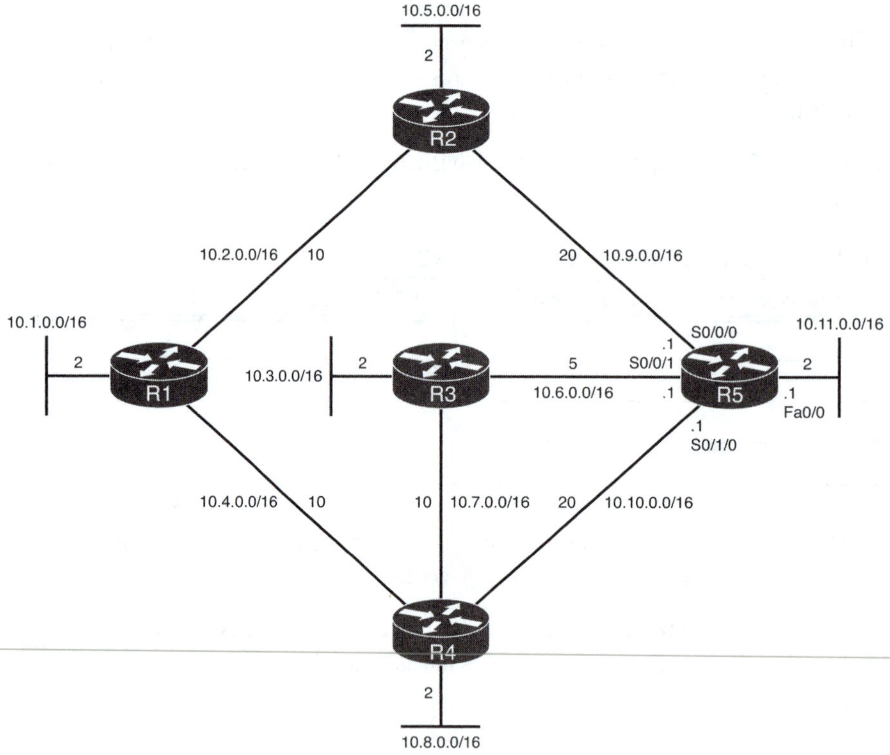

Table 18-12 shows partial information in the link-state database for R5 after all LSPs have been received and R5 is ready to calculate the SPF algorithm. Fill in the missing information

Table 18-12   Link-State Database for R5

LSPs from R1		
- Connected to neighbor	on network	, cost of
- Connected to neighbor	on network	, cost of
- Has a network	, cost of	

LSPs from R2		
- Connected to neighbor R1 on network 10.2.0.0/16, cost of		
- Connected to neighbor R5 on network	, cost of	
- Has a network	, cost of	

LSPs from R3		
- Connected to neighbor	on network	, cost of
- Connected to neighbor	on network	, cost of
- Has a network	cost of	

LSPs from R4		
- Connected to neighbor	on network	, cost of
- Connected to neighbor	on network	, cost of
- Connected to neighbor	on network	, cost of
- Has a network	, cost of	

R5 Link States		
- Connected to neighbor	on network	, cost of
- Connected to neighbor	on network	, cost of
- Connected to neighbor	on network	, cost of
- Has a network	, cost of	

Because all LSPs have been processed using the SPF algorithm, R5 has now constructed the complete SPF tree. Table 18-13 repeats the SPF tree for R5 that you determined earlier. Fill in the table again here.

Table 18-13   SPF Tree for R5

Destination	Shortest Path	Cost
R1 LAN		
R2 LAN		
R3 LAN		
R4 LAN		

Using this tree, the SPF algorithm results indicate the shortest path to each network. Only the LANs are shown in the table, but SPF can also be used to determine the shortest path to each WAN link network shown in Figure 10-3 earlier. Complete the missing information in the following list for R5's shortest path to each network:

- Network 10.1.0.0/16 via ___ serial _____ at a cost of ___
- Network 10.2.0.0/16 via ___ serial _____ at a cost of ___
- Network 10.3.0.0/16 via ___ serial _____ at a cost of _
- Network 10.4.0.0/16 via ___ serial _____ at a cost of ___

- Network 10.5.0.0/16 via __ serial _____ at a cost of __
- Network 10.7.0.0/16 via __ serial _____ at a cost of __
- Network 10.8.0.0/16 via __ serial _____ at a cost of __

Using Link-State Routing Protocols

List three advantages and disadvantages of using link-state routing protocols when compared to distance vector routing protocols.

Advantages

-
-
-

-

Disadvantages

-
-
-

The Routing Table

The structure or format of the routing table might seem obvious until you take a closer look. Understanding the structure of the routing table will help you verify and troubleshoot routing issues because you will understand the routing table lookup process. You will know exactly what the Cisco IOS does when it searches for a route.

Identifying Elements of the Routing Table

The purpose of this exercise is to practice how to correctly identify the route source, administrative distance, and metric for a given route based on output from the **show ip route** command.

The output is not common for most routing tables. Running more than one routing protocol on the same router is rare. Running three, as shown here, is more of an academic exercise and has value in that it will help you learn to interpret the routing table output.

Using the **show ip route** information in Example 18-1, fill in the missing spaces in Table 18-14.

Note: The output is from IOS 12 so local routes are not shown.

Example 18-1   **Multiple Routing Sources in the Routing Table**

```
R2# show ip route
Codes: C - connected, S - static, I - IGRP, R - RIP, M - mobile, B - BGP
       D - EIGRP, EX - EIGRP external, O - OSPF, IA - OSPF inter area
       N1 - OSPF NSSA external type 1, N2 - OSPF NSSA external type 2
       E1 - OSPF external type 1, E2 - OSPF external type 2, E - EGP
       i - IS-IS, L1 - IS-IS level-1, L2 - IS-IS level-2, ia - IS-IS inter area
       * - candidate default, U - per-user static route, o - ODR
       P - periodic downloaded static route


Gateway of last resort is not set


     10.0.0.0/16 is subnetted, 1 subnets
S       10.4.0.0 is directly connected, Serial0/0
     172.16.0.0/24 is subnetted, 3 subnets
C       172.16.1.0 is directly connected, FastEthernet0/0
C       172.16.2.0 is directly connected, Serial0/0
D       172.16.3.0 [90/2172416] via 172.16.2.1, 00:00:18, Serial0/0
C     192.168.1.0/24 is directly connected, Serial0/1
O     192.168.100.0/24 [110/65] via 172.16.2.1, 00:00:03, Serial0/0
O     192.168.110.0/24 [110/65] via 172.16.2.1, 00:00:03, Serial0/0
R     192.168.120.0/24 [120/1] via 172.16.2.1, 00:00:18, Serial0/0
```

Table 18-14   Route Sources, AD Values, and Metrics

Route	Route Source	AD	Metric
10.4.0.0/16			
172.16.1.0/24			
172.16.2.0/24			
172.16.3.0/24			
192.168.1.0/24			
192.168.100.0/24			
192.168.110.0/24			
192.168.120.0/24			

Dynamically Learned IPv4 Routes

The Cisco IP routing table is not a flat database, but a _____ structure that is used to speed up the lookup process when locating routes and forwarding packets. This structure includes several levels. For simplicity, we will discuss all routes as one of two levels: level 1 or level 2.

Briefly describe an ultimate route.

Briefly describe a level 1 route.

List the three types of level 1 routes.

List the three sources of level 1 routes.

The level 1 route can be further defined as an ultimate route.

Indicate which of the following routes are level 1 routes by writing yes or no in the blank in front of the route.

Level 1 route?

____   192.168.1.0/24

____   192.168.1.32/27

____   192.168.4.0/22

____   172.16.0.0/14

____   172.16.0.0/16

____   172.16.1.0/24

____   10.1.0.0/16

____   10.0.0.0/8

What is the main difference between a parent route and an ultimate route?

What is the relationship between parent and child routes?

In the partial output of the routing table in Example 18-2, indicate whether each route is a parent route or a child route by checking the appropriate column.

Example 18-2   Parent and Child Routes: Classful

```
        172.16.0.0/16 is subnetted, 2 subnets
C           172.16.1.0/24 is directly connected, GigabitEthernet0/0
L           172.16.1.1/32 is directly connected, GigabitEthernet0/0
R           172.16.2.0/24 [120/1] via 209.165.200.226, 00:00:12, Serial0/0/0
```

Route	Parent	Child
172.16.0.0		
172.16.1.0		
172.16.1.1		
172.16.2.0		

In Example 18-2, notice that our child routes do not share the same subnet mask, as was the case in the classful example. In this case, we are implementing a network addressing scheme with VLSM.

In the partial output of the routing table in Example 18-3, indicate whether each route is a parent route or a child route by checking the appropriate column.

Example 18-3   Parent and Child Routes: Classless

```
        172.16.0.0/16 is variably subnetted, 5 subnets, 3 masks
C         172.16.1.0/24 is directly connected, GigabitEthernet0/0
L         172.16.1.1/32 is directly connected, GigabitEthernet0/0
R         172.16.2.0/24 [120/1] via 209.165.200.226, 00:00:12, Serial0/0/0
R         172.16.3.0/24 [120/2] via 209.165.200.226, 00:00:12, Serial0/0/0
R         172.16.4.0/28 [120/2] via 209.165.200.226, 00:00:12, Serial0/0/0
```

Route	Parent	Child
172.16.0.0		
172.16.1.0		
172.16.1.1		
172.16.2.0		
172.16.3.0		
172.16.4.0		

The IPv4 Route Lookup Process

When a router receives a packet on one of its interfaces, the routing table lookup process compares the destination IP address of the packet with the entries in the routing table. The best match between the packet's destination IP address and the route in the routing table is used to determine which interface to forward the packet.

Routing Table Lookup Chart

Figure 18-10 shows an incomplete version of the chart used to explain the routing table lookup process. Write in the correct labels for the chart.

Figure 18-10 Routing Table: Parent/Child Relationship

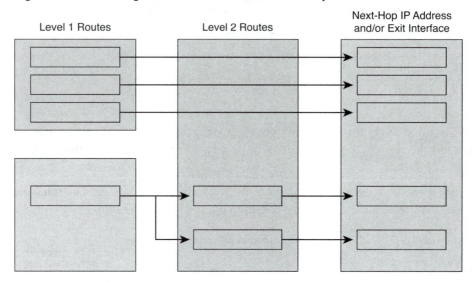

Routing Table Lookup Exercise

Use the routing table shown in Example 18-4 for this exercise.

Note: The output is from IOS 12 so local routes are not shown.

Example 18-4   Routing Table for B2

```
B2# show ip route
Codes: C - connected, S - static, I - IGRP, R - RIP, M - mobile, B - BGP
<output omitted>


Gateway of last resort is not set

     10.0.0.0/30 is subnetted, 3 subnets
R        10.10.10.0 [120/1] via 10.10.10.5, 00:00:21, Serial0/0/0
C        10.10.10.4 is directly connected, Serial0/0/0
R        10.10.10.8 [120/1] via 10.10.10.5, 00:00:21, Serial0/0/0
     172.16.0.0/16 is variably subnetted, 8 subnets, 6 masks
R        172.16.0.0/18 [120/1] via 10.10.10.5, 00:00:21, Serial0/0/0
C        172.16.68.0/22 is directly connected, FastEthernet0/0
C        172.16.72.0/23 is directly connected, FastEthernet0/1
R        172.16.128.0/20 [120/1] via 10.10.10.5, 00:00:21, Serial0/0/0
R        172.16.160.0/21 [120/2] via 10.10.10.5, 00:00:21, Serial0/0/0
R        172.16.176.0/22 [120/2] via 10.10.10.5, 00:00:21, Serial0/0/0
R        172.16.188.0/23 [120/2] via 10.10.10.5, 00:00:21, Serial0/0/0
R        172.16.190.0/24 [120/2] via 10.10.10.5, 00:00:21, Serial0/0/0
```

The router, B2, receives a packet from 172.16.68.10 destined for 172.16.142.10. Use binary to prove which route in Example 18-4 is the longest match. Make sure that you designate the bits that must match between the IP address and the longest match route. If no route matches, simply state "No Match."

The router, B2, receives a packet from 172.16.72.10 destined for 172.16.179.10. Use binary to prove which route in Example 18-3 is the longest match. Make sure that you designate the bits that must match between the IP address and the longest match route. If no route matches, simply state "No Match."

The router, B2, receives a packet from 172.16.69.10 destined for 172.16.65.10. Use binary to prove which route in Example 18-4 is the longest match. Make sure that you designate the bits that must match between the IP address and the longest match route. If no route matches, simply state "No Match."

Analyze an IPv6 Routing Table

Refer to the output in Example 18-5 and analyze the IPv6 routing table. In Table 18-15, fill in the missing information.

Example 18-5   IPv6 Routing Table for R1

```
R1# show ipv6 route
<Output omitted>
C    2001:DB8:CAFE:1::/64 [0/0]
      via GigabitEthernet0/0, directly connected
L    2001:DB8:CAFE:1::1/128 [0/0]
      via GigabitEthernet0/0, receive
D    2001:DB8:CAFE:2::/64 [90/3524096]
      via FE80::3, Serial0/0/1
D    2001:DB8:CAFE:3::/64 [90/2170112]
      via FE80::3, Serial0/0/1
C    2001:DB8:CAFE:A001::/64 [0/0]
      via Serial0/0/0, directly connected
L    2001:DB8:CAFE:A001::1/128 [0/0]
      via Serial0/0/0, receive
D    2001:DB8:CAFE:A002::/64 [90/3523840]
      via FE80::3, Serial0/0/1
C    2001:DB8:CAFE:A003::/64 [0/0]
      via Serial0/0/1, directly connected
L    2001:DB8:CAFE:A003::1/128 [0/0]
      via Serial0/0/1, receive
L    FF00::/8 [0/0]
      via Null0, receive
```

Table 18-15   IPv6 Route Sources, AD Values, and Metrics

Route	Route Source	AD	Metric
2001:DB8:CAFE:A001::/64			
2001:DB8:CAFE:1::1/128			
2001:DB8:CAFE:A002::/64			

CHAPTER 19

Single-Area OSPF

Open Shortest Path First (OSPF) is a link-state routing protocol that was developed as a replacement for the distance vector routing protocol RIP. RIP was an acceptable routing protocol in the early days of networking and the Internet. However, RIP's reliance on hop count as the only metric for determining best route quickly became problematic. Using hop count does not scale well in larger networks with multiple paths of varying speeds. OSPF has significant advantages over RIP in that it offers faster convergence and scales to much larger network implementations.

Characteristics of OSPF

In 1991, OSPFv2 was introduced in RFC 1247 by John Moy. OSPFv2 offered significant technical improvements over OSPFv1. It is classless by design; therefore, it supports VLSM and CIDR.

OSPF Terminology

OSPF introduces many new terms to our discussion of networking. Match the definition on the left with a term on the right.

Definitions

a. Responsible for updating all other OSPF routers when a change occurs in the multiaccess network.

b. OSPF packet used to reply to LSRs as well as to announce new information.

c. Attaches to multiple areas, maintains separate link-state databases for each area it is connected to, and routes traffic destined for or arriving from other areas.

d. Describes the details of OSPF link-state concepts and operations.

e. Sent by an OSPF router to confirm receipt of an LSU.

f. Monitors the DR and takes over as DR if the current DR fails.

g. When a failure occurs in the network, such as when a neighbor becomes unreachable, these are flooded throughout an area.

h. An open standard, link-state routing protocol designed to address the limitations of RIP.

i. An OPSF router that is neither DR or BDR but particpates in the OSPF process on a multiaccess network.

j. A network that cycles between an up state and a down state.

k. Connects to an external routing domain that uses a different routing policy.

l. Contains an abbreviated list of the sending router's link-state database and is used by receiving routers to check against the local link-state database.

m. When this is not equal, the router with the highest number will be the DR regardless of router ID values.

n. This is the router ID for an OSPF router if no loopbacks are configured.

o. Asks for more information about any entry in the DBD.

Terms

_____ Area Border Router (ABR)

_____ Autonomous System Boundary Router (ASBR)

_____ backup designated router (BDR)

_____ database description (DBD)

_____ designated router (DR)

_____ DRothers

_____ flapping link

_____ highest IP address

_____ link-state acknowledgment (LSAck)

_____ link-state advertisement (LSA)

_____ link-state request (LSR)

_____ link-state update (LSU)

_____ Open Shortest Path First (OSPF)

_____ RFC 2328

_____ router priority

OSPF Concepts

The initial development of OSPF began in 1987 by the _____ _____ ____ _____ (____) OSPF Working Group. At that time, the Internet was largely an academic and research network funded by the U.S. government.

In 1998, the OSPFv2 specification was updated to the current version reflected in RFC _____. Because OSPF is an open standard, you can easily find the RFC online. List one website where the OSPF RFC can be found.

_____

The data portion of an OSPF message is encapsulated in a packet. This data field can include one of five OSPF packet types. Figure 19-1 shows an example of an encapsulated OSPF message. Fill in the missing field contents.

Figure 19-1   Encapsulated OSPF Message

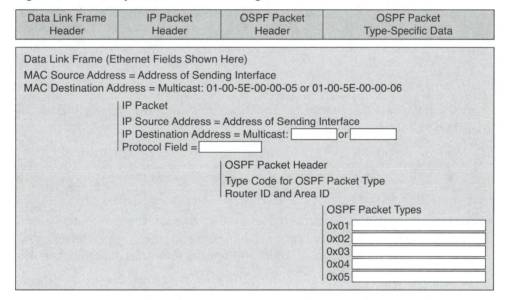

The following list describes the five different types of OSPF LSPs. Each packet serves a specific purpose in the OSPF routing process. Fill in the name for each packet type.

1. _____: Used to establish and maintain adjacency with other OSPF routers

2. _____ _____ (___): Contains an abbreviated list of the sending router's link-state database and is used by receiving routers to check against the local link-state database

3. ___-___ _____ (___): A request for more information about any entry in the DBD

4. ___-___ _____ (___): Used to reply to LSRs as well as to announce new information

5. ___-___ _____ (_____): Confirms receipt of an LSU

Every OSPF message includes the header, as shown in Figure 19-2. Also shown in the figure are the fields of the OSPF Hello packet. Fill in the missing field contents.

Figure 19-2 OSPF Message Format

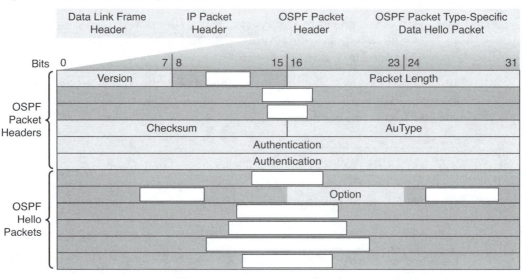

OSPF Hello packets are transmitted to multicast address _____ in IPv4 and _____ in IPv6 (all OSPF routers) every

- 10 seconds (default on multiaccess and point-to-point networks)

- 30 seconds (default on nonbroadcast multiaccess [NBMA] networks; for example, Frame Relay)

The _____ interval is the period, expressed in seconds, that the router will wait to receive a Hello packet before declaring the neighbor down. If the _____ interval expires before the routers receive a Hello packet, OSPF will remove that neighbor from its link-state database. Cisco uses a default of 4 times the Hello interval:

- 40 seconds (default on multiaccess and point-to-point networks)

- 120 seconds (default on NBMA networks; for example, Frame Relay)

OSPF Operation

Receiving an OSPF Hello packet on an interface confirms for a router that there is another OSPF router on this link. OSPF then begins the process of establishing adjacency with the neighbor.

Routers initially exchange Type _____ packets, which is an abbreviated list of the sending router's LSDB and is used by receiving routers to check against the local LSDB.

A Type _____ packet is used by the receiving routers to request more information about an entry in the DBD.

The Type _____ packet is used to reply to an LSR packet.

Then, a Type _____ packet is sent to acknowledge receipt of the LSU.

In Table 19-1, indicate which OSPF packet type matches the LSA purpose.

Table 19-1   Identify OSPF Packet Types

| | OSPF Packet Type | | | | |
LSA Purpose	Hello	DBD	LSR	LSU	LSAck
Discovers neighbors and builds adjacencies between them.					
Data field is empty.					
Asks for specific link-state records from router to router.					
Sends specifically requested link-state records.					
Contains list of sending router's LSDB.					
Can contain seven different types of LSAs.					
Checks for database synchronization between routers.					
Confirms receipt of a link-state update packet.					
Maintains adjacency with other OSPF routers.					

In Figure 19-3, record the five states that occur between the *down state* and the *full state*.

Figure 19-3   Transitioning Through the OSPF States

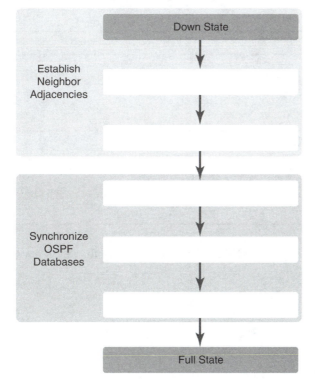

In Table 19-2, indicate which OSPF state matches the state description.

Table 19-2   Identify the OSPF States

	OSPF States						
State Description	Down	Init	Two-Way	Ex-Start	Exchange	Loading	Full
Routes are processed using the SPF algorithm.							
A neighbor responds to a Hello.							
Hello packets are received from neighbors, containing the sending router ID.							
On Ethernet links, elect a designated router (DR) and a backup designated router (BDR).							
No Hello packets received.							
Router requests more information about a specific DBD entry.							
Routers exchange DBD packets.							
Routers have converged.							
The LSDB and routing tables are complete.							
A new OSPF router on the link sends first Hello.							
Initiates the exchange of DBD packets.							
Negotiate master/slave relationship and DBD packet sequence number.							

Describe the two challenges regarding OSPF LSA flooding in multiaccess networks.

■

■

For each multiaccess topology in Figure 19-4, indicate how many adjacencies would be formed if DB/BDR process wasn't part of OSPF operations.

Figure 19-4   Multiaccess Topologies

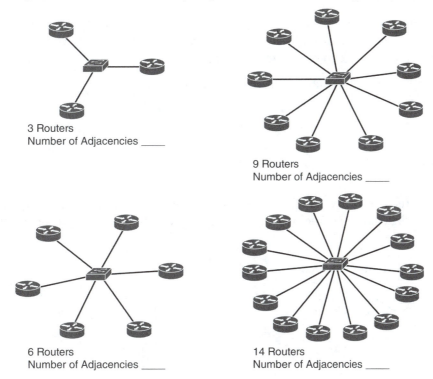

3 Routers
Number of Adjacencies _____

9 Routers
Number of Adjacencies _____

6 Routers
Number of Adjacencies _____

14 Routers
Number of Adjacencies _____

Briefly describe the DR/BDR election process.

Video Demonstration - Observing OSPF Protocol Communications (RSE 8.1.3.6/RP 6.1.3.6)

Configuring Single-Area OSPFv2

Now that you have a good understanding of how OSPF works, it is time to learn the configuration commands we use for OSPF as well as how to verify OSPF is operating as expected.

The Router ID

Every router requires a router ID to participate in an OSPF domain. The router ID can be defined by an administrator or automatically assigned by the router. The router ID is used by other OSPF routers to uniquely identify neighbors.

Explain the role of the router ID in multiaccess networks.

Complete the flowchart in Figure 19-5 to indicate the order of precedence used by the router to choose the router ID. The two diamond shapes are questions. The rectangle at the bottom is a decision.

Figure 19-5   Router ID Order of Precedence

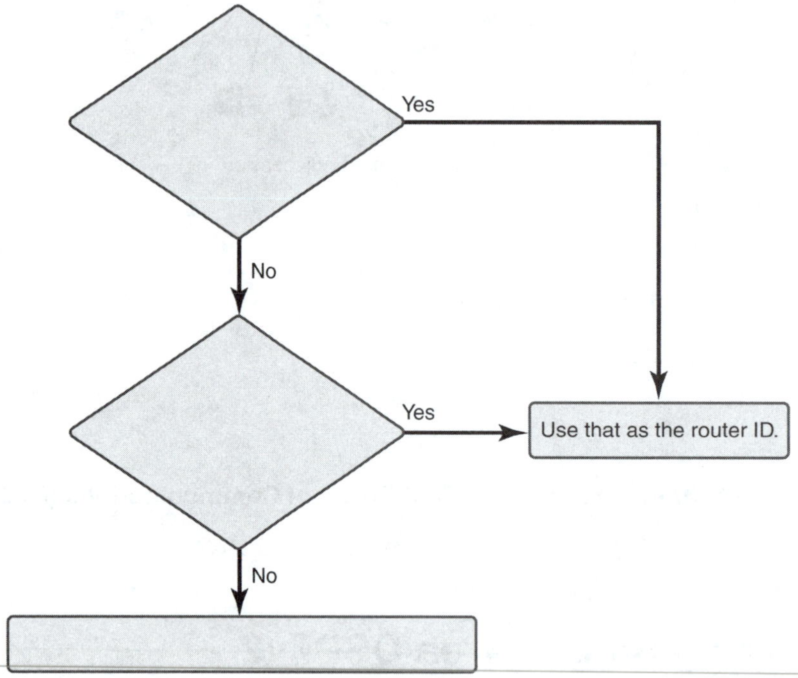

Record the router prompt and command syntax to configure the router ID.

When would it be appropriate to configure a loopback interface to serves as a router ID?

Single-Area OSPFv2 Basic Configuration Scenario

Figure 19-6 shows the topology that we will use to configure OSPFv2 and OSPFv3. This first topology shows IPv4 network addresses. The IPv4 addressing scheme is in Table 19-3.

Figure 19-6   OSPFv2 Topology with IPv4 Network Addresses

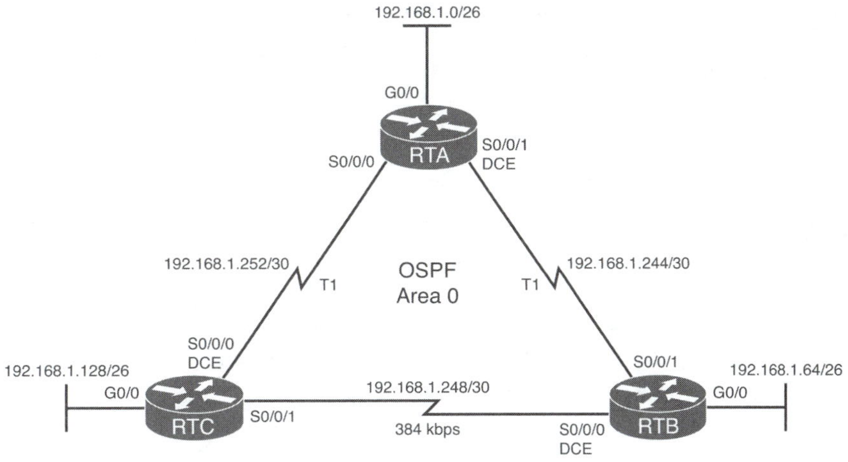

Table 19-3   IPv4 Addressing Scheme for OSPFv2

Device	Interface	IPv4 Address	Subnet Mask
RTA	G0/0	192.168.1.1	255.255.255.192
	S0/0/0	192.168.1.253	255.255.255.252
	S0/0/1	192.168.1.245	255.255.255.252
	Router ID	1.1.1.1	
RTB	G0/0	192.168.1.65	255.255.255.192
	S0/0/0	192.168.1.249	255.255.255.252
	S0/0/1	192.168.1.246	255.255.255.252
	Router ID	2.2.2.2	
RTC	G0/0	192.168.1.129	255.255.255.192
	S0/0/0	192.168.1.254	255.255.255.252
	S0/0/1	192.168.1.250	255.255.255.252
	Router ID	3.3.3.3	

Record the command syntax, including router prompt, to configure the OSPF routing process.

The value for *process-id* can be any number between _____ and _____.

The command syntax, including router prompt, for adding network statements to the OSPF routing process is as follows:

For single area OSPF configurations, the *area-id* is normally set to 0.

The *wildcard-mask* argument is simply the inverse of the subnet mask. For example, the bit pattern for 11110000 (240) becomes 00001111 (15). List the subnet mask and corresponding wildcard mask for each of the following network addresses.

Network Address	Subnet Mask	Wildcard Mask
192.168.14.64/26		
10.1.1.16/28		
172.24.4.0/23		
192.168.200.128/20		
172.17.2.128/25		
192.168.226.96/27		
10.0.0.0/8		
10.100.200.48/30		
172.18.0.0/15		
10.128.0.0/10		

In the space provided, document the correct commands, including router prompt, to configure the routers in Figure 19-6 with OSPFv2. Include commands to configure the router ID and disable updates on the LAN interface.

Adjusting OSPF Cost

The OSPF metric is called cost. From RFC 2328:

> *A cost is associated with the output side of each router interface. This cost is configurable by the system administrator. The lower the cost, the more likely the interface is to be used to forward data traffic.*

Notice that RFC 2328 does not specify which values should be used to determine the cost. So the implementation of the cost metric is up to the operating system that is running OSPF.

The Reference Bandwidth

What is the formula used to calculate OSPF cost in the Cisco IOS?

What is the default value for the reference bandwidth?

In Table 19-4, record the Cisco IOS Cost for each of the interface types.

Table 19-4   Cisco ISO Default OSPF Cost Values

Interface Type	Reference Bandwidth / Default Interface Bandwidth	Cost
10GE	100,000,000 / 10,000,000,000	
Gigabit Ethernet	100,000,000 / 1,000,000,000	
Fast Ethernet	100,000,000 / 100,000,000	
Ethernet	100,000,000 / 10,000,000	
Serial 1.544 Mbps	100,000,000 / 1,544,000	
Serial 128 Kbps	100,000,000 / 128,000	
Serial 64 Kbps	100,000,000 / 64,000	

If you did the calculations right you can see that, by default, 10GE, Gigabit Ethernet, and Fast Ethernet all have the same cost value. The IOS rounds to the nearest integer, so the cost value cannot be less than 1.

What is the router prompt and command syntax to change the reference bandwidth to a higher value so that 10 GigE, Gigabit Ethernet, and Fast Ethernet will all have different values?

The value is entered in M/bs, so what is a good value to enter to change the resulting cost values?

Record the command to set the reference bandwidth on RTA. All three routers would then be configured with the same value.

```
% OSPF: Reference bandwidth is changed.
        Please ensure reference bandwidth is consistent across all routers.
```

The Default Interface Bandwidth

However, adjusting the reference bandwidth may not be enough to ensure that OSPF is accurately advertising the cost of its links. Table 19-3 shows the default interface bandwidth that the Cisco IOS uses to calculate the OSPF cost. But these interface bandwidths may not reflect that actual bandwidth for serial interfaces since bandwidth is determined by the agreed-upon rate with the ISP.

What is the router prompt and command syntax to change the interface bandwidth value used by OSPF to calculate cost?

In Figure 19-6, RTC and RTB share a link that is contracted at the rate of 384 kbps. Record the command to change the bandwidth.

Modifying the OSPF Cost Metric

Instead of configuring the bandwidth, you could configure the cost directly. This would allow the IOS to bypass the metric calculation.

What is the router prompt and command syntax to manually configure the cost value?

In what situation is this command useful?

Record the commands to configure the link between RTB and RTC with the actual cost. Remember to take into account the new reference bandwidth value you configured earlier.

Verify the OSPF Configuration

Fill in the missing command to complete the following sentences:

The _____ command can be used to verify and troubleshoot OSPF neighbor relationships.

The _____ command is a quick way to verify vital OSPF configuration information, including the OSPF process ID; the router ID; networks the router is advertising; the neighbors the router is receiving updates from; and the default administrative distance, which is 110 for OSPF.

The _____ command can also be used to examine the OSPF process ID and router ID. In addition, this command displays the OSPF area information as well as the last time the SPF algorithm was calculated.

The quickest way to verify Hello and Dead intervals is to use the _____ command.

The quickest way to verify OSPF convergence is to use the _____ command to view the routing table for each router in the topology.

Lab - Configuring Basic Single-area OSPFv2 (RSE 8.2.4.5/RP 6.2.4.5)

Packet Tracer - Configuring OSPFv2 in a Single Area (RSE 8.2.2.7/RP 6.2.2.7)

Configure Single-Area OSPFv3

OSPFv3 is the OSPFv2 equivalent for exchanging IPv6 prefixes. Recall that in IPv6, the network address is referred to as the prefix and the subnet mask is called the prefix-length. Similar to its IPv4 counterpart, OSPFv3 exchanges routing information to populate the IPv6 routing table with remote prefixes.

Comparing OSPFv2 and OSPFv3

As with all IPv6 routing protocols, OSPFv3 has separate processes from its IPv4 counterpart. The processes and operations are basically the same as in the IPv4 routing protocol but run independently. OSPFv2 and OSPFv3 each have separate adjacency tables, OSPF topology tables, and IP routing tables.

In Table 19-5, indicate whether a function or feature belongs to OSPFv2, OSPFv3, or both.

Table 19-5   Compare OSPFv2 and OSPFv3

Function or Feature	OSPFv2	OSPFv3	Both
Uses the SPF algorithm to calculate best paths.			
Uses 5 basic packet types.			
Uses 224.0.0.6 for DR and BDR multicasts.			
Uses cost as its metric.			
Uses IPsec for authentication.			
Link-State Routing Protocol.			
Unicast routing enabled by default.			
Dynamic Routing Protocol.			
Uses FF02::6 for DR and BDR multicasts.			
Uses MD5 or plain-text authentication.			
Elects a DR and a BDR.			
IP unicast routing must be enabled.			

Configuring OSPFv3

Figure 19-7 shows the same topology we used for OSPFv2, but with IPv6 network addresses. Table 19-6 shows the IPv6 addressing scheme.

Figure 19-7   OSPFv3 Topology with IPv6 Network Addresses

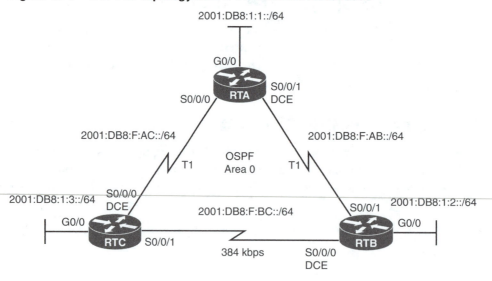

Table 19-6   IPv6 Addressing Scheme for OSPFv3

Device	Interface	IPv6 Address/Prefix
RTA	G0/0	2001:DB8:1:1::1/64
	S0/0/0	2001:DB8:F:AC::1/64
	S0/0/1	2001:DB8:F:AB::1/64
	Link local	FE80::A
	Router ID	1.1.1.1
RTB	G0/0	2001:DB8:1:2::1/64
	S0/0/0	2001:DB8:F:BC::1/64
	S0/0/1	2001:DB8:F:AB::2/64
	Link-local	FE80::B
	Router ID	2.2.2.2
RTC	G0/0	2001:DB8:1:3::1/64
	S0/0/0	2001:DB8:F:AC::2/64
	S0/0/1	2001:DB8:F:BC::2/64
	Link local	FE80::C
	Router ID	3.3.3.3

The routers are already configured with interface addressing. Record the correct commands, including router prompt, to configure the routers with OSPFv3. Include commands to enable IPv6 routing, configure the router ID, change the reference bandwidth to 10000, and disable updates on the LAN interface. Except for the router ID, the commands are the same for all three routers. So you only need to document one router.

Verifying OSPFv3

Fill in the missing command to complete the following sentences:

The _____ command can be used to verify and troubleshoot OSPF neighbor relationships.

The _____ command is a quick way to verify vital OSPF configuration information, including the OSPF process ID, the router ID, and interfaces the router is advertising.

The _____ command can also be used to examine the OSPF process ID and router ID. In addition, this command displays the OSPF area information as well as the last time the SPF algorithm was calculated.

To view a quick summary of OSPFv3-enabled interfaces, use the _____ command. However, the quickest way to verify Hello and Dead intervals is to use the _____ command.

The quickest way to verify OSPF convergence is to use the _____ command to view the routing table for each router in the topology.

Lab - Configuring Basic Single-Area OSPFv3 (RSE 8.3.3.6/RP 6.3.3.6)

Packet Tracer - Configuring Basic OSPFv3 (RSE 8.3.3.5/RP 6.3.3.5)

Packet Tracer - Skills Integration Challenge (RSE 8.4.1.2/RP 6.4.1.2)

CHAPTER 20

Access Control Lists

One of the most important skills a network administrator needs is mastery of access control lists (ACLs). An ACL is a sequential list of permit or deny statements that apply to addresses or upper-layer protocols. ACLs provide a powerful way to control traffic into and out of a network. ACLs can be configured for all routed network protocols. In this chapter, you learn how to use standard and extended ACLs on a Cisco router as part of a security solution.

IP ACL Operation

An ACL is a series of IOS commands that control whether a router forwards or drops packets based on information found in the packet header. ACLs are among the most commonly used features of Cisco IOS software.

Packet Tracer
☐ Activity

Packet Tracer - ACL Demonstration (RSE/RP 9.1.1.7)

Standard Versus Extended IPv4 ACLs

In Table 20-1, indicate whether the description applies to standard, extended, or named ACLs.

Table 20-1   Standard, Extended, and Named ACLs

ACL Type Descriptions	Standard	Extended	Named
Uses ACL numbers 100–199.			
Uses ACL numbers 1300–1999.			
Uses ACL numbers 1–99.			
Entries can be added or deleted within the ACL.			
Simplest type of ACL; used for smaller networks.			
Filters traffic solely based on source address.			
Uses a numeric identifier and filters on protocol numbers.			
Should be typed with ALL CAPITAL LETTERS.			
Starts with a number and filters by destination address.			
Can be used inclusively for ACL numbers 1–199.			

Calculating Wildcard Masks

A wildcard mask is a string of 32 binary digits used by the router to determine which bits of the address to examine for a match before permitting or denying the packet.

As with subnet masks, the numbers 1 and 0 in the wildcard mask identify how to treat the corresponding IP address bits. However, in a wildcard mask, these bits are used for different purposes and follow different rules. Subnet masks use binary 1s and 0s to identify the network, subnet, and host portion of an IP address. Wildcard masks use binary 1s and 0s to filter individual IP addresses or groups of IP addresses to permit or deny access to resources.

When filtering traffic for a network, the *wildcard-mask* argument is simply the inverse of the subnet mask. For example, the bit pattern for 11110000 (240) becomes 00001111 (15).

For the ACL statements in Table 20-2, record the wildcard mask used to filter the specified IPv4 address or network.

Table 20-2   Determine the Correct Wildcard Mask

ACL Statement	Wildcard Mask
Permit all hosts from the 192.168.1.0/25 network	
Permit all hosts from the 10.0.0.0/16 network	
Deny all hosts from the 10.10.100.0/24 network	
Deny all hosts from the 10.20.30.128/26 network	
Permit all hosts from the 172.18.0.0/23 network	
Permit all hosts from the 192.168.5.0/27 network	
Deny host 172.18.33.1	
Deny all hosts from the 172.16.1.192/29 network	
Permit all hosts from the 172.31.64.0/18 network	
Permit host 10.10.10.1	
Deny all hosts from the 172.25.250.160/28 network	
Deny all hosts from the 172.30.128.0/20 network	
Deny all hosts from 10.10.128.0/19 network	
Permit all hosts from the 172.18.0.0/16 network	
Permit all hosts from the 192.168.200.0/30 network	

Wildcard Mask in Operation

In Table 20-3, for each of the ACL statements and corresponding source addresses, choose whether the router will either permit or deny the packet.

Table 20-3   Determine the Permit or Deny

ACL Statement	Source Address	Permit or Deny
access-list 33 permit 198.168.100.0 0.0.0.63	198.168.100.3	
access-list 20 permit 192.168.223.64 0.0.0.15	192.168.223.72	
access-list 21 permit 192.0.2.11 0.0.0.15	192.0.2.17	
access-list 39 permit 198.168.100.64 0.0.0.63	192.168.22.100.40	
access-list 66 permit 172.16.0.0 0.0.255.255	172.17.0.5	
access-list 65 permit 172.16.1.1 0.0.0.0	172.16.1.1	
access-list 16 permit 10.10.10.0 0.0.0.255	10.10.10.33	
access-list 60 permit 10.10.0.0 0.0.255.255	10.10.33.33	
access-list 50 permit 192.168.122.128 0.0.0.63	192.168.122.195	
access-list 55 permit 192.168.15.0 0.0.0.3	192.168.15.5	
access-list 30 permit 192.168.223.32 0.0.0.31	192.168.223.60	
access-list 1 permit 192.168.155.0 0.0.0.255	192.168.155.245	
access-list 25 permit 172.18.5.0 0.0.0.255	172.18.6.20	
access-list 50 permit 192.168.155.0 0.0.0.255	192.168.156.245	
access-list 18 permit 10.10.10.0 0.0.0.63	10.10.10.50	

Guidelines for ACL Creation

Complete the ACL Operation sentences on the left using words from the Word Bank on the right. Not all words are used.

ACL Operation

a. An access control list (ACL) controls whether the router will _____ or ____ packet traffic based on packet header criteria.

b. A router with three interfaces and two network protocols (IPv4 and IPv6) can have as many as __ active ACLs.

c. ACLs are often used in routers between internal and external networks to provide a ____ ____.

d. For inbound ACLs, incoming packets are processed _____ they are sent to the outbound interface.

e. For outbound ACLs, incoming packets are processed ____ they are sent to the outbound interface.

f. For every ACL, there is an implied deny statement; if a packet does not match any of the ACL criteria, it will be _____.

g. ACLs can filter data traffic per protocol, per direction, and per _____.

h. ACLs can filter traffic based on source/ destination address, _____, and port numbers.

Word Bank

___ Discarded

___ Four

___ Firewall

___ Interface

___ Pathway

___ Deny

___ After

___ Processing

___ 6

___ Protocol

___ 12

___ Forwarded

___ Permit

___ Switch

___ Before

Guidelines for ACL Placement

Every ACL should be placed where it has the greatest impact on efficiency. The basic rules are as follows:

- Locate _____ ACLs as close to the destination as possible because these ACLs do not specify destination addresses.

- Locate _____ ACLs as close as possible to the source of the traffic to be filtered.

Use the information shown in Figure 20-1 to determine the router, interface, and direction for each scenario in Table 20-4.

Figure 20-1   ACL Placement Topology

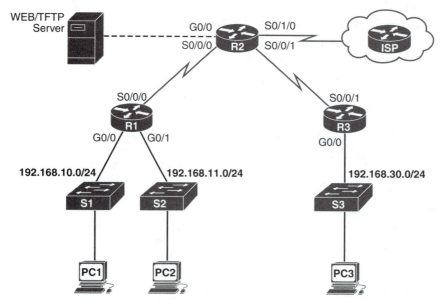

Table 20-4   ACL Placement Scenarios

Scenario	Router	Interface	Direction
Use a standard ACL to stop the 192.168.10.0/24 network from accessing the Internet through the ISP.	R2	S0/1/0	Outbound
Use a standard ACL to stop the 192.168.11.0/24 network from accessing the 192.168.10.0/24 network.	R1	G0/0	Outbound
Use an extended ACL to allow only TFTP and web traffic to access the WEB/TFTP server.	R2	G0/0	Outbound
Use an extended ACL to stop the 192.168.30.0/24 network from accessing the web/TFTP server.	R3	G0/0	Inbound

Standard IPv4 ACLs

To use numbered or named standard ACLs on a Cisco router, you must first create the standard ACL. Then you must apply the ACL to one of the router's processes such as an interface or Telnet lines.

Configuring Standard IPv4 ACLs

The full command syntax to configure a standard ACL is as follows:

```
Router(config)# access-list access-list-number { deny | permit | remark } source
[ source-wildcard ][ log ]
```

The following ACL statement would first add a remark and then permit traffic from the
172.16.0.0/16 network:

```
Router(config)# access-list 1 remark Permit traffic from HR LAN, 172.16.0.0/16

Router(config)# access-list 1 permit 172.16.0.0 0.0.255.255
```

In this case, the remark is not that helpful. However, in more complex configuration scenarios,
the remark option can help to quickly communicate the purpose of an ACL statement.

If the policy calls for filtering traffic for a specific host, you can use the host address and
0.0.0.0 as the wildcard mask. But if you do, the IOS will drop the 0.0.0.0 and just use the host
address as shown in Example 20-1.

Note: Older IOS versions convert 0.0.0.0 to the keyword **host** and prepend it before the IP address,
such as **host 172.16.1.10**.

Example 20-1   Filtering One IP Address

```
R1(config)# access-list 1 deny 172.16.1.10 0.0.0.0

R1(config)# do show access-lists

Standard IP access list 1

    10 deny   172.16.1.10

R1(config)#
```

If the policy calls for filtering traffic for all sources, you can configure 0.0.0.0
255.255.255.255 as the source address and wildcard mask. The IOS will convert it to the
keyword **any**, as shown in Example 20-2.

Example 20-2   Filtering All Addresses

```
R1(config)# access-list 1 deny 172.16.1.10 0.0.0.0

R1(config)# access-list 1 permit 0.0.0.0 255.255.255.255

R1(config)# do show access-lists

Standard IP access list 1

    10 deny   172.16.1.10

    20 permit any

R1(config)#
```

Note: The sequence numbers before each statement can be used to edit the statement, as discussed later.

An ACL has no impact unless it is applied to some process. To filter inbound or outbound traffic, an ACL must be applied to an interface and the direction of traffic specified. The command syntax to apply an ACL to an interface is as follows:

```
Router(config-if)# ip access-group { access-list-number | access-list-name } { in | out }
```

Naming an ACL makes it easier to understand its function. For example, an ACL configured to deny FTP could be called NO_FTP. The command syntax to enter named ACL configuration mode is as follows:

```
Router(config)# ip access-list [ standard | extended ] name
```

The *name* can be any alphanumeric string that does not begin with a number. Once in named ACL configuration mode, the router prompt changes depending on whether you chose standard or extended. The syntax for named standard ACL configuration mode is as follows:

```
Router(config-std-nacl)# [ permit | deny | remark ] { source [source-wildcard] } [log}
```

So, to reconfigure Example 20-2 with a named standard ACL and a remark, we could do something like Example 20-3.

Example 20-3 Standard Named ACL

```
R1(config)# ip access-list standard NOT_BOB

R1(config-std-nacl)# remark Stop Bob

R1(config-std-nacl)# deny host 172.16.1.10

R1(config-std-nacl)# permit any

R1(config-std-nacl)# exit

R1(config)# interface g0/0

R1(config-if)# ip access-group NOT_BOB in

R1(config-if)# do show access-lists

Standard IP access list NOT_BOB

    10 deny host 172.16.1.10

    20 permit any

R1(config-if)#
```

Use the information in Figure 20-2 to write ACL statements for the following three scenarios. Include the router prompt in your configurations.

Figure 20-2   Topology for Standard ACL Configuration Scenarios

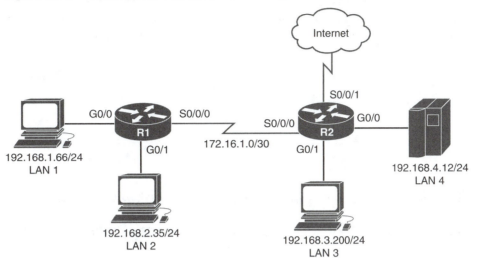

Standard ACL Scenario 1

Record the commands to configure and apply a standard ACL that will filter traffic into the 192.168.1.0 LAN. The 192.168.3.77 host should not be able to access this LAN, but all other hosts on the 192.168.3.0 and 192.168.4.0 networks should be permitted. All other traffic should be blocked.

Standard ACL Scenario 2

Record the commands to configure and apply a standard ACL that will filter traffic to host 192.168.4.12. Both the 192.168.1.66 host and all hosts in the 192.168.2.0 LAN should be permitted access to this host. All other networks should not be able to access the 192.168.4.12 host.

Standard ACL Scenario 3

Record the commands to configure and apply a standard ACL that will filter traffic to LANs. Internet traffic should only be allowed to access the 192.168.4.12 server.

Packet Tracer - Configuring Standard ACLs (RSE/RP 9.2.1.10)

Packet Tracer - Configuring Named Standard ACLs (RSE/RP 9.2.1.11)

Modifying IPv4 ACLs

The IOS automatically adds a sequence number before the ACL statement, as you can see in the previous examples that used the **show access-lists** command. These sequence numbers can be used to delete an erroneous ACL statement and add back a correct ACL statement. The rules for using sequence numbers to edit a standard or extended numbered ACL are as follows:

1. Enter named ACL configuration mode for the ACL even if it is a numbered ACL.

2. Delete the sequence number that is in error.

3. Use the deleted sequence number to add in the correct ACL statement.

Note: For standard and extended numbered ACLs, you cannot add a new sequence number statement in the middle of the ACL.

In Example 20-4, the wrong address is currently being denied. Enter the commands to delete the erroneous statement and add back a statement to deny 192.168.1.66.

Example 20-4   Standard Numbered ACL with Error

```
R1(config)# access-list 1 deny 192.168.1.65
R1(config)# access-list 1 permit any
R1(config)# do show access-lists
Standard IP access list 1
    10 deny   192.168.1.65
    20 permit any
R1(config)#
```

Lab - Configuring and Verifying Standard ACLs (RSE/RP 9.2.2.8)

Securing vty Ports with a Standard IPv4 ACL

Filtering Telnet or Secure Shell (SSH) traffic is usually considered an extended IP ACL function because it filters a higher-level protocol. However, because the **access-class** command is used to filter incoming or outgoing Telnet/SSH sessions by source address, you can use a standard ACL.

The command syntax of the **access-class** command is:

```
Router(config-line)# access-class access-list-number { in [ vrf-also ] | out }
```

The parameter **in** restricts incoming connections between the addresses in the access list and the Cisco device, and the parameter **out** restricts outgoing connections between a particular Cisco device and the addresses in the access list.

Record the commands to configure an ACL to permit host 192.168.2.35 and then apply the ACL to all Telnet lines.

```
R1(config)#
```

Lab - Configuring and Verifying VTY Restrictions (RSE/RP 9.2.3.4)

Packet Tracer - Configuring an ACL on VTY Lines (RSE/RP 9.2.3.3)

Extended IPv4 ACLs

For more precise traffic-filtering control, extended IPv4 ACLs can be created. Extended ACLs are numbered 100 to 199 and 2000 to 2699, providing a total of 799 possible extended numbered ACLs. Extended ACLs can also be named.

Configuring Extended IPv4 ACL Statements

The procedural steps for configuring extended ACLs are the same as for standard ACLs. The extended ACL is first configured, and then it is activated on an interface. However, the command syntax and parameters are more complex to support the additional features provided by extended ACLs. The command syntax for an extended ACL with some of the available options is as follows:

```
Router(config)# access-list access-list-number { deny | permit | remark } protocol
source [source-wildcard] destination [destination-wildcard] [operand] [port-number or
name] [established]
```

Use the operand to compare source or destination ports. Possible operands are **lt** (less than), **gt** (greater than), **eq** (equal), **neq** (not equal), and **range**.

For example, to allow host 172.16.1.11 web access to 10.10.10.10, you might use the following ACL statement:

```
R1(config)# access-list 100 permit tcp host 172.16.1.11 host 10.10.10.10 eq 80
```

Note: You must either use the **host** keyword or **0.0.0.0** for the wildcard mask when configuring an extended ACL to filter one IP address.

The steps for configuring, applying, and editing named and numbered extended ACLs is the same as standard ACLs.

Extended ACL Configuration Scenarios

Refer to the topology in Figure 20-3. Then use the bank of ACL statement components to construct an ACL statement for the following scenarios. Some components may be equivalent. Some components will not be used.

Figure 20-3   Topology for Extended ACL Configuration Scenarios

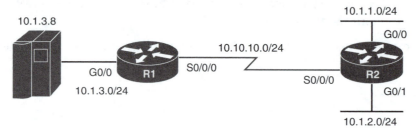

ACL Components

10.1.3.0	50	udp	10.1.2.0	99	any
eq 21	0.0.0.0	eq 53	deny	host	10.1.3.8
101	150	ip	10.1.1.0	122	10.10.10.0
permit	eq 80	access-list	0.0.0.255	10.1.2.9	tcp

Extended ACL Scenario 1

Record the command to configure a numbered ACL statement that will only allow users on the 10.1.1.0/24 network to have HTTP access to the web server on the 10.1.3.0/24 network. The ACL is applied to R2 G0/0 inbound.

Extended ACL Scenario 2

Record the command to configure a numbered ACL statement that will block host 10.1.2.9 from having FTP access to the 10.1.1.0/24 network. The ACL is applied to R2 G0/1 inbound.

Extended ACL Scenario 3

Record the command to configure a numbered ACL statement that will allow only host 10.1.3.8 on the 10.1.3.0/24 network to reach destinations beyond that network. The ACL is applied to R1 G0/0 inbound.

Evaluating Extended IPv4 ACL Statements

Refer to the topology in Figure 20-4. Each of the following scenarios applies an extended ACL to R1 G0/0 for inbound traffic. Evaluate the scenarios to determine whether the packets listed in the scenario's table will be permitted or denied. Each scenario is independent of the other two scenarios.

Figure 20-4   Evaluating an Extended ACL

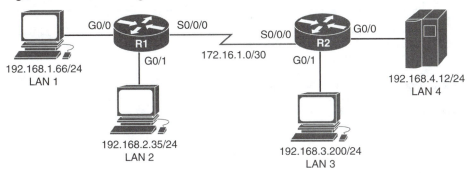

Extended ACL Evaluation Scenario 1

```
R1# show access-lists
Extended IP access list 103
    permit ip host 192.168.1.66 host 192.168.4.12
    permit ip host 192.168.1.77 host 192.168.4.12
    deny ip 192.168.1.0 0.0.0.255 192.168.4.0 0.0.0.255
    permit ip 192.168.1.0 0.0.0.255 192.168.2.0 0.0.0.255
```

Inbound Packets for Scenario 1

Source	Destination	Permit	Deny
192.168.1.66	192.168.3.51		
192.168.1.33	192.168.2.34		
192.168.1.88	192.168.4.39		
192.168.1.77	192.168.3.75		
192.168.1.88	192.168.2.51		
192.168.1.66	192.168.3.75		

Extended ACL Evaluation Scenario 2

```
R1# show access-lists
Extended IP access list 104
    deny tcp host 192.168.1.66 host 192.168.4.12 eq www
    permit tcp host 192.168.1.77 host 192.168.3.75 eq 22
    deny ip 192.168.1.0 0.0.0.255 192.168.3.0 0.0.0.255
    permit ip 192.168.1.0 0.0.0.255 192.168.4.0 0.0.0.255
```

Inbound Packets for Scenario 2

Source	Destination	Protocol	Permit	Deny
192.168.1.66	192.168.3.200	http		
192.168.1.88	192.168.2.75	http		
192.168.1.77	192.168.3.75	ssh		
192.168.1.77	192.168.3.75	http		
192.168.1.66	192.168.4.92	http		
192.168.1.66	192.168.4.75	ssh		

Extended ACL Evaluation Scenario 3

```
R1# show access-lists
Extended IP access list 105
    permit tcp 192.168.1.0 0.0.0.255 host 192.168.3.200 eq www
    permit ip host 192.168.1.66 host 192.168.3.200
    permit tcp 192.168.1.0 0.0.0.255 host 192.168.4.12 eq 22
    permit tcp host 192.168.1.66 192.168.2.0 0.0.0.255 eq telnet
```

Inbound Packets for Scenario 3

Source	Destination	Protocol	Permit	Deny
192.168.1.77	192.168.2.75	Telnet		
192.168.1.67	192.168.2.88	http		
192.168.1.66	192.168.3.200	Telnet		
192.168.1.66	192.168.2.75	Telnet		
192.168.1.77	192.168.3.75	http		
192.168.1.66	192.168.4.12	ssh		

Extended ACL Quiz

Refer to the topology in Figure 20-5 and the following scenario to answer the five questions.

Figure 20-5   Extended ACL Quiz Topology

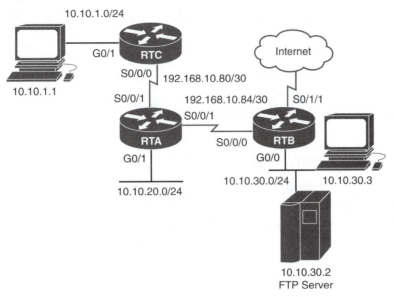

Scenario

A single access list needs to be created to deny the 10.10.1.0 /24 network and the 10.10.20.0 /24 network from reaching the 10.10.30.0 /24 network. The host 10.10.1.1 should have access to the FTP server only. The rest of the 10.0.0.0 network should have access to the 10.10.30.0 /24 network. All devices should be able to access the Internet.

Question 1

What should be the first line of the new access list described in the practice scenario just described?

a.   `access-list 101 permit ip 10.10.1.1 0.0.0.0 10.10.30.0 0.0.0.255`

b.   `access-list 101 deny ip 10.10.1.0 0.0.0.255 10.10.30.0 0.0.0.255`

c.   `access-list 10 deny 10.10.1.0 0.0.0.255`

d.   `access-list 101 permit ip host 10.10.1.1 host 10.10.30.2`

Question 2

What should be the second line of the new access list described in the practice scenario just described?

a.   `access-list 101 permit ip host 10.10.1.1  host 10.10.30.0 0.0.0.255`

b.   `access-list 101 deny ip 10.10.1.0 0.0.0.255 10.10.30.0 0.0.0.255`

c.   `access-list 101 deny ip 10.10.1.0 0.0.0.255 any`

d.   `access-list 101 permit ip host 10.10.1.1 host 10.10.30.1`

Question 3

What should be the third line of the new access list described in the practice scenario just described?

a.   `access-list 101 deny ip 10.10.20.0 0.0.0.255 10.10.30.0 0.0.0.255`

b.   `access-list 101 permit ip host 10.10.1.1 10.10.30.0 0.0.0.255`

c.   `access-list 101 deny ip 10.20.1.0 0.0.0.255 any`

d.   `access-list 101 permit ip host 10.10.1.1  host 10.10.30.1 eq ftp`

Question 4

What should be the fourth line of the new access list described in the practice scenario just described?

a.   `access-list 10 permit ip host 10.0.0.0 0.0.0.255`

b.   `access-list 101 permit ip 10.0.0.0 0.0.0.0 10.10.30.0 0.0.0.255`

c.   `access-list 101 deny ip 10.10.1.0 0.0.0.255 10.10.30.0 0.0.0.255 eq any`

d.   `access-list 101 permit ip any any`

Question 5

Where should the new access list described in the practice scenario just described be placed to ensure its effectiveness?

a.   G 0/0 on RTB as an outbound list

b.   G 0/1 on RTA as an inbound list

c.   S 0/1/1 on RTB as an outbound list

d.   S 0/0/1 on RTA as an outbound list

Lab - Configuring and Verifying Extended ACLs (RSE/RP 9.3.2.13)

Packet Tracer - Configuring Extended ACLs - Scenario 1 (RSE/RP 9.3.2.10)

Packet Tracer - Configuring Extended ACLs - Scenario 2 (RSE/RP 9.3.2.11)

Packet Tracer - Configuring Extended ACLs - Scenario 3 (RSE/RP 9.3.2.12)

Troubleshoot ACLs

When troubleshooting ACLs, it is important to first understand precisely how the router processes and filters packets. In addition, you should check for several common errors. The most common errors are entering ACLs in the wrong order and not applying adequate criteria to the ACL rules.

When processing packets, a router looks twice to see whether an ACL needs to be evaluated—inbound and outbound. In Figure 20-6, label each stage in the ACL processing flowchart with one of the processing steps. All processing steps are used. Some processing steps are used more than once.

Figure 20-6   Processing Flowchart for an ACL

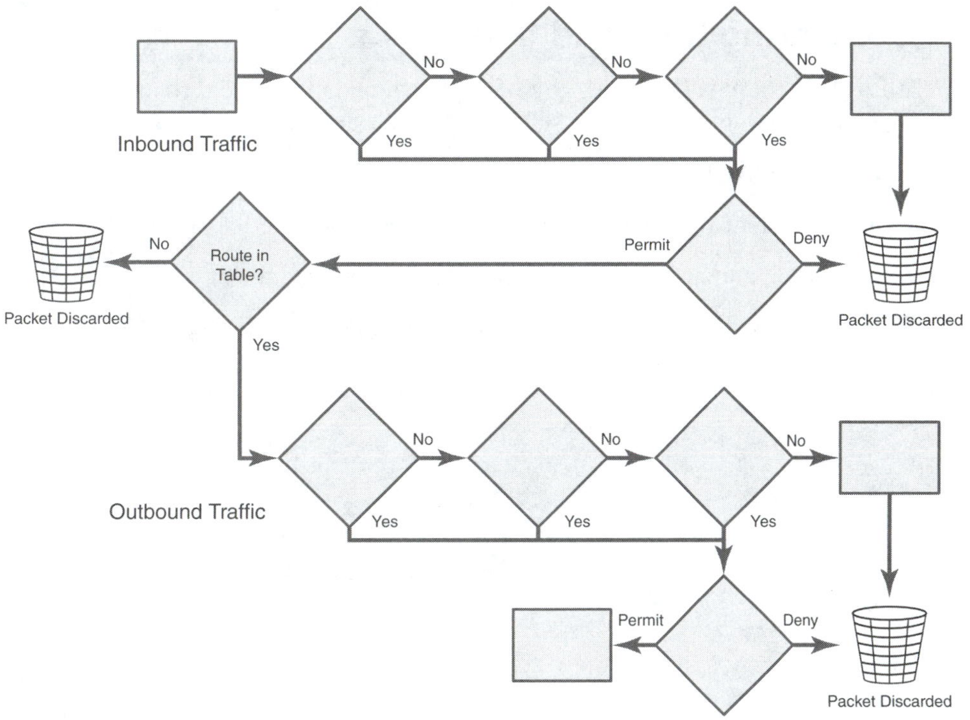

Processing Steps

Implicitly Deny Any

Inbound Interface

Match 1st ACL Statement

Match 2nd ACL Statement

Match 3rd ACL Statement

Outbound Interface

Permit or Deny

Lab - Troubleshooting ACL Configuration and Placement (RSE/RP 9.4.2.7)

Packet Tracer - Troubleshooting ACLs (RSE/RP 9.4.2.6)

Packet Tracer - Skills Integration Challenge (RSE/RP 9.4.2.8)

IPv6 ACLs

IPv6 ACLs are similar to IPv4 ACLs in both operation and configuration. Being familiar with IPv4 access lists makes IPv6 ACLs easy to understand and configure.

Comparing IPv4 and IPv6 ACLs

With IPv6, there is only one type of ACL, which is equivalent to an IPv4 extended named ACL. There are no numbered ACLs in IPv6. To summarize, IPv6 ACLs are

- Named ACLs only
- Equivalent to the functionality of an IPv4 extended ACL

An IPv4 ACL and an IPv6 ACL cannot share the same name.

What are three significant differences between IPv4 and IPv6 ACLs?

-

-

-

Configuring IPv6 ACLs

What is the command syntax to enter IPv6 ACL configuration mode?

What is the command syntax to configure an IPv6 ACL statement?

What is the command syntax to apply an IPv6 ACL to an interface?

Refer to Figure 20-7. This is the same OSPFv3 topology we used in Chapter 19.

Figure 20-7   Topology for IPv6 ACL Configuration Scenario

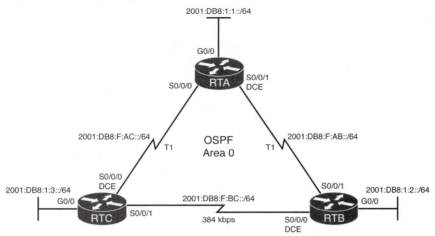

Record the commands to configure and apply the IPv6 ACL name NO-RTC that will block the RTC LAN from accessing the RTB LAN using port 80 but will allow all other traffic.

 Lab - Configuring and Verifying IPv6 ACLs (RSE/RP 9.5.2.7)

 Packet Tracer - Configuring IPv6 ACLs (RSE/RP 9.5.2.6)

CHAPTER 21

DHCP

Every device that connects to a network needs a unique IP address. Because computers and users in an organization often change locations, it can be difficult and time-consuming to manage static IP address assignments. Although some devices should always be statically assigned IP addressing information, Dynamic Host Configuration Protocol (DHCP) installed on a server helps manage the addressing of the majority of devices in the enterprise. DHCP is available for both IPv4 (DHCPv4) and for IPv6 (DHCPv6).

Dynamic Host Configuration Protocol v4

DHCPv4 assigns IPv4 addresses and other network configuration information dynamically. Because desktop clients usually make up the bulk of network nodes, DHCPv4 is an extremely useful and timesaving tool for network administrators.

DHCPv4 Operation

DHCPv4 uses four messages between the DHCP server and a client set to use DHCP for IPv4 addressing configuration. In Figure 21-1, label each DHCP message type sent between the server and client when originating a lease.

Figure 21-1   DHCPv4 Lease-Origination Operation

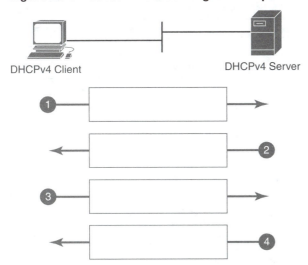

Configuring a Cisco Device as a DHCPv4 Server

Use the following steps to configure a Cisco router or switch to act as a DHCPv4 server:

Step 1. Exclude statically assigned IPv4 addresses.

Typically, some IPv4 addresses in a pool are assigned to network devices that require static address assignments. To exclude these addresses, use the **ip dhcp excluded-address** *first-address* [*last-address*] global configuration command.

Step 2. Configure a DHCPv4 pool name.

Use the **ip dhcp pool** *pool-name* global configuration command to create a pool with the specified name. The router will then be in DHCPv4 configuration mode as indicated by the prompt changing to Router(dhcp-config)#.

Step 3. Configure the DHCPv4 pool settings.

Some settings are required and others are optional. In Table 21-1, record the command syntax for the two required DHCPv4 settings and four optional DHCPv4 settings.

Table 21-1   DHCPv4 Pool Settings

Required Tasks	Command Syntax
Define the address pool.	**network** *network* [*mask* | */prefix-length*]
Define the default router or gateway.	**default-router** *address* [*add2...add8*]
Optional Tasks	**Command Syntax**
Define a DNS server.	**dns-server** *address* [*add2...add8*]
Define a domain name.	**domain-name** *domain*
Define the duration of the DHCP lease.	**lease** { *days* [*hours*] [*minutes*] | **infinite** }
Define the NetBIOS WINS server.	**netbios-name-server** *address* [*add2...add8*]

Refer to Figure 21-2. Record the commands to configure R1 as the DHCP server for the 172.16.1.0/24 LAN. Exclude the first ten IP addresses. Use an appropriate name. Include a setting for the DNS server and the domain R1.com.

Figure 21-2   DHCPv4 Configuration Topology

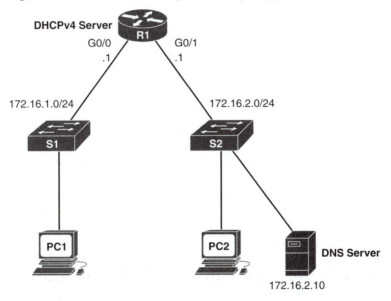

```
R1(config)#
```

To verify DHCP settings, use the **show run** command to see the configuration. There are also two other DHCP show commands you can use. Record the commands that display the following information:

```
R1#
Bindings from all pools not associated with VRF:
IP address          Client-ID/              Lease expiration        Type
                    Hardware address/
                    User name
172.16.1.11         0100.5056.be0b.b4       Sep 03 2013 07:33 PM    Automatic
R1#
Memory usage        32253
Address pools       1
Database agents     0
Automatic bindings  1
Manual bindings     0
Expired bindings    0
Malformed messages  0
```

```
Secure arp entries    0


Message                Received
BOOTREQUEST            0
DHCPDISCOVER           1
DHCPREQUEST            1
DHCPDECLINE            0
DHCPRELEASE            0
DHCPINFORM             2


Message                Sent
BOOTREPLY              0
DHCPOFFER              1
DHCPACK                3
DHCPNAK                0
R1#
```

Configuring a Router to Relay DHCPv4 Requests

Refer to Figure 21-3. It is just like Figure 21-2 except that now there is a DHCP server on the 172.16.2.0/24 LAN that provides addressing services to both 172.16.1.0/24 and 172.16.2.0/24.

Figure 21-3   DHCPv4 Topology with a Dedicated DHCPv4 Server

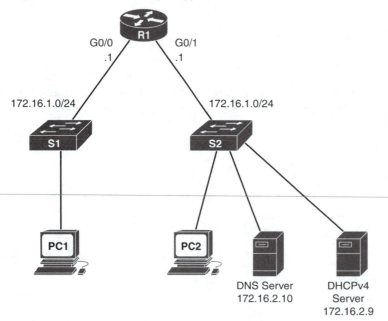

Assume the DHCP pool for 172.16.1.0/24 has been removed from R1. Record the commands to configure R1 to send DHCP requests to the new DHCP server.

```
R1(config)#
```

What eight UDP services does this command forward?

Configuring a Router as a DHCPv4 Client

Commonly, routers receive IP addressing from a DHCP server. This is particularly true in small office/home office (SOHO) networks. Refer to Figure 21-4. Record the commands to configure SOHO to request IPv4 addressing for its G0/1 interface.

Figure 21-4   Configuring a Router as a DHCPv4 Client

```
SOHO(config)#
```

Lab - Configuring Basic DHCPv4 on a Router (RSE 10.1.2.4/SwN 7.1.2.4)

Lab - Configuring Basic DHCPv4 on a Switch (RSE 10.1.2.5/SwN 7.1.2.5)

Packet Tracer - Configuring DHCPv4 Using Cisco IOS (RSE 10.1.3.3/SwN 7.1.3.3)

Troubleshooting DHCPv4

DHCPv4 problems are most commonly the result of configuration issues. Because of the number of potentially problematic areas, use a systematic approach to troubleshooting.

Troubleshooting Task 1: Resolve IPv4 Address Conflicts

Why might an address conflict occur?

What command will display DHCP address conflicts?

Troubleshooting Task 2: Verify Physical Connectivity

What commands are helpful to ensure interfaces are active?

Troubleshooting Task 3: Test Connectivity Using a Static IP Address

When troubleshooting any DHCPv4 issue, verify network connectivity by configuring static IPv4 address information on a client workstation. If the workstation is unable to reach network resources with a statically configured IPv4 address, the root cause of the problem is not DHCPv4. At this point, network connectivity troubleshooting is required.

Troubleshooting Task 4: Verify Switch Port Configuration

What are some potential reasons why a switch in between the DHCPv4 server and client might be the cause of the problem?

Troubleshooting Task 5: Test DHCPv4 Operation on the Same Subnet or VLAN

It is important to distinguish whether DHCPv4 is functioning correctly when the client is on the same subnet or VLAN as the DHCPv4 server. If DHCPv4 is working correctly when the client is on the same subnet or VLAN, the problem may be the DHCP relay agent. If the problem persists even with testing DHCPv4 on the same subnet or VLAN as the DHCPv4 server, the problem may actually be with the DHCPv4 server.

 Lab - Troubleshooting DHCPv4 (RSE 10.1.4.4/SwN 7.1.4.4)

Dynamic Host Configuration Protocol v6

Similar to IPv4, IPv6 global unicast addresses can be configured manually or dynamically. However, there are two methods in which IPv6 global unicast addresses can be assigned dynamically:

- Stateless Address Autoconfiguration (SLAAC), as shown in the figure
- Dynamic Host Configuration Protocol for IPv6 (stateful DHCPv6)

SLAAC and DHCPv6

SLAAC uses ICMPv6 Router Solicitation and Router Advertisement messages to provide addressing and other configuration information that would normally be provided by a DHCP server. Briefly describe these two messages.

Explain the two ways a client can create its own unique interface ID from the information in an RA.

Once the client creates an interface ID, what process does it use to ensure that it is unique?

A router will always respond to an RS from a client. However, the RA message reply can have one of three options for the client. Briefly describe these three options.

■

■

■

What are the default values for the M and O flags in the RA message, and what do they mean?

What is the command to configure an interface for stateless DHCPv6?

What does this command do to the RA message?

What is the command to configure an interface for stateful DHCPv6?

What does this command do to the RA message?

In Figure 21-5, label each DHCPv6 message type sent between the server and client when originating a lease.

Figure 21-5   DHCPv6 Lease-Origination Operation

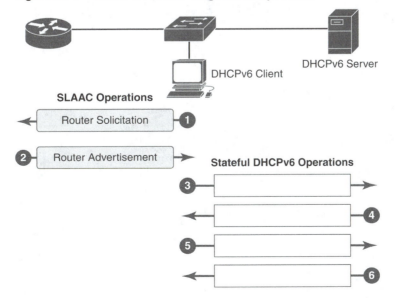

Configuring a Router as a Stateless DHCPv6 Server

To configure a router as a DHCPv6 server, you must complete four steps:

Step 1.   Enable IPv6 routing.

The **ipv6 unicast-routing** command is required before the router will send ICMPv6 RA messages.

Step 2.   Configure a DHCPv6 pool.

Use the **ipv6 dhcp pool** *pool-name* global configuration command to create a pool and enter DHCPv6 configuration mode, which is identified by the Router(config-dhcpv6)# prompt.

Step 3.   Configure the DHCPv6 settings.

The stateless DHCPv6 server can be configured to provide other information that might not have been included in the RA message such as DNS server address (**dns-server** *dns-server*) and the domain name (**domain-name** *domain-name*).

Step 4.   Configure the DHCPv6 interface.

Bind the pool to the interface with the **ipv6 dhcp server** *pool-name* command, and change the O flag with **ipv6 nd other-config-flag** command.

Refer to Figure 21-6. Record the commands to configure R1 as the DHCPv6 server for the 2001:DB8:1:1::/64 LAN. Use an appropriate name. Include a setting for the DNS server and the domain R1.com.

Figure 21-6   DHCPv6 Configuration Topology

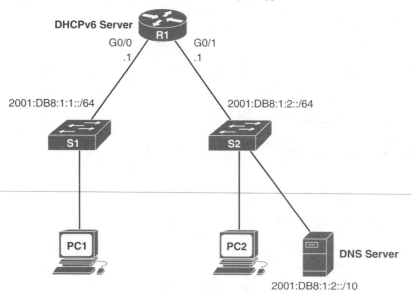

```
R1(config)#
```

What are the commands to configure a router interface as a DHCPv6 client?

Configuring a Router as a Stateful DHCPv6 Server

Configuring a router as a stateful DHCPv6 server is similar to configuring a stateless server. The most significant difference is that a stateful server also includes IPv6 addressing information similar to a DHCPv4 server and you set the M flag instead of the O flag.

What is the command to the DHCPv6 pool with IPv6 addressing information?

For the previous configuration, add the commands to configure the IPv6 addressing information for infinite lifetime, set the O flag back to 0, and set the M flag to 1.

```
R1(config)#
```

If the DHCPv6 server is located on a different network than the client, you can configure the IPv6 router as a DHCPv6 relay agent. What is the command to configure a router as a DHCPv6 relay agent?

Lab - Configuring Stateless and Stateful DHCPv6 (RSE 10.2.3.5/SwN 7.2.3.5)

Lab - Troubleshooting DHCPv6 (RSE 10.2.4.4/SwN 7.2.4.4)

Packet Tracer Skills Integration Challenge (RSE 10.3.1.2/SwN 7.3.1.2)

CHAPTER 22

Network Address Translation for IPv4

All public IPv4 addresses that transverse the Internet must be registered with a Regional Internet Registry (RIR). Only the registered holder of a public Internet address can assign that address to a network device. With the proliferation of personal computing and the advent of the World Wide Web, it soon became obvious that 4.3 billion IPv4 addresses would not be enough. The long-term solution was to eventually be IPv6. But for the short term, several solutions were implemented by the IETF, including Network Address Translation (NAT) and RFC 1918 private IPv4 addresses.

NAT Operation

There are not enough public IPv4 addresses to assign a unique address to each device connected to the Internet. Networks are commonly implemented using private IPv4 addresses.

NAT Characteristics

Fill in the table with the private addresses defined by RFC 1918.

Class	Address Range	CIDR Prefix
A		
B		
C		

Briefly explain the following terms:

- Inside local address:

- Inside global address:

- Outside global address:

- Outside local address:

In Figure 22-1, label each type of NAT address.

Figure 22-1   Identify NAT Address Types

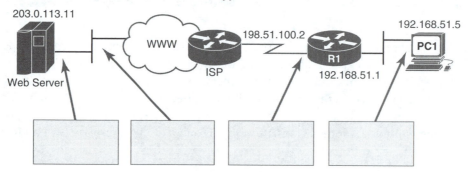

Types and Benefits of NAT

Briefly describe the three types of NAT:

   ■   Static address translation (static NAT):

   ■   Dynamic address translation (dynamic NAT):

   ■   Port Address Translation (PAT):

When is it appropriate to use static NAT?

What is the difference between dynamic NAT and PAT?

List and explain at least three advantages and three disadvantages to using NAT.

Advantages

   ■

   ■

   ■

   ■

Disadvantages

   ■

   ■

   ■

   ■

   ■

Packet Tracer
☐ Activity

Packet Tracer - Investigating NAT Operation (RSE 11.1.2.6/WAN 5.1.2.6)

Configuring NAT

Configuring NAT is straightforward if you follow a few simple steps. Static NAT and dynamic NAT configurations vary slightly. Adding PAT to a dynamic NAT is as simple as adding a keyword to the configuration.

Configuring Static NAT

Use the following steps to configure static NAT:

Step 1. Create a map between the inside local IP address and the inside global IP address with the **ip nat inside source static local-ip global-ip** global configuration command.

Step 2. Configure the inside interface of the LAN the device is attached to participate in NAT with the **ip nat inside** interface configuration command.

Step 3. Configure the outside interface where NAT translation will occur with the **ip nat outside** interface configuration command.

Refer to the topology in Figure 22-2 to configure static NAT.

Figure 22-2 Static NAT Configuration Topology

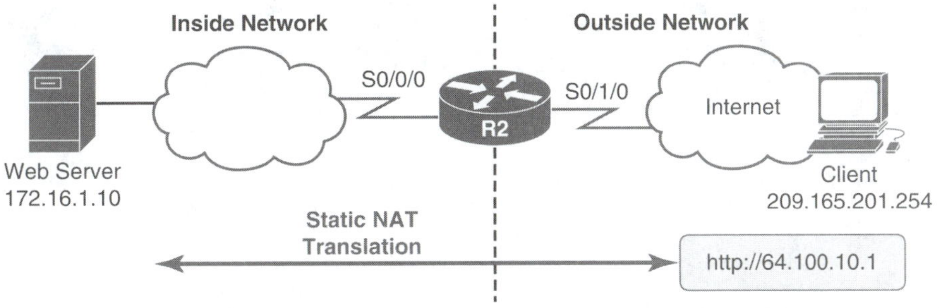

The web server uses an inside local address 172.16.1.10 that needs to be translated to the inside global address 64.100.10.1. Record the command including router prompt to configure the static translation on R2.

Record the commands including router prompt to configure the inside interface.

Record the commands including router prompt to configure the outside interface.

Packet Tracer
☐ Activity

Packet Tracer - Configuring Static NAT (RP 11.2.1.4/WAN 5.2.1.4)

Configuring Dynamic NAT

Use the following steps to configure dynamic NAT:

Step 1. Define the pool of addresses that will be used for dynamic translation using the **ip nat pool** *name start-ip end-ip* {**netmask** *netmask* | **prefix-length** *prefix-length*} global configuration command.

Step 2. Configure an ACL to specify which inside local addresses will be translated using a standard ACL.

Step 3. Bind the NAT pool to the ACL with the **ip nat inside source list** *ACL-number* **pool** *name* global configuration command.

Step 4. Configure the inside interface of the LAN the device is attached to participate in NAT with the **ip nat inside** interface configuration command.

Step 5. Configure the outside interface where NAT translation will occur with the **ip nat outside** interface configuration command.

Refer to the topology in Figure 22-3 to configure dynamic NAT.

Figure 22-3   Dynamic NAT Configuration Topology

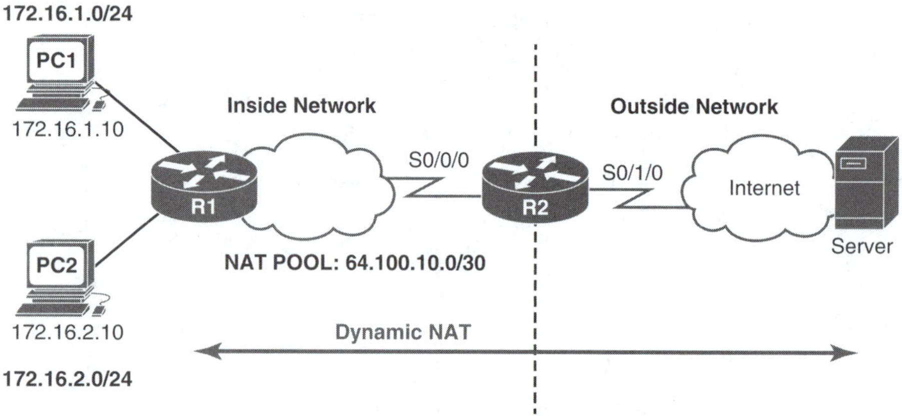

The pool of available addresses is 64.100.10.0/30. Record the command including router prompt to configure the NAT pool with an appropriate name.

The two LANs, 172.16.1.0/24 and 172.16.2.0/24, need to be translated. No other addresses are allowed. Record the command including router prompt to configure the ACL.

Record the command including router prompt to bind the NAT pool to the ACL.

Record the commands including router prompt to configure the inside interface.

Record the commands including router prompt to configure the outside interface.

Lab - Configuring Dynamic and Static NAT (RP 11.2.2.6/WAN 5.2.2.6)

Packet Tracer - Configuring Dynamic NAT (RP 11.2.2.5/WAN 5.2.2.5)

Configuring Port Address Translation

Configuring Port Address Translation (PAT) is just like configuring dynamic NAT except you add the keyword **overload** to your binding configuration:

```
Router(config)# ip nat inside source list ACL-number pool name overload
```

However, a more common solution in a small business enterprise network is to simply overload the IP address on the gateway router. In fact, this is what a home router does "out of the box."

To configure NAT to overload the public IP address on an interface, use the following command:

```
Router(config)# ip nat inside source list ACL-number interface type number overload
```

In this case, of course, there is no pool configuration.

Refer to the topology in Figure 22-4 to configure PAT.

Figure 22-4   Dynamic NAT Configuration Topology

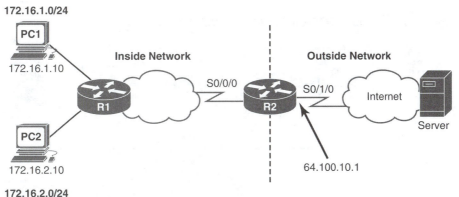

R1 is using the public IP address 64.100.10.1 on the Serial 0/1/0 interface. Record the command including router prompt to bind the ACL you configured for dynamic NAT to the Serial 0/1/0 interface.

That's it! The rest of the commands are the same as dynamic NAT. However, the process of translating inbound and outbound packets is a bit more involved. PAT maintains a table of inside and outside addresses mapped to port numbers to track connections between the source and destination.

The series of Figures 22-5 through 22-8 illustrate the PAT process overloading an interface address. Use the options in Table 22-1 to fill in the source address (SA), destination address (DA), and corresponding port numbers as the packet travels from source to destination and back.

Table 22-1   Addresses and Port Numbers

64.100.10.2	192.168.51.5	1268	209.165.201.11
1150	53	192.168.51.1	80

Figure 22-5   Hop 1: PC1 to NAT-Enabled R1

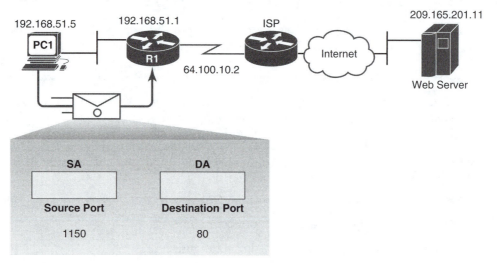

Figure 22-6   Hop 2: NAT-Enabled R1 to Web Server

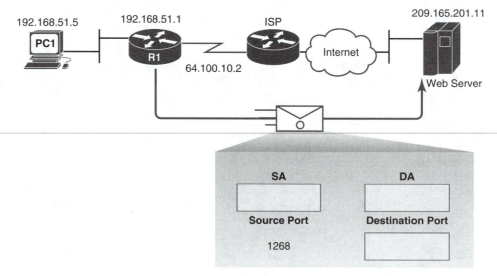

Figure 22-7   Hop 3: Web Server to NAT-Enable R1

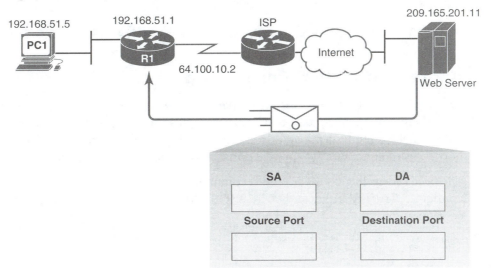

Figure 22-8   Hop 4: NAT-Enabled R1 to PC1

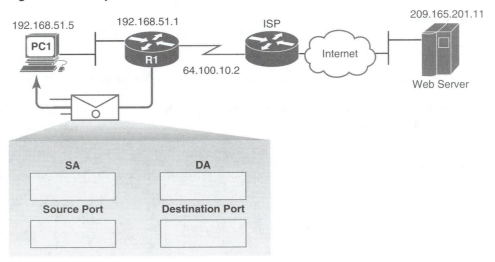

Lab - Configuring NAT Pool Overload and PAT (RP 11.2.3.7/WAN 5.2.3.7)

 Packet Tracer - Implementing Static and Dynamic NAT (RP 11.2.3.6/WAN 5.2.3.6)

A Word About Port Forwarding

Because NAT hides internal addresses, peer-to-peer connections work only from the inside out, where NAT can map outgoing requests against incoming replies. The problem is that NAT does not allow requests initiated from the outside. To resolve this problem, you can configure port forwarding to identify specific ports that can be forwarded to inside hosts.

The port forwarding configuration is commonly done in a GUI. However, you can also configure port forwarding in the Cisco IOS adding the following command to your NAT configuration:

```
Router(config)# ip nat inside source {static {tcp | udp local-ip local-port global-ip global-port} [extendable]
```

Packet Tracer - Configuring Port Forwarding on a Linksys Router (RP 11.2.4.4/WAN 5.2.4.4)

Configuring NAT and IPv6

IPv6 includes both its own IPv6 private address space and NAT, which are implemented differently than they are for IPv4. IPv6 uses a unique local address (ULA) for communication within a local site.

In Figure 22-9, label the missing parts of the IPv6 ULA address structure.

Figure 22-9   IPv6 Unique Local Address Structure

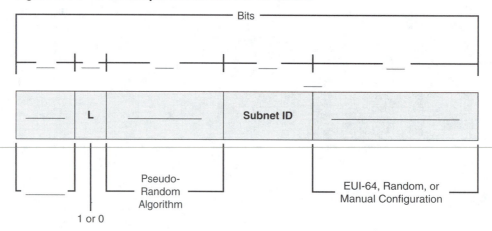

ULAs are also known as local IPv6 addresses. Briefly describe three characteristics of ULAs.

■

■

■

What is the main purpose of NAT for IPv6?

Briefly describe the three transition strategies to move from IPv4 to IPv6.

Troubleshooting NAT

When there are IPv4 connectivity problems in a NAT environment, it is often difficult to determine the cause of the problem. The first step in solving the problem is to rule out NAT as the cause. Follow these steps to verify that NAT is operating as expected:

Step 1. Review the purpose of the NAT configuration. Is there a static NAT implementation? Are the addresses in the dynamic pool actually valid? Are the inside and outside interfaces correctly identified?

Step 2. Verify that correct translations exist in the translation table using the **show ip nat translations** command.

Step 3. Use the **clear ip nat translations** * and **debug ip nat** commands to verify that NAT is operating as expected. Check to see whether dynamic entries are re-created after they are cleared.

Step 4. Review in detail what is happening to the packet, and verify that routers have the correct routing information to move the packet.

 Lab - Troubleshooting NAT Configurations (RP 11.3.1.5/WAN 5.3.1.5)

 Packet Tracer - Verifying and Troubleshooting NAT Configurations (RP 11.3.1.4/ WAN 5.3.1.4)

Packet Tracer - Skills Integration Challenge (RP 11.4.1.2/WAN 5.4.1.2)